The Nurture Notebook for
Mom and Baby

Thriving Together Through Postpartum Recovery and Interactive Play

I0547550

Written by a Team of Respected Pediatric and Women's Health Professionals

Internet addresses given in this book were accurate at the time it went to press.

This book is intended as a reference volume only, not as a medical manual. The information given here is designed to inspire and inform. It is not intended as a substitute for any treatment that may have been prescribed by your doctor. If you suspect that you have a medical problem, we urge you to seek competent medical help.

All activities in this book are interactive. You must physically support your baby during all activities. You and your baby must both be cleared by your personal care teams to participate in all the activities in this book. This book's authors, co-authors, and contributing authors are not liable for the safety of you or your baby.

If you notice signs indicating a possible delay in your baby's development, discuss these concerns with your baby's pediatrician. You may request information on a developmental screening. Your baby's pediatrician may refer you to a specialist. You might also find information about your state's early intervention (EI) program. The earlier intervention is received, the better the long-term outcomes for your baby.

The authors do not endorse, recommend, nor sponsor any manufacturer or product in this book. The specific products used in this book were presented only due to the availability of products at the time or utilization of resources available to the authors. Because new products are constantly produced, we support asking professionals for their current recommendations pertaining to specific toys and products when you are ready to purchase products. We encourage you to educate yourself by researching available products.

Talk with your doctor before starting this or any exercise program.

Printed in the United States of America

Published in Hellertown, PA

Cover and interior design by Christina Gaugler

Photographs by Brianna Davis, Jennifer Bainbridge of the Bainbridge Studio, and Kim Bandi

Front cover photo by Bree is for Beauty Photography

Back cover photo by Thomas Finan

Library of Congress Control Number available upon request

ISBN 979-8-89420-010-1

For more information or to place bulk orders, contact the author or the publisher at Jennifer@BrightCommunications.net.

Bright
COMMUNICATIONS

To every parent who strives to nurture themselves and their children,
to my team who passionately share their knowledge to improve the lives of others,
and to my family for supporting my dream of writing this book

Contents

Introduction

The Nurture Notebook is a unique, holistic approach to pressing parenting issues and common concerns delivered by trustworthy experts. With support for nurturing both the new mom and her baby, through every month, it is designed to bring structure and joy to the first year of life.

As a pediatric specialist and mom of three, I believe there is a critical gap between supporting our baby's development and our own postnatal recovery and wellness. After talking to various parents over the past 18 years, in both my profession and as a parent myself, I know I am not alone. What we all have in common is this: We love our children. We want the best for our children. We carry them in our hearts everywhere we go. And whether we stay at home or work, we often put our health and wellness on the backburner because that's what parents do to fulfill their baby's needs, right? But what if you can do both? What if you can find time to take care of both you and your baby? Our goal for this book is just that—to support your journey through the first year of your life together.

Why start in your baby's first year of life? Because your baby needs you to be holistically healthy so you can live your best life, and in turn, support them in their best life. So, I can't think of a better year to start modeling and teaching your baby the importance of developing self-love, and it is for that reason that

The Nurture Notebook team was developed.

In this book, Julie Spencer, DPT, PCES, women's health specialist and owner of integrative health center The Restoration Space, starts each month with an affirmation focused on supporting the typical feelings a mom might be experiencing. Dr. Spencer follows that with a recovery progression she uses with new moms to promote strength, endurance, and emotional health for a safe recovery, returning to exercises and activities, while preventing future injuries.

Then experts, including pediatric occupational therapists, professors, speech pathologists, and innovators in the field, offer wisdom, insight, and developmentally based activities. New moms will feel increased confidence and insight into their baby's monthly milestones with the information presented in a friendly, accessible format.

The Nurture Notebook includes contributions from more than a dozen medical experts in a wide range of fields, including:

- Kim Bandi, OTR/L (pediatric occupational therapist), founder of The Nurture Notebook, director of Valley Family Therapeutics, Orton-Gillingham practitioner, and photographer
- Sonja Burmeister, OTD, MSPA-C (physician's assistant), OTR/L (pediatric occupational therapist), EICP-OT Certified Specialist in Pediatric Early Intervention, certified autism

specialist, owner of Valley Family Therapeutics, co-owner of Connective Interventions, co-founder of MyHealthcareKit

- Julie Spencer, PT, DPT, PCES (women's health physical therapist, pregnancy and postpartum corrective exercise specialist), co-founder of The Restoration Space
- Jaime Henry-Heimer, MS CCC-SLP/L (pediatric speech and language pathologist), owner and CEO of Radical Speech Therapy Solutions
- Emily Cupples, DPT, pediatric physical therapist
- Erin Jenewein, OD, MS, FAAO, diplomate-binocular vision, perception, Pediatric Optometry Associate Professor Pennsylvania College of Optometry Salus University
- Kim DeWire, DMD, owner of DeWire Dental
- John Page, PHD, audiologist
- Tracy Walters, MA, LPC (licensed professional counselor)
- Alison Unger, MPH, RDN, LDN, CDCES
- Danielle Kinney, homeschool mom, founder and CEO of the Confident Baker
- Beth Kushner-Giovenco, RN, BSN, IBCLC (lactation consultant)

When looking for a women's health therapist (PT) to support you postpartum, make sure to find one who specializes in pelvic floor therapy, pregnancy and/or postpartum, and/or women's health. Not all PTs are comfortable treating pregnant/postpartum moms. Similarly, many PTs who have a background in orthopedics alone treat a woman who is struggling with issues related to pregnancy and postpartum as they would any other patient with back pain, which is like treating an apple as an orange: Both are fruits, but many differences can be overlooked.

If possible, we highly recommend a PT who is trained in utilizing biofeedback for your pelvic floor. (Most PTs that specialize in pelvic floor therapy and women's health have this training, but not all.) Using biofeedback software is useful to determine the baseline of your pelvic floor. Are you too tense or are you too relaxed? Do you have strength but "appear" weak because your muscle tone is too high? Or is it hard to even find these muscles to engage them in the first place?

It is important to note that biofeedback is not about Kegel training. In fact, more often than not it is to help one release their muscles and find relaxation versus finding strength and tension.

- Jolie Maehrer, RN, BSN, IBCLC (lactation consultant)
- Briana Davis, Jennifer Bainbridge, and Kim Bandi, photographers, capture the first year of life, providing visual guidance for the exercises and activities.

Visit *The Nurture Notebook* website for extensive biographies of our team.

As health and wellness experts and parents ourselves, we understand how limited time is and the balancing acts and variety of challenges day-to-day life with children brings; therefore, we provide facts and tips in tandem with simple developmental, routine-based activities for your baby.

Readers looking for more advice in specific areas will find bonus chapters and resources on our website, including additional information on:

- Parents' emotional well-being in the first year
- Nutrition
- Breastfeeding
- Your baby's health in the first year

A note on the developmental milestones and activities in *The Nurture Notebook*: Each area of your baby's development works together and facilitates growing awareness of their body. These skills will someday lead to mastery of their environment. Believe it or not, your baby's current development impacts their future successes in academics, athletics, social skills, and much more. You are your baby's strongest advocate,

hero, protector, most-loved role model, first coach, and teacher. Enjoying these milestones with your baby builds the bond between the two of you, creating your baby's sense of security and even impacting your baby's reactions to stressful events. We feel it is important that you understand that these skills help your baby now and that they are also foundational skills for future growth.

Your role is to encourage the next step in development, wherever your baby's might be. You can always go back a chapter, continuing to work on the same activities until your baby has mastered them, or move ahead if they are mastering skills sooner.

With that all said, remember: An abundance of toys is not necessary for your baby's healthy development. The focus should be placed on quality opportunities for communication; sensorimotor play—activities that promote the interaction between your baby's motor and sensory functions; exposure to a variety of play positions—developmental and foundational positions in which you encourage your baby to play, such as on their back, side-lying, tummy, and supported sitting; and facilitation of movement patterns—the way in which your baby moves and transitions between positions to facilitate higher-level motor skills and coordination.

Why do we focus on these areas within our book? Because in this technology-driven, fast-paced world we live in, sometimes we forget to enjoy quality experiences and communication and simple opportunities for sensorimotor play, play positions, and movement patterns that don't require a lot of money; rather, these experiences help you as parents focus on being present in the moment with your baby, during their activities. This book breaks them down, focusing on utilizing your resources and your routines, as well as having an awareness of the small celebrations that create the big milestone moments in your baby's life.

Points to Consider Prior to Reading the Book

- *The Nurture Notebook* is intended to be read at a monthly pace with chapters coinciding with each month of you and your baby's first year together. Additional resource chapters and information are available on our website.

- This book is NOT to be used in lieu of medical advice for your or your baby.

- Check with your OB-GYN for clearance to participate in all activities.

- Check with your baby's pediatrician for clearance to participate in all activities.

- If you have postnatal concerns about your healing process, seek medical attention from your obstetrician-gynecologist (OB-GYN), primary caregiver, physical therapist, and/or a women's health specialist.

- The order of postnatal exercises and movement was designed on purpose and in a specific sequence for postnatal recovery. You might feel ready to progress through the recommended exercises more quickly than in the months in which they are described. This might be okay with clearance from your doctor. However, even with clearance, we strongly encourage you to follow and master each step of the sequence outlined prior to adding on, even if you are moving through the sequence more quickly.

Note: The exercises are designed for recovery from both the vaginal and Cesarean section deliveries. Talk with your doctor before starting this or any exercise program. Clearance from your doctor and setting the correct foundation is crucial. These are based on years of experience treating and rehabilitating postpartum women. Because the exercises focus on the correct sequence or strategy needed for our bodies to work correctly, they lay the foundation for any other progression or advancement of future exercises. If you do not lay this foundation and your body is not taught nor reminded of how it is meant to work, you are setting your body up for injury and dysfunction.

- Development occurs in ranges and is different for every baby. In this book, we presented milestones at the earliest time we might see them emerge so that you are aware of what you may see and how to enrich those experiences. Please do not panic if you see a milestone listed in one month, but your baby has not yet met that milestone. This does not mean your baby is delayed or will struggle in their future. Normal development has significant ranges. For example, walking can occur anytime between a several-month span before it is considered a delay.

- In this book, activities have not been labeled with one set area of development, such as fine-motor skills, because each activity involves multiple developmental skills. For example, speech and language development should be incorporated into all activities. We want to encourage parents not to focus on a specific area such as fine motor, but, rather, to make every activity an opportunity to enrich all areas of development.

- All activities in this book are interactive. You must physically support your baby during all activities. You and your baby must both be cleared by your personal care teams to participate in all the activities in this book. This book's authors, co-authors, and contributing authors are not liable for the safety of you or your baby.

- Build activities into your daily routine to promote engagement and consistency with the exercises for both you and your baby. We give tips on how to do this throughout our book.

- Embrace the quality of all your baby's experiences, rather than the speed at which they master milestones.

- It is common for a baby to stop focusing on a skill when they are developing a new skill. For example, your baby may stop babbling or speaking while they attempt to master walking.

- Regression is when a baby has mastered a milestone and then stops doing the skill all together. If a skill was not mastered, regression has not truly occurred. However, true regression can be a red flag for other developmental concerns and should be discussed with your baby's pediatrician.

- You will learn a lot about your baby in this first year, including how to anticipate their needs. For example, while you're doing activities in this book, recognizing your baby will be hungry after a three-hour nap and planning accordingly will help them to feel secure and nurtured and will decrease their stress.

- If you notice signs indicating a possible delay in your baby's development, discuss these concerns with your baby's pediatrician. You may request information through a developmental screening. Your baby's pediatrician may refer you to a specialist. You might also find information about your state's early intervention (EI) program. The earlier intervention is received, the better the long-term outcomes for your baby.

- Due to a variety of reading styles and our attempts to reach a very broad population, our goal is to appeal to different readers' preferences and learning styles. We have tried to make things simple and lighthearted yet educational, with added information in our blogs and on our website for parents who want more detailed, research-based information.

- Many milestones might seem insignificant to some people; however, they are foundational stepping-stones necessary to help your baby reach the next milestone successfully. Celebrate the development of all accomplishments, big and small.

- We do not endorse, recommend, or sponsor any manufacturer or product in this book. Because new products are constantly produced, we support asking professionals for their current recommendations pertaining to specific toys and products when you are ready to purchase products. We encourage you to educate yourself by researching available products.

- In addition to the wealth of information provided in this book, we offer a great deal more information on our website.

Thank you for trusting us to share in your postnatal recovery and first year of making memories with your sweet baby. We encourage you to reach out to us with your personal journey and feedback about your first year together.

A Note for You

"Dare to be the adults we want our children to be."—Brené Brown, PhD

Do you know the key to being your best parenting self and giving your baby everything to survive and thrive? *Taking care of yourself first*. You need to be healthy, *both physically and emotionally*, to properly care for and bond with your baby. And there is nothing selfish about that.

You spent nine-plus crazy, yet amazing, months watching your body grow and change—feeling life grow and move inside you. People love pregnant women. They open the doors for you; they offer you seats in crowded rooms. You have parking spaces even designated just for you. You have a prenatal massage, prenatal yoga, and pre-natal boutiques sporting better maternity options than your prior nonmaternity wardrobes possibly held . . . there are endless prenatal options now. You may see your doctor more than 10 times in nine months to check on you and your baby. You are treated like a modern-day goddess, even when you don't feel like one. You are told you glow, and even on the non-glowy days, just those words alone can make you believe it.

Then your baby comes, and all the attention focuses on your perfect new human. And you? Well, you are pretty much forgotten by every-one *except* for your baby. For your baby, you are *everything*: food source, bathing source, soother, entertainer, provider, and scheduler, and it's *exhausting*. Your body no longer holds your baby inside, but your body may quite possibly feel worse than it did during pregnancy. And your adorable pregnancy belly now may feel like an out-of-shape blob that is just plain judged.

You are tired and trying to understand and adapt to this new life, your new role, and the changes in your body at the same time. You may mourn your independence and freedom from your pre-mommy life, but at the same time, you can't imagine what your life was just a few short days/weeks/months ago without your new love. And your hormones? Well, they are *raging*. It may feel like PMS times 1,000, mixed in with a demanding boss whose expectations feel impos-sible at times.

Now you may have a handle on this, but it is common to feel as if you've been hit by a Mack truck, feeling unsure how you are going to regain some semblance of normalcy. It's time to find yourself again and refamiliarize yourself with your body. (Yes, those muscles are still there.) Find moments of peace and moments of empow-erment because without you, there is no Mommy. It is impossible to be the best version of you for your baby if you're not taking care of your. So do not put yourself down on your priority list; make the women's health information presented here as important as the rest. These exercises and activities are intended to be easy, achievable, and time-efficient while also effective in helping you regain strength and endurance. *Please take care of yourself so you can take care of everything else.*

Items for Suggested Exercises

- Yoga mat or anti-skid surface

- Slider (Options: exercise sliders, furniture sliders, washcloths or pillowcases, Swiffer pads, or fuzzy socks for hands and/or feet)

- Exercise bands

- Light hand weights (two to three pounds) or household items, such as soup cans

- Yoga block (or a small step stool or a thick book with an anti-slip surface under it)

- Small ball (or pillow)

The First Four Weeks

© Bree Is For Beauty Photography

MOMMY MOVEMENTS

In the first four weeks postpartum, you will likely feel a variety of emotions, and your body needs to heal, breathe, and regain body awareness. Each of us has unique experiences, so you must stay in contact with your OB-GYN for guidance regarding your specific healing process and a referral to a pelvic floor therapist. After you have clearance from your OB-GYN, utilize the month-to-month women's health exercises in this book as a guide to recovery.

The Diaphragmatic Breathing and Pelvic Floor Contraction exercises are now the focus for supporting your recovery. Be sure to listen to your body, go at your own comfortable pace.

Postnatal Rest and Recovery

Some people feel as if we have to strive for perfection in all aspects of life, but the pressure seems 10-fold for a parent welcoming a newborn into the world. Maybe it's a perfectionistic inner dialogue, new moms showcasing perfectly clean homes and three-course meals on social media, or family members telling you how to raise your baby the right way. Whenever you are feeling defeated this way, breathe and remind yourself,

"I am enough!"

The pure act of being with your baby is invaluable to them. You are their reason for existence, and that miracle alone is an accomplishment in itself. That's why it's so important to begin your own healing process soon after giving birth. You can start by bringing awareness to your breath and your muscles with the following foundational exercises.

Diaphragmatic Breathing

Think of your ribcage opening in all directions front, back, and sides, as you inhale, like opening an umbrella.

Inhale deeply for six seconds. Relax your belly muscles, relax your pelvic floor muscles, and envision filling your whole ribcage with air, front, sides, and back.

Exhale for six seconds. Slowly exhale out, letting everything simply returning back to your starting position.

Standing with your hands on your ribcage take a 360-Degree Breath as above to help guide your breath and complete the sequence five times.

Pelvic Floor Contractions (aka Kegels)

Pelvic Floor Contractions (PFCs), also known as Kegels, will help you recover your vaginal strength postpartum, but they are also the groundwork for all other exercises—and really all other movements. This exercise is about finding the correct muscles and waking them up.

While lying on your back, place your hand on your belly button and walk your fingers straight down toward your pelvic bone.

Slide your fingers slightly back up toward your belly button so that you fall just off the pelvic bone. The muscle beneath your fingers is your transversus abdominis (TA). Lightly close your vaginal and rectal openings, and then gently pull them up and in toward your core, as if you are holding your urine or stopping your urine stream. If you are doing these correctly, the vaginal and rectal muscles are the only muscles engaged. Do not hold your breath. Do not squeeze your butt (gluteal muscles) or your legs. You will feel slight movement beneath the fingers that are above your pubic bone.

Movement always occurs on the exhale.

Diaphragmatic Breathing with Pelvic Floor Contractions

Once you have mastered true diaphragmatic breathing and identified where your pelvic floor muscles are, it is time to combine them as follows. Inhale deeply, expanding your rib cage. Exhale, close and lift your pelvic floor, and hold for five seconds. Relax and take one or two six-second diaphragmatic breaths to reset your breath and your body. Relaxing the pelvic floor is as important as the contraction. That's one cycle. Aim for completing this exercise three times a day, for five to 10 cycles, one time lying down, one time sitting down, and other times in the position of your choice.

Embedding PFCs into your daily routine, such as when you are feeding your baby, allows for several check-ins with your body and your pelvic floor throughout the day. However, you can also find other times during the day, such as at a stop light or every time you brush your teeth, to relax and strengthen your pelvic floor muscles in a variety of functional positions, including standing.

It is most important to do a full cycle (contract/relax) to reset and rehab your pelvic floor, so focus on quality over quantity.

BABY'S DEVELOPMENT

The milestones listed below are based on when they might first be noticed, not when they should be mastered. Development is not one size fits all. Every baby develops at their own pace, and milestones build upon each other and occur at different ages.

Let's talk about your baby's earliest development. The second your baby was born, a variety of sensations begin bombarding them. There are no more waves of amniotic fluid to buffer the cold, loud, bright, chaotic world into which they have arrived. The most commonly known senses are sight (vision), sound (auditory), taste (gustatory), touch (tactile), and smell (olfactory).

In addition, body position (proprioception), movement (vestibular), and internal awareness (interoception) are hidden senses that provide input to your brain about your body within your environment. The sense of proprioception is found in your muscles and joints to identify where a body part is in space. The vestibular sense is found in your inner ear and detects head movements needed to maintain balance throughout the day. The interoception sense is found in your organs and sends information to your brain about your vital functions such as, but not limited to, hunger, thirst, pain, respiration, digestion, and bladder and bowel needs. Unlike an adult, your baby experiences all of their senses as a whole right now, not individually. Making "sense" of their senses will evolve as they learn about their new world.

Consider these sensory impacts of your baby's environment and novel experiences when you are unable to identify why your baby is crying.

Motor Development

After birth, your baby's arms and legs are held in tightly to their body. Over the first month, gravity, along with active movement, help to elongate their muscles. This relaxation and extension of your baby's body will enable them to begin to kick their legs, raise and turn their head during tummy time, and start to move their arms together spontaneously. As they gain strength, babies are able to explore the tactile sense through their hands, and they might even find comfort in bringing them to their mouth and sucking them. All these large movements are important because they help your baby get into a variety of positions to experience the world through all their bodily senses.

Visual Development

Your baby's field of vision (how far into the periphery your baby can see), visual acuity (sharpness), and the ability to see all the colors of the rainbow are different than for an adult. A baby's line of sight (visual field) is smaller than an adult's.

Visual acuity (clarity) in the first month is generally no better than 20/200, compared with an adult without any visual issues at a visual acuity of 20/20. That means an adult has approximately 10 times the ability to see objects as your newborn does. This is because your baby's retinal structures are still immature. In fact, your baby can see only about eight to 12 inches away from their face.

Regarding color, your baby is more easily able to see black and white right now, particularly in patterns. Processing the contrast of the outer

Note: If you notice that your baby's eyes turn in or out, this is normal. Most babies do not display normal ocular (eye) alignment until around five weeks of age.

portions of your face first (hairline, chin) enables your baby to recognize you as the primary caregiver, often within a few days of birth.

Cognitive Development

Cognition is the mental process of gaining knowledge. Your baby's ability to understand this acquired knowledge is enriched through their experiences and senses as their brain rapidly makes connections. While observing your baby, you can pick up on how the senses facilitate cognitive growth, such as the physical response of their eyes widening to sounds and voices, indicating their increasing auditory awareness.

Social-Emotional Development

Socio-emotionally, your baby establishes initial but fleeting eye contact with you, relaxes in your arms, reflexively smiles, and communicates with you through their cry. They desire, love, and accept positive physical contact frequently. Your baby is dependent on you to nurture them and provide life-sustaining help. As they grow and learn more about their body, they begin to discover strategies to meet their own needs. Until then, remember that "recreating the womb" through low lights, quiet noise, and gentle rocking help your baby to feel soothed until they develop their own self-soothing strategies.

Self-Care Development

For the purpose of this book, self-care refers to your baby's growing ability to work toward independently completing necessary daily tasks, such as eating, drinking, and dressing. Right now, your baby is fully dependent on you, and your bond will be strengthened through your growing intuition, understanding, responsiveness, and awareness of their needs. Most notable this month is feeding; they reflexively open and close their mouth in response to your breast or a bottle nipple. They also reflexively turn to the side where their cheek is stimulated (rooting reflex) to latch onto a nipple.

When drinking, your baby firsts sucks in breast milk or formula multiple times before being able to swallow it in order to protect their airway and prevent choking. This pattern later progresses to coordinating sucking, swallowing, and breathing rhythmically during feeding.

Speech and Language Development

Speech and language can be broken down into two separate areas: expressive, which is talking, and receptive, which is hearing and understanding. Initially, your baby's sounds will range from their first instinctual cry, which is music to your ears, to their sweet little baby noises. You will hear them start making unintentional comforting sounds (i.e. sucking) and express themselves through crying. Their cries will start as one long cry, similar to that of a sheep's "baa," and slowly change in pitch, tone, and intensity to indicate their specific needs, such as hunger, sleepiness, or the need for a diaper change.

Oral motor skills revolve around your baby's reflexive ability to latch on and drink from either your breast or a bottle nipple to feed right now. If your baby is struggling to latch on and coordinate their sucking and breathing, consult your baby's pediatrician or a lactation specialist.

Primitive reflexes are the automatic reactive movements vital for survival and development.

Tonic labyrinthe reflex (TLR): This reflex is foundational for large muscle groups and postural stability. The TLR helps your baby to adjust to gravity after birth and impacts the development of tone, balance, spatial awareness, and posture. This is one of the reasons tummy time is important.

Moro reflex (aka startle reflex): This reflex is a sympathetic nervous system response linked to fight or flight. This reflex is important for bonding with your baby, gravitational security (comfort with movements) and organizing, self-regulating, and concentrating.

Rooting reflex: This reflex is an automatic (autonomically based internal regulation) reaction a baby has of locating food at this age by breast or bottle. This reflex is stimulated when their cheek is touched and is essential for feeding at this age. It is important for sucking, chewing, swallowing, and overall eating.

Palmar grasp reflex: When your baby's palm is stimulated, they will automatically (autonomically) bend (flex) their fingers in a grasping pattern. This reflex is important for the development of gross motor coordination of the hand, required for grasping and maintaining objects in their hands, as well as manipulating larger items.

Asymmetrical tonic neck reflex (ATNR): This reflex helps your baby with their passage through the birth canal during delivery. It involves opposite sides (contralateral) movement patterns (i.e. crawling and walking patterns) where the limbs on the same side of their body extend, and they turn their head. It also provides the foundation for hemispheric brain dominance and speech and language development, as well as supports postural control.

Spinal galant: This reflex also helps you and your baby during the birthing process assisting with descending into the birth canal, helps activate the semicircular canals in the ears to support vestibular movement (balance) later in life, enhances proprioceptive system development (which goes hand-in-hand with the vestibular system). It provides a solid foundation for standing and walking.

Developmental Play

All the activities presented throughout each month of this book are intended to be interactive between you and your baby to promote bonding through communication and touch.

Auditory Play

Although it might sound obvious or even silly, actively and intentionally communicating with your baby throughout their day (daily commentary) lays the groundwork for speech and language development. Your baby will learn (encode) this vocabulary, building the foundation for a lifetime of strong communication and connection.

Here are three simple ways to integrate daily commentary into your daily routine and engage all of your baby's senses.

1. Introducing your baby to your home, family, and pets

2. Labeling the sights, smells, sounds, and textures they encounter throughout their day

3. Doing daily tasks with your baby positioned safely next to you and describing what you are doing.

Note: As you talk with your baby throughout your day, consider how they also communicate with you. Crying is their primary way to communicate and create a connection with you. It is typical for a crying baby to cause feelings of anxiety and stress, and this tension can actually be internalized by your baby. Try your best to establish a tranquil environment for your baby's social/emotional well-being, as well as your own. Maintaining a soft voice will inspire a peaceful atmosphere. Ambient sounds (i.e. "Shhhh") calm your baby and help them to maintain breathing rhythms. If you are feeling upset, there is no shame in putting your baby down in a safe place (i.e. crib), walking away, and taking deep breaths to calm yourself.

Phone calls: Your baby can't tell you what sounds they hear yet, but you can stimulate their auditory (hearing) system by embedding phone calls into their daily routine. While on phone calls, make eye contact with your baby while talking, put your phone on speaker, and place it away from your baby. This practice will allow your baby to hear and distinguish the sound of different voices, known as auditory discrimination. As your baby develops, exposure to a variety of voices is enriching and will help them learn to distinguish a very important one—yours.

Body sounds: Another way to stimulate your baby's hearing system is to make a clicking noise with your fingers or mouth to create a light noise on one side of your baby's body, then pause. Your baby will turn their head to the sound, indicating that they have heard it. Repeat the sound on the other side. While staying within eight to 12 inches from your baby, slowly move in an arch over their head to the other ear to engage their visual system when switching sides.

Reading: It's never too early to start reading to your baby! Reading fosters closeness and emotional connection, as caregivers hold their infants close and engage them in the reading experience. This interaction lays the foundation for healthy attachment and social development. The sound of your voice is powerful, and the purpose of reading at this age is to give your baby the chance to both hear your voice and make eye contact with the book.

Your baby enjoys books that provide repetition and are black and white with simple pictures or interesting patterns. An easy way to enrich their bedtime ritual is to read the same book every day and change how you read the book as your baby evolves. For example, if you are looking at a picture of a house, start by labeling it (house). Over time, expand on it (black-and-white house). As your baby's attention further develops, add motor skills (knock on the book while stating "knock, knock, knock").

Singing: Your baby loves your voice whether you can hold a tune or not. You can sing anything. It's not important what you sing but how you sing it and that you encourage eye contact when you can. You can turn any phrase or tune into a lullaby just by singing it slowly and with a soft voice, such as "I love you today. I love you tomorrow. I love you, love you, love you, love you always, my darling."

Many studies have shown the positive effects of music exposure on various parts of the brain. In fact, the University of Washington conducted a study that showed music might have the ability to enhance infants' speech processing, which means music can help babies learn the rhythm and timing of speech.

POSITIONAL PLAY

Frequent opportunities for exposure to a variety of natural play positions, such as lying on their tummy, back, and sides, generate critical sensory experiences for your baby's learning and development.

Tummy Time Play Position

The American Academy of Pediatrics (AAP) is an organization formed by pediatricians devoted to striving for and supporting the health, safety, and well-being of children, infants through young adulthood. The AAP (2022 Guide) reported the importance of supervised tummy time, while your baby is awake, starting the day your baby comes home from the hospital. They recommend working up to 15 to 30 minutes daily by 7 weeks old.

As pediatric specialists, we encourage parents to schedule tummy time into their baby's routine, such as with every diaper change and before and after naptimes, gradually increasing the amount of time they maintain the position in small increments.

Supervised, awake tummy time is recommended to facilitate infant development and to minimize development of positional plagiocephaly.

Tummy time can initially be a challenging activity. As your baby learns to coordinate their body to lift their head, parents should provide consistent, frequent opportunities. With practice, babies will begin to happily explore their world from this position.

To provide an enriched sensory experience, start your baby on their back and slowly roll them onto their side and then to their tummy. Place your baby's forearms underneath them with their elbows bent, to encourage weight bearing through their forearms, which will start to strengthen your baby's arms. Allow your baby's lower body to be in whatever position is comfortable. Initially, your baby might seem most comfortable with their knees also tucked under them. Alternate which side you roll your baby to each time.

Naptime Diaphragmatic Breathing

Tummy time looks different at various stages in development. It can be incorporated into a variety of daily activities, such as the way you hold your baby, to increase frequency.

Remember the diaphragmatic breathing you learned during postnatal rest and recovery? You are going to put that to use here while your baby is practicing tummy time. While your baby is lying on you and starting to fall asleep, observe their breathing pattern. Watch their rib cage expand and contract. Begin your breathing exercise by mimicking their breathing pattern, in sync with them. Observe your baby's breathing pattern with your eyes closed and continue to practice deep breathing.

Now lie down on your back with your head supported and your baby on top of you, belly to belly. When you feel your baby's belly rise, relax

When your baby is completing tummy time on a firm, safe surface, get down at their level, within eight to 12 inches from their face, to keep them engaged and able to tolerate the position longer.

your belly muscles and inhale, feeling your belly meet theirs. Your baby's breathing will naturally be faster than yours, but for a few minutes, try to synchronize your belly (inhale) with each inhale of theirs. This exercise helps train your breath, your abdominals, and your pelvic floor, while providing tummy time and nurturing your bond with your baby, recalling a time during pregnancy when your breath was their breath.

Baby Feeding and Pelvic Floor Contractions

Embedding pelvic floor contractions (Kegels) into your daily routine, such as when you are feeding your baby, allows for several check-ins with your body and your pelvic floor throughout the day. However, you can also find other times during the day, such as at a stoplight or every time you brush your teeth, to strengthen your pelvic floor muscles in a variety of functional positions, like standing. Aim to complete this exercise three times a day, for five to 10 cycles—one time lying down, one time sitting down, and other times in the position of your choice. However, doing a full cycle (contract/relax) is most important to reset and rehab your pelvic floor, so think quality over quantity.

Back Play Position

Whenever your baby is lying on their back, whether it is to sleep or play for a period of time, alternate their head to their left and right sides periodically to promote preservation of skin, bone, and fontanelle (soft spot) integrity. This also helps to ensure baby's head shape is symmetrical.

High-Contrast Fixation

Stimulate your baby's ability to fixate visually on an object and promote future eye-hand coordination needed for reaching, grasping, and pointing by using high-contrast toys.

While your baby is lying in your lap or on a safe, firm surface on the floor, hold a black-and-white object eight to 12 inches away from your baby's face, about the distance from your arms to your face when you are holding your baby. Move it slowly and fluidly in an arch from your baby's left ear, over their face, to their right ear, as if you are making a rainbow.

Next, place the black-and-white object eight to 12 inches in front of their nose. Make an arch toward the top of their head and then back down, ending below their chin.

Place the black-and-white object on your baby's shoulder and then create a diagonal arch over their face, aiming for the space over the top, opposite side of their head. Repeat on the other side.

Playing with high-contrast toys in back play presents a perfect opportunity to socialize with your baby. Talk, sing, and label items using expressive, almost exaggerated, intonation (e.g. "Ooooohhhhhhh!! Look baby, here is a black-and-white bear; grrhh."). As your baby shows sustained visual attention, encourage them to respond to your facial expressions.

Positive Touch

The Cleveland Clinic, a nonprofit academic medical center and leader in research, education, and health information, reports that skin-to-skin contact between baby and parent provides a calm, warm environment that decrease your baby's fussiness and promote more stable blood sugar levels. Research further indicates that skin-to-skin contact upon returning home promotes the baby's brain development.

As you create bonding and enriched sensory experiences through skin-to-skin contact (with baby's uncovered chest against their mother's or father's uncovered chest), observe your baby's response to this sensory experience and follow their signs, specifically the impact on their level of alertness and calm.

Once your baby is comforted by skin-to-skin contact, the International Association of Infant Massage encourages the slow introduction of gentle strokes to your baby's back and legs.

When you massage your baby, use a firm, open hand. Maintain contact with your baby as on-and-off touch is startling, especially because your baby is still learning about their environment and senses.

To provide a positive whole-body sensory experience, play calm music or quietly sing a lullaby.

When to massage your baby and what to use makes a difference. We suggest massage after their bath as an optimal time because their muscles are relaxed and they are more likely to be in a calm emotional state.

Your baby's skin provides a protective barrier

between their internal and the external environment. This protective barrier regulates things such as hydration and body temperature. Within the first year, your baby's skin will change, so be mindful to not use scented products due to a newborn's sensitivity to scents and research current products on the market for viability and safety.

Natural Mystery Scents

Your baby has been exposed to tastes in utero and has an extraordinary sense of smell that has been observed within an hour of birth through what's called the breastfeeding crawl—their ability to locate your breasts through their sense of smell when placed on your abdomen and in between your breasts. In other words, when your baby is first born, they open their eyes and smell you, and if placed in this position, they might start to move their hands and feet to draw closer to your breast using their sense of smell.

During your baby's first month, you can start to introduce them to various safe natural scents to expose and stimulate their olfactory sense (sense of smell).

As stated above, it is believed that infants are more sensitive to chemicals, so we recommend using natural scents for this activity. For example, use a fresh orange. Do not use powders, spices, nor anything that might be inhaled into your baby's nasal passage. Carefully pass the scent under your baby's nose, staying close so the smell will emanate, yet be far enough away to avoid accidental inhalation of an object. Watch your baby's reaction. Do they turn away, widen their eyes, coo, or have a reflexive smile?

The First Four Weeks

Fill in the answers to reflect on the past month and to track.

How do you feel?

_____

_____

What exercises did you work on?

_____

_____

What is your baby doing now?

_____

_____

What was your baby's favorite activity this month?

_____

_____

What questions do you have for your ob-gyn and your baby's pediatrician?

_____

_____

Notes:

_____

_____

_____

_____

Parents' Emotional Well-Being in the First Year

Contributed by Tracy Walters, MA, LPC

Having a baby is arguably one of the most profound experiences of your life. There is often a huge emphasis on the physical changes that come during and after pregnancy and less on the emotional changes that accompany this transition. Knowing a little more about what to expect with the potential rollercoaster of emotions will hopefully set your mind at ease in these early sleep-deprived days.

It may surprise you to hear that both positive and negative life experiences cause a stress response in your body. That's right; stress does not discriminate. What that means is that even if you are over the moon with the new baby you have always dreamed of having, you can still experience a stress response. This is important to keep in mind as you move through the first year of your baby's life. Even positive, happy changes in life still register as *stress*. When it comes to a stress response, your body and mind are less concerned with the specifics of the change and more concerned with the amount of disruption to your daily routine. Keep this in mind the next time you hear your inner critic suggesting there's something wrong with you for being stressed out about such a joyful time in your life.

Postpartum

Baby blues or something more? Your doctor has probably talked to you about the baby blues and postpartum depression (PPD). The hormonal changes (specifically, the dramatic drop in estrogen and progesterone after birth), lack of sleep, getting to know your baby, and learning how to take care of them, all while negotiating life as a new parent, are a perfect recipe for mood changes. In the months after childbirth, 50 to 75 percent of all new moms and up to 25 percent of new dads experience some form of baby blues. These symptoms include crying (with no identifiable reason), mood swings, feeling overwhelmed, and changes in eating and sleeping habits. The above symptoms are common and normal as you adapt to your new life with your baby. When and if you experience the above, stay calm and do the following: get extra sleep if possible (maybe a good time for your partner to take over bottle duty) and call on your support system so you can recharge a bit. Baby blues may come and go over the first year of your baby's life, but the symptoms should be mild and alleviated with rest and breaks from parent duty.

If your baby blues persist for longer than a week or two and the symptoms above become more intense and frequent, it is important to report this to your doctor. Up to 15 percent of women develop PPD within the first year of their baby's life. These symptoms are similar to the baby blues, only more intrusive and intense. Symptoms include fatigue, feeling very sad or hopeless, loss of interest in activities you used to enjoy, feelings of guilt, withdrawal from family and friends, little or no interest in your baby, and thoughts of hurting yourself or your baby. The good news is that postpartum depression is temporary and treatable! Your doctor should be able to refer you to a therapist who specializes in supporting new parents or suggest medications to help (including ones that don't interfere with breastfeeding).

The most severe, and thankfully rarest, form of PPD is called postpartum psychosis (PPP). Affecting about one to two out of every 1,000 new mothers, it has a rapid onset, typically within the first few weeks postpartum. As the name implies, symptoms of PPP include a break from reality, which can include bizarre thoughts, hallucinations (visual or auditory), thoughts of self-harm or harming your baby, and rapid cycling of moods (very high/hyperactive mood followed by a low or tired mood, for example). PPP is treated as an emergency medical condition, meaning you will need to be seen by a healthcare provider immediately to ensure your baby's safety.

A little less common but still important to have on your radar are postpartum anxiety (PPA), postpartum obsessive-compulsive disorder (PPOCD), and postpartum posttraumatic stress disorder (PPPTSD). PPA affects about 10 percent of all postpartum women. Again, anxiety can be a normal response to being a new parent. A certain amount of worry is natural and normal as you recognize this amazing gift (but also the immense responsibility) of taking care of your baby. However, if you find yourself dealing with constant worry, racing thoughts about something bad happening to your baby, or physical symptoms of panic, including dizziness,

nausea, or chest pain, it is time to reach out to your doctor.

PPOCD affects about 3 to 5 percent of new moms. Frequently, obsessive and compulsive behaviors arise from a desire to reduce anxiety. You may fear for your baby's safety (anxiety-based) and may create rituals or repetitive behaviors. These may include cleaning and recleaning, organizing and reorganizing, and checking and rechecking. PPOCD can also include obsessive thoughts about your baby and spill over to impacting your baby's care. An example may be weighing your baby several times a day, each day, to make sure your baby is gaining weight the way they are supposed to, even after getting reassurance from your baby's pediatrician that their weight gain is normal.

PPPTSD is experienced by about 1 to 6 percent of women. PPPTSD typically arises when a parent's birth plan doesn't go as planned. This may occur in the event of an unplanned cesarean section, maternal distress, or fetal distress, such as your baby going to the NICU for monitoring after birth. Poor communication from the support team and an overall sense of powerlessness are also factors in developing PPPTSD. Symptoms may include flashbacks to the real or perceived trauma, anxiety, panicking, feeling detached from reality, a sense of hypervigilance, and an avoidance of anything that may trigger a memory of the event (such as smells, sounds, or locations).

For all of the above mood disorders, there is treatment, support, and help. These are treatable, temporary issues; the sooner you let your doctor know, the sooner you can feel better.

Postpartum mood disorders can occur even if you have no history of anxiety, depression, or obsessive/compulsive thoughts or behaviors. You can take good care of yourself and your baby while still experiencing these symptoms. Sometimes, it can be hard to tell if what you're feeling is typical for the hormonal healing process. Ask yourself this question: Is this impacting my ability to care for myself and/or care for my baby? If so, discuss these feelings with your doctor. Do not feel embarrassed or guilty about your feelings; you are not alone. Reporting your symptoms to your doctor is the best thing you can do for yourself and your baby.

An extended version of the Parents' Emotional Well-Being in the First Year chapter is available with the purchase of *The Nuture Notebook for Mom and Baby* online at TheNurtureNotebook.com, at the "Bonus Extended Chapters" section, using the password BonusPEW*3. The extended version includes the information in paperback as well as the following: Paternal Postpartum Depression, Breast-Feeding and Weaning, Steps to Minimize the Intensity of Emotional Distress, Caring for Your Emotional Well-Being, Setting Boundaries, the Myth of Perfectionism, Taming Your Inner Critic, Grieving the Loss of Your Old Life, Practicing Mindfulness, and Awareness, Compassion, Acceptance.

Nutrition

Contributed by Alison Unger, MPH, RDN, LDN, CDCES and Danielle Kinney

Nutrition is a key component involved in leading a healthy lifestyle. As a parent, you will shape your baby's eating habits, both directly and indirectly. Being responsible for the demands involved in parenting, such as nutrition, can feel overwhelming. Even though you take steps to protect and care for your baby, you may still find yourself asking, and re-asking, questions that pertain to both your and your baby's diet. Rest assured that it is completely normal to feel anxious or unprepared. Our goal is to equip you with the tools needed to navigate through this first year with confidence, making mealtime a positive shared experience for both you and your family.

Imagine proper nutrition as a path on which you expand throughout different stages of your life. The correct balance of foods can support your and your baby's needs now and reduce the risk of some chronic diseases in the future.

Postnatal Nutrition

Your body changes both physically and emotionally during pregnancy and after you give birth. Your body expends a lot of energy simply keeping your baby safe and healthy during pregnancy. Now that your baby is born, your body will continue to change as you produce milk and go through the emotional ups and downs of extra stress. But, whether you carried your baby in your womb or not, remember your own nutrition is important too. Making healthy choices will replenish nutrient stores, heal the wounds of giving birth, assist your body with adequate nutrients for lactation, help you return to your prepregnancy weight, and facilitate caring for your baby with more focus and energy.

In addition, a healthy diet and hydration may alleviate some of the postpartum discomforts experienced by new moms such as constipation and hemorrhoids. Eating foods rich in fiber (such as vegetables, fruits, and whole grains) can help to prevent or relieve constipation when paired with plenty of water. This is essential for your body's storage of nutrients, such as calcium, iron, vitamin D, vitamin B_6, vitamin B_{12}, omega-3 fatty acids, and folate to be replenished during the postpartum period. Dietary supplements should never take the place of a balanced diet; however, you may want to consider a pre- or postnatal supplement or a daily multivitamin. Talk to your OB-GYN or RDN in detail about your pregnancy, postpartum nutrition for recommended lifestyle guidelines to follow, and postnatal vitamin options that can support lactation and postpartum deficiencies.

Make time to rest, sleep, and ask for help when you need it. Remember that it is okay to take a break if you are feeling physically and emotionally overwhelmed. Be sure to attend all of your postpartum checkups, even if you're feeling fine. Postpartum checkups are a great time to reassess your overall health.

Set reasonable goals, plan, and take steps to simplify your meals, so you can thrive and enjoy this time with your baby. Incorporate lean proteins, fruits, vegetables, whole grains, dairy, and healthy fats daily as part of a balanced diet.

When deciding to eat healthier, consider organizing your kitchen and pantry to provide easily accessible, healthy choices that will both motivate you and help you to carry over your lifestyle intentions.

Fluid Consumption

Drink plenty of unsweetened fluids to quench your thirst and stay hydrated. Light yellow or clear urine is indicative of being well hydrated. Add variety to your water intake by infusing it with fruit or vegetable slices. Unsweetened flavored seltzers and 100 percent fruit or vegetable juice in moderation are other beverage alternatives.

Breastfeeding mothers should drink an eight- to ten-ounce glass of water with meals and before or after each breast-feed. You may also drink moderate amounts of caffeinated beverages (i.e. one or two cups) unless your baby appears more restless after breastfeeding. Avoiding alcohol is the safest option for your baby.

NUTRITION FOR YOUR BABY

Whether you choose to breast- or formula-feed your baby, know that your experience will be unique to you and your family. You may have many questions including how much to feed your baby. At birth, your baby's stomach can hold approximately one to two teaspoons. This capacity increases to one to two ounces by approximately day 10. The volume or frequency of your baby's feedings will vary as your baby grows older. They are likely consuming enough breast milk or formula if they appear content after feeding and are steadily gaining weight after the first week of age. If your baby is breastfeeding, see the Breastfeeding chapter for "Signs Your Baby is Receiving Adequate Nutrition." It will be important to visit a pediatrician for routine checkups to monitor your baby's weight, height, and head circumference.

Your baby will continue to drink primarily breast milk or iron-fortified formula until they turn one year old. Due to its low iron content, cow's milk should not be used as an alternative under the age of 12 months. In addition, because your baby's digestive system is still developing, it may be unable to tolerate cow's milk protein in large amounts.

An extended version of the Nutrition chapter is available with the purchase of *The Nuture Notebook for Mom and Baby* online at TheNurtureNotebook .com, at the "Bonus Extended Chapters" section, using the password BonusNUT*2.

Breastfeeding

Contributed by Beth Kushner-Giovenco, RN, BSN, IBCLC (lactation consultant) and Jolie Maehrer, RN, BSN, IBCLC (lactation consultant)

Choosing a feeding method for your baby is a very important and personal decision. If you have decided to provide your baby with human milk, congratulations! Knowledge is power. The more information you have before beginning your breastfeeding journey, the more prepared you will feel. Take a class, join a breastfeeding support group, or talk to a friend who has had a positive breastfeeding experience. You will gain self-confidence and a support system that will help guide you through the early days and weeks of breastfeeding.

In its most recent policy statement, the American Academy of Pediatrics (AAP) reaffirmed its recommendation of "exclusive breastfeeding for about six months, followed by continued breastfeeding as complementary foods are introduced, with the continuation of breastfeeding for one year or longer as mutually desired by mom and infant." (AAP, 2012)

Breast milk contains all the required, perfectly matched nutrients to promote the proper growth and development of your baby. The benefits of breast milk are plentiful.

Benefits for Your Baby

- Digests easily
- Leads to fewer gastro-intestinal (GI), ear, respiratory infections
- Provides an abundance of antibodies
- Protects against sudden infant death syndrome
- Decreases the risk of obesity and type 1 and type 2 diabetes

Benefits for the Breastfeeding Mom

- Saves time and money
- Associated with weight loss
- Helps to shrink uterus back to prepregnancy size
- Lowers the risk of breast and uterine cancer
- Decreases the risk of type 2 diabetes

Breastfeeding is the next step in the birthing process. Think about it: Formula was not always available; babies are born to breastfeed, and your body has been preparing for the process of making milk for the past nine months. Your breasts start making breast milk, called colostrum, as early as 16 weeks of pregnancy. Some women may actually notice drops of fluid on the nipple during pregnancy. Your body will make and store colostrum prior to your baby's arrival, and this early milk will contain all the nutrients your baby will need for the first two to three days after delivery.

Colostrum is both high in protein and rich in antibodies that will help to protect your baby from infection. Yellow to clear in color, it loosens mucus in your baby's GI tract and serves as a laxative to eliminate your baby's meconium (first stools) more easily. Your baby does not need significant amounts of colostrum for feeding. In fact, a newborn baby's tummy is the size of a marble, and most babies consume only a few drops to one teaspoon of milk with each early feeding. Transitional milk follows the colostrum, and by days two to four, your mature milk will become plentiful. By the end of your baby's first week, their tummy, which has grown to the size of a golf ball, can hold one to one and a half ounces of milk.

Stimulation of the nipple during breastfeeding sends a message to your pituitary gland to release milk. A hormone called oxytocin is released by the pituitary, causing contraction of the cells surrounding the milk ducts. These contractions squeeze the milk down through the milk ducts and out of the nipple to your baby. This process is called the let-down or milk-ejection reflex. Oxytocin, sometimes called the "love hormone," helps mothers feel very relaxed and even sleepy when breastfeeding. If you do feel tired during feedings, get up and walk around, and have a drink and snack to wake up. Do not, however, feed your baby in your bed.

Oxytocin may cause you to feel thirsty, decrease postpartum bleeding, and facilitate the contraction of the uterus, helping it to return to its prepregnancy size. You may notice a tingling sensation in your breasts or a warmth during the let-down of milk. The hormone prolactin stimulates the breast to produce milk and is released from your pituitary gland.

Tips for Successful Breastfeeding After Delivery

When learning to breastfeed, remember that your baby must learn how to coordinate their sucking, swallowing, and breathing, all while adjusting to life outside of the womb. You are the only home your baby knows, and the most comfortable place for them is to be close to you either while nursing or cuddling, skin to skin, on your chest.

After delivery, request to hold your baby skin to skin as soon as possible. Skin-to-skin is when your baby lies on your bare chest, belly down, only in their diaper, with a blanket covering their back.

Skin-to-skin has a calming effect on your baby and helps to stabilize their vital signs and blood sugars. Because your baby will be in a quiet, alert state, lying skin to skin, they will likely breastfeed more easily, paving the way for future feedings. Skin-to-skin contact in the early days of your baby's life with both you and your partner offers invaluable bonding experiences.

Getting Started with Breastfeeding

If possible, offer breast milk in the first hour of life while your baby is most alert and interested in feeding. Because life doesn't always go as planned, you may encounter a medical indication for supplementing breastfeeding with expressed breast milk, donor milk, or formula. Your lactation team can help you navigate these potential challenges, teaching you how to protect your milk supply and breastfeeding relationship.

Remember that every baby is different, and not all experiences are the same. You are doing an amazing job, no matter how much milk you are able to provide for your baby.

If you have a low milk supply, even a few ounces of breast milk are beneficial. You may still be able to provide your baby with the benefits of breast milk and sustain breastfeeding for your intended duration. So, if breastfeeding is your goal, consult with your lactation specialist. They will be able to advise you about how to properly and safely continue your personal breastfeeding journey.

In the early weeks, rest as much as you can, limit your visitors, accept help around the house, stay hydrated, and eat a balanced diet.

Feed your baby on demand at least eight to twelve times per day. Look for your baby's early hunger cues to help guide you instead of the clock. These cues include bringing their fists to their mouth, sucking on their hands, smacking their lips, opening their mouths, turning their head and looking for your breast, actively moving, or fidgeting. Crying is a late cue, so try to catch your baby's early signs of hunger. If your baby is not waking frequently, have a discussion with your lactation team to find what works best; you may need to wake them to ensure they are receiving enough calories and nutrients. Often, skin-to-skin contact and gentle rousing are enough to interest your baby in nursing.

Feeding frequently based on your baby's cues will enable you to produce a plentiful milk supply. Your body's milk production is dependent on supply and demand, and the more milk that is removed from your breast, the more milk your breasts will produce. This minimizes the risk of engorgement as well. When your baby empties your breast, your body knows to make more.

Let your baby decide how long to breastfeed on each breast. Offer the first breast until your baby is finished. You will know they're done when your baby either pulls off your breast, falls asleep, or has a fluttery-type comfort suck. You can then burp your baby and offer the second side, again, for as long as the baby wants. If your baby does not want the second side, start on that side at the next feeding. Again, look to your baby to guide you.

Ask for help with proper positioning and latching if you are struggling. The way to hold your baby during breastfeeding and the latching process may seem overwhelming at first, but they will become more natural with practice. Be patient with yourself, and keep your resource phone numbers (i.e., board-certified lactation consultant and an experienced breastfeeding mother) on hand for questions and concerns. Every new mom will benefit from some form of support in the days following delivery.

Signs Your Baby Is Receiving Adequate Nutrition

- Feeding eight to twelve times per day
- Apparent satisfaction after feeding and self-detaches
- Swallows are heard during feedings
- Breasts feel softer after feeding
- Consistent weight gain once milk is plentiful of three-fourths to one ounce per day
- Return to birth weight by two weeks of age
- Adequate urine (i.e., day one: one wet diaper, day three: three wet diapers, one week and after six wet diapers per day)
- Adequate bowel movements (Three to four bowel movements per day. Initially, the stool will be black and tarry meconium but will change to a mustard color by day four or five.)

Menstrual Cycle

If you are not breastfeeding, your first menses are likely to return by six to eight weeks postpartum. However, the range for breastfeeding mothers is much greater. Your menses may return a couple of weeks after delivery or not until after weaning, which may be 18 months or longer. Most breastfeeding moms will not get their menses during the first six months if they are exclusively breastfeeding.

An extended version of the Breastfeeding chapter is available with the purchase of *The Nuture Notebook for Mom and Baby* online at TheNurtureNotebook.com, at the "Bonus Extended Chapters" section, using the password BonusBRE*4.

One Month Old

MOMMY MOVEMENTS

Welcome to the classic version of "fake it till you make it." The babymoon is wearing off as you are trying to keep up with your busy life, with little to no sleep. Between fatigue and mommy brain, it is normal to feel as if it takes maximum effort to get out of bed in the morning, let alone make any attempt to exercise. You might need a reminder that what you think about, you bring about. Whatever your story, set your mind. You have passed the 30-day mark; you've got this! Now press "play" on your most upbeat playlist and declare "I am energized," as you start easing back into cardiovascular activity.

POSTNATAL CARDIOVASCULAR ACTIVITY

The benefits of moving your body go beyond the physical benefits of losing weight and increasing muscle tone. Cardiovascular (or aerobic) activity is key to improving confidence, emotional health, digestion, sleep quality, and coordination and to boost your immune system. One of the best side effects of cardio exercise is the release of endorphins. These special, seemingly magical hormones are the best antidote to stress and/or a bad mood. Simply put, regular cardiovascular exercise will make you a better version of you, for yourself and your baby.

Find a cardiovascular activity that your body feels comfortable performing and that brings you joy, so you will be more likely to stick with it. Walking, biking, swimming, or even light dancing are some examples of post-pregnancy cardiovascular activities.

Start with 10 minutes of cardiovascular activity three days a week and build up to five days a week. Once you are able to complete the cardiovascular activity without being out of breath, add five minutes. Your goal is to increase your cardiovascular activity to 30 minutes per day, three to five days per week.

Remember, you have plenty of time to get back to an exercise routine, so pace yourself. Do not get anxious, stuck on frequency, or feel guilty and defeated if you skip a day. Forgive yourself quickly and continue to progress forward. Exercise should not add to your stress; it should help relieve it. Set small goals to get your body used to moving again and remember the importance of practicing self-care by incorporating you time into your day.

Monitor yourself during cardiovascular exercise to keep on track safely. You can use a tool called the rate of perceived exertion (RPE) scale to rate your physical sensations and determine how hard you are working and how you are feeling while you are exercising.

Rate of Perceived Exertion (RPE) Using the Modified Borg Scale

The following scale will help you to rate your physical sensation and determine how hard you work and how you feel while you are exercising. The maximal exercise in pregnancy and postpartum should occur at an RPE of three to six, which is equal to 50 to 80 percent of aerobic capacity (moderate intensity).

Months Postpartum	Rate of Perceived Exertion
Birth to Two Months	**One RPE** You might be able to tolerate and sustain very, very easy intensity activities, light physical activities that involve very, very little exertion levels, allowing you to breathe normally/very lightly, such as light laundry. **Two RPE** You might be able to engage in very easy intensity activities, light warm-up, or cardio activities, such as walking slowly through your neighborhood, that involve only very little exertion and light breathing. Your maximum heart rate (MHR) should stay at or below 60 beats per minute (BPM).
Two to Four Months	**Three RPE** You might be able to tolerate and maintain easy intensity activities in longer intervals involving little exertion, where your breathing is elevated but comfortable and you recover easily, such as a brisk walk for a light cardio workout. Your MHR should stay below 60 BPM.
Four to Six Months Complete numerical RPE progression at your pace. Consider involving a specialist trained in postpartum recovery at this time.	**Three RPE** You might need to stay at three RPE. (See above.) Only when you are ready and cleared by your doctor should you increase your activity level. **Four RPE** You might start to work back up to activities of moderate intensity with recovery intervals between easy steady cardio states, where you can hold a conversation but have a noticeably quicker breathing pattern. You might start to feel as if you can work out again for longer spurts of time. Your MHR should be between 60 and 65 BPM. **Five RPE** You might be able to maintain a steady aerobic state comfortably during somewhat harder intensity activities while holding short conversations and demonstrating heaving breathing. You might feel as if you are getting in a good workout and might be able to stick with it for an hour. Your MHR should stay below 70 BPM. **Six RPE** You might be able to participate in harder intensity activities. They are challenging to maintain a steady cardio state. Your breathing is likely very heavy, and you can speak in some sentences. You feel as if you are getting a good workout and can maintain it for about 30 to 40 minutes. This is not recommended unless you are used to competing at a higher level. Your MHR should stay below 75 BPM.

From birth to two months postpartum, you might be able to tolerate and sustain very, very easy intensity activities and light physical activities that involve very, very little exertion, allowing you to breathe normally/very lightly, for example doing light laundry). This level of activity is a one out of 10 on the RPE scale.

You might be able to engage in very easy intensity activities and light warm-up or cardio activities, such as walking slowly through your neighborhood, that involve only very little exertion and light breathing. This level activity is a two out of 10 on the RPE scale.

Most new moms have an OB-GYN appointment between four and six weeks postpartum. That's a great time to talk about exercise. When you feel ready for and are cleared by your doctor to increase your exercising to moderate intensity, you might benefit from seeking the guidance of specialists trained and educated in core and pelvic postpartum recovery to prevent future injury or dysfunction, such as urinary incontinence and pelvic organ prolapse.

Don't push yourself; there is no need to rush. If getting back to moderate intensity is your goal, you will get there. There is no reward for pushing to get yourself there sooner than your body is ready and willing to.

BABY'S DEVELOPMENT

You survived the first four weeks, and you are committed to maximizing the health and wellness of both you and your baby. Your baby's personality might start to peek through this month. They are more alert now, and their vocalizations might vary slightly as they continue to attempt to communicate with you. Remember, every baby develops at their own pace.

Motor Development

At one month old, your baby is relaxing out of the fetal position (called physiological flexion), allowing their arms and legs to begin to extend, improving their range of motion and mobility. Your baby appears more active, and their nerves continue to constantly communicate with their brain, developing stronger neural pathways with age and practice. These connections send messages to their brain even more rapidly as their gross motor skills develop at a steady pace. Your baby's movements are random and symmetrical; they move both arms or legs at the same time, appearing uncoordinated. As your baby continues to grow and develop, these irregular movements become more controlled and refined. They might even move in response to seeing a toy.

Your baby is getting stronger, which enables them to turn their head to each side, maintain control of their head in the midline (middle, front of your baby) briefly, and even start to bring their hands to the middle of their body, all while lying on their back.

While your baby is on their tummy, they are able to lift their head momentarily, extending their neck to 45 degrees, and turn their head to either side, allowing their ear instead of their cheek to rest on the surface. By turning their head, they allow their nose to be to the side, protecting their airway.

Last month, when your baby was on their tummy, their weight was displaced forward toward their head because their knees were bent under them. In contrast, this month their legs are more likely extended behind with their thighs resting on the supporting surface because the weight has shifted off of their head and behind their pelvis and thighs. This head-to-pelvis weight shift is important in development because it will assist your baby as they push up through their forearms and hands in preparation for sitting and crawling.

Overall, your baby holds their head to both sides now more consistently rather than favoring one side. You should see this in all positions, including in their car seat, bouncer, and crib.

All of these changes encourage your baby to be more alert, noticing their environment and the people in it more, motivating them to lift and move their head, and promoting their future eye-hand coordination.

Note: When lying on their back your baby is not able to lift their head up when they are lifted from a surface upon which they are lying. Due to this lack of head control (head lag), you must continue to support their head and neck when they are being lifted and held. Do not pull up on their arms.

Visual Development

Visual development is focused around your baby making more sustained eye contact with you, so as their visual system gets stronger, so does your bond. Their eyes have started to work together, and at around five weeks, you should notice that their eyes are aligned most of the time. Until now, your baby might have been focusing mostly on the outer portions of your face, but, now they might begin to look at other facial features like your mouth and hairline and might even make eye contact. As their eyes develop and their vision continues to improve, they might follow moving objects with their eyes and even coordinate their eyes together inwardly to look at nearby objects (which is called convergence).

Your baby's color vision is rapidly developing, and, they might be able to distinguish additional colors.

Cognitive Development

Your baby's cognition continues to develop through their sensory experiences, and this new awakening helps them start to understand some basic patterns of their body and surroundings. Your baby might show an interest in an object or person for up to 60 seconds. They continue to respond to your voice and might attend to your voice for up to 30 seconds, which strengthens your bond because they appear to be listening to you more. This increased attention allows you to engage your baby's interest while you are holding them, smiling, and singing to them. All the sensory input you provide them will help expand upon their cognitive progression and those rich connections in their brain. As your baby starts to anticipate something, they may even show excitement, which makes holding and talking with your baby more fun. You can start to build anticipation and excitement for them with your words and body language.

Social-Emotional Development

Socially and emotionally, your baby will continue to calm when cuddled, communicate with you and gain your attention through crying. If they are already sharing reactionary, reflexive smiles, you might now see their first social smile, which is voluntary.

Self-Care Development

Every baby has different sleeping patterns, possibly sleeping up to four to 10 hours at a stretch now. Your baby will likely nap often but cry less when they are awake. However, it is typical for your baby to cry for approximately 90 minutes per day, often during the evening hours in the first three months.

Change your baby's environment during the "witching hour," that time in the evening when your baby might be fussy due to sensory overload. Consider taking your baby out into the fresh air, walking around to different rooms, or even undressing them if they are overheated.

At this stage of your baby's development, they develop a normal pattern of sucking, swallowing, and breathing while they are drinking, and their efficiency for feeding improves.

Speech and Language Development

Remember that speech and language development are broken down into two separate abilities: expressive and receptive language. Receptive language refers to your baby's ability to hear and understand the meaning of words. Expressive language refers to your baby's ability to respond verbally.

At this age, your baby might alter the length, volume, and pitch of their cries, make sucking sounds for the first time to express themselves. It is important that you respond to them whenever they attempt to communicate with you, whether their form of communication is crying or smiling. When your baby begins to make sounds, imitate the sounds back to them. In these moments, you are teaching them about back-and-forth conversation and reinforcing that sounds have meaning, enabling your baby to start to understand that their attempts to communicate are effective and are not arbitrary.

Have you caught yourself speaking to your baby, and maybe even a pet, in a sing-song voice, exhibiting hyper-articulation (over-enunciating sounds) and slow repetition? This is called "parentese." It is instinctual,

Note: Parentese should not be confused with "baby talk," which are silly nonsense words. For example, baby talk sounds like this, "Does baby-waby want a bottle-waddle?" Whereas, parentese sounds like this, "Does baaaby want a booottle?" Baby talk does not promote the understanding of the language as parentese does.

and it is the earliest language a baby hears. Research suggests that parentese promotes joint attention (which is when you and your baby are both paying attention to the same thing, jointly) and increases your baby's understanding of language. A study at McGill University found that babies will listen to the high-pitch sounds of parentese 40 percent longer than "regular" speech patterns.

The building blocks of language start early. Using parentese will help your baby hear the beginnings and endings of words. By speaking slowly and with exaggerated tones of voice and elongated vowels (which is also called intonation), parentese helps your baby decode the language you are speaking.

Developmental Play

An increase in sustained eye contact allows increased engagement in activities, such as singing, talking, reading, and playing, all of which help your baby encode language. This sets the stage for bonding, attention span, memory, language, social communication (pragmatics), and literacy for the future. Remember, when your baby makes sounds, encourage eye contact and imitate the sounds back. This teaches your child about the back-and-forth of conversation and reinforces the sounds.

Every baby is unique, and you know your baby best, so carry over the activities you want from month to month, depending on your baby's interests, preferences, and abilities.

PLAY POSITIONS

Starting this month, you will notice the term "play positions" being used more. Play positions start to become increasingly important as your baby gets older. Varying your baby's position helps them become more comfortable with conquering movement against gravity and stimulates their balance center, promoting global gross motor development.

These changing play positions allow your baby's senses to experience the world in different ways, promoting stronger sensorimotor development—your baby's sensory and motor interactions with the world. It is believed that through sensorimotor interactions cognitive growth occurs. If your baby is placed in a stationary position, such as in a car seat or bouncer all day, they will not experience the various positions required for all of their senses to interact fully with the world. Conversely, if they are given the opportunity to explore the world in various play positions, their body will experience the world differently and uniquely, and their development will be more enriched.

Supervised Tummy Time Play Position

Tummy time is one of the most important skills your baby will develop in early infancy. It is not uncommon for your baby to dislike tummy time at first, but stick with it. They will eventually grow to enjoy this position as they begin to see their world more clearly. Remember: Optimal tummy time starts with your baby on a firm surface on their back, slowly rolling them to their side (alternating sides each time) and then their tummy.

Tummy time should be practiced multiple times throughout your day (e.g. increase your baby's opportunity for tummy time from last months recommended two to three times daily to three to four times daily now, for a total of at least 30 to 60 minutes each day in daily increments). Tummy time helps to improve upon their upper-body strength for future crawling and also assists in the integration of primitive reflexes. Remember to ensure that your baby's face is lifted off the surface or positioned to the side to promote proper breathing and avoid airway obstruction.

One variation is reclined tummy time. This alternative position requires less strength because it reduces their position against the natural weight of gravity. Place your baby on their forearms with their elbows bent so that their arms are tucked under their body for the optimal position. It might be a difficult position at this age; just try your best.

You can also do tummy time when you are sitting upright. Hold your baby facing you so they can push off to see you. Engage your baby's interest by holding them, smiling, and singing to them.

Build tummy time into your daily routine (i.e. after diaper change, before feeding, when they wake up, before they go to bed) to increase the likelihood of your ability to carry this critical activity over.

Be creative and think of different safe ways to promote this position. If you notice your baby has trouble maintaining tummy time, is excessively fussy, or spits up a lot during or after tummy time, consult your baby's pediatrician.

Rocking and Rolling

Rhythmic movement while in tummy time provides gentle weight bearing through various parts of your baby's body. Here are a couple of ways to do this.

Either recline or lie down, placing your baby on your chest with their elbows bent and propped on their forearms. Rock your body slowly from side to side. Put on some music or simply let your baby listen to your heartbeat while they are in this position.

Grab an exercise ball. Position it safely between your legs to secure it and place your baby on top of the ball, holding them along their torso. An exercise ball provides great proprioceptive feedback, gentle pressure through the joints of your baby's body, as well as vestibular experiences, balance, and movement exploration. An exercise ball can be used for many future exercises as your baby gets older, too.

Gently rock your baby from side to side. A rocking motion helps stimulate their balance system, calm their nervous system, and prepare them for whole-body movement.

Don't have an exercise ball? Pull out a firm pillow and place it on your lap or somewhere you can safely play with your baby and complete this same activity.

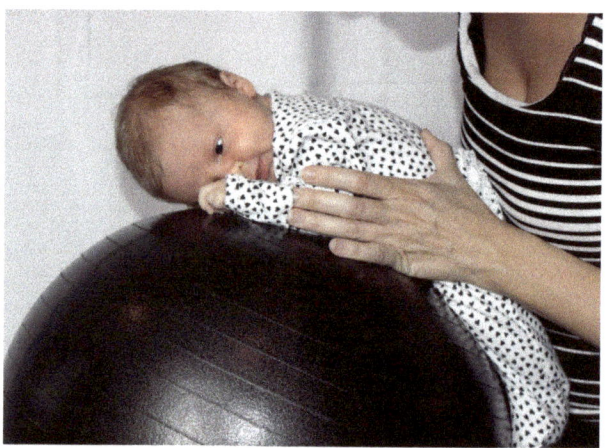

Back Play Position

In this play position, your baby gets to experience the nature of gravity gently applying pressure on their body and enabling relaxation and muscle elongation. Placing your baby on their back on a blanket or play mat allows them to turn their head to either side and explore their environment visually, as well as to move their extremities against gravity. Your hands will be free, enabling you to dangle a soft object above them in all planes.

Note: Positioning your baby in a new corner of the crib once a week can change where they look. Consequently, this practice will alter where pressure occurs on the back of their head, promoting a rounder shape skull and avoiding flat spots (which is also called plagiocephaly).

Traction Pulls

Traction to your baby's jaw is a great activity to work on jaw strength, which is needed for your baby to sustain sucking and promote prolonged latch on the pacifier. The ability to maintain a latch enables your baby to self-soothe instead of accidentally pushing the pacifier out, especially at night. Traction also develops the oral-motor skills crucial for future chewing and talking.

Note: Always remember to check pacifiers and bottle tips for rips. Immediately throw them away if you see a rip because this can pose a choking hazard.

If your baby sucks on a pacifier or bottle, gently tugging on it outwardly without breaking the seal will help work on this. Do these three to five times each feed, with a pacifier after breastfeeding or with a bottle during bottle-feeding.

Say and Sway

Reinforce the activities you started last month, such as reading, singing, talking, and sound play. Each month, your baby will engage differently with the common activities you have carried over. For example, last month you swayed your head while singing to your baby, understanding that they were unable to track you visually and that you were simply trying to gain and sustain some eye contact. This month, when you sway your head slowly from side to side, you are doing so with the intention of encouraging your baby to track you, which means to follow visually.

Hands Apart and Together

It is important for your baby to explore their environment through their hands. For this reason, keep their nails trimmed to avoid scratching themselves and limit the use of protective mitts to only when necessary.

Encouraging your baby to bring their hands to midline and then to their mouth is a calming position that promotes body awareness. Lay your baby on your lap on their back to allow visual interaction with you. Bilateral integration, such as bringing your baby's hands together to engage in an activity, is a critical milestone needed to function well throughout life. Add a toy that makes noise, has textures, vibrates, or lights up to encourage visual attention to task during this activity. Gently push your

baby's hands together on the toy in midline.

Facilitate midline play by cupping your hands over your baby's and bringing them together if needed. Incorporate this into your daily routine by holding their hands around your breast while they nurse or around a bottle while they drink from it.

Back Rolling

Secure an exercise ball or pillow between your legs. Place your baby on their back and gently rock them from side to side, forward, backward, clockwise, and counter-clockwise.

A Splash of Color

Start adding contrasting colors such as red to your baby's toy and book collection. Your baby will now use the visual skill of convergence, which allows their eyes to work together and focus on objects moving close and far away. This skill is an essential milestone for future reading and handwriting progress.

Hold a high-contrast toy eight inches away from your baby's face and move it slowly throughout the following sequence: Start parallel to their left ear and move the toy in an arch over to their right side, stopping at their midline on the way. Move the toy closer to your baby's nose, then back eight inches. See if your baby brings their eyes inward toward their nose, converging, to follow it. Respond to your baby's gaze by smiling and talking to them.

© Jennifer Bainbridge

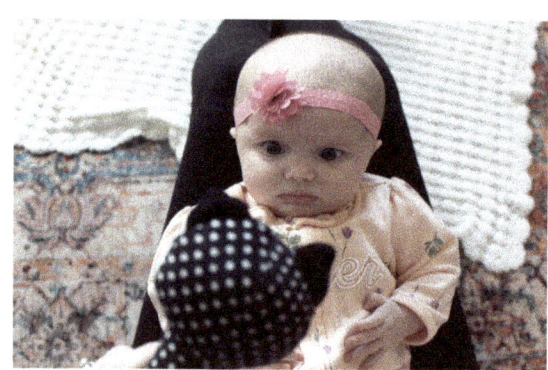

© Jennifer Bainbridge

Spontaneous Swat

While your baby is on their back playing, you might notice that they engage with a toy by swatting at it. Encourage them by dangling a sound-producing toy above their head. Provide your baby with adequate time to respond to the toy, allowing their eyes and brain to process the information. Next, touch the toy to their hand and then slowly move it away to see if they will reach for it. If your baby does not respond by moving their hand, then offer hand-over-hand help.

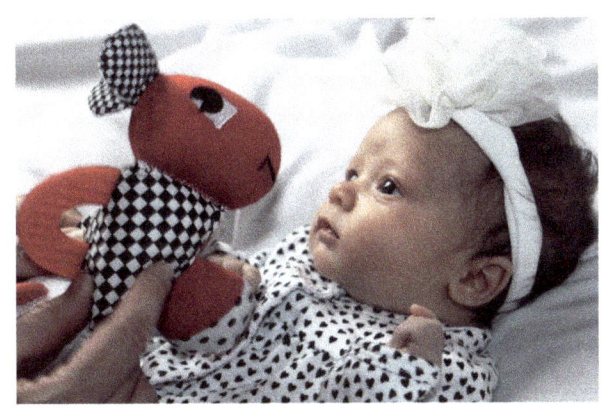

To use the hand-over-hand technique, place your hand on your baby's hand to help them to complete an activity. Gently hold their hand and guide them through the motion of reaching for the toy, alternating hands.

Often parents use their dominant hand to do hand-over-hand. Although that strategy is a good way to start, you must understand that you don't know which side will be your baby's dominant side. Remember to use both sides of their body during activities.

Some babies don't like the gentle guidance of hand-over-hand. If that's the case with your baby, here are a couple tips. Gently tap a toy on their hand and then place it back down in their line of vision. Tap your baby behind the elbow to bring their forearm/hand into their visual field to encourage them to reach for the toy. Gently squeeze their upper arm, elbow, forearm, and hand to bring awareness to their arm to encourage them to reach for the toy.

Ultimately, the goal is spontaneous movement that enables your baby to learn how their body interacts with the world, so do not force anything. Give your baby frequent opportunities, and they will eventually accidentally touch the toy. This spontaneous touch helps produce future intentional reach and grasp.

Note: Every baby processes information from their environment differently, requiring varying amounts of wait time.

What is wait time? Wait time is when you pause allowing time for your baby to naturally respond. It is a great tool for keeping your baby involved. Take the game peekaboo as an example. Putting a toy under a blanket and pulling it off over and over again is not very effective repetitively. You want your baby involved, so you must interact directly with them and observe them. When you complete the peekaboo sequence, before pulling the blanket off, observe and wait for your baby's anticipation of the blanket's removal. Keep them engaged. Give them just enough time to process what you are asking, whether it is 10 seconds or 30 seconds, and then react.

Finger Strengthening

Your baby's little hands are going to become so skilled over this first year. This exercise will strengthen their hands and aid in their future fine motor abilities, which are skills requiring the use of the smaller body parts such as fingers.

Place your finger on the palm of your baby's hand and allow your baby to reflexively close their hand around your finger, which is called the palmar grasp reflex. This reflex is present at birth and typically goes away between three and six months as evidenced by baby being able to purposefully and voluntarily release objects.

Allow your baby to grasp your finger. Give gentle tugs on your baby's fingers when the palmar grasp reflex is engaged. Move your fingers out against theirs in gentle tugs. Use the same amount of pressure that you would use to squeeze a fruit to test if it is ripe. This act provides input to help raise your baby's awareness of their hands and fingers. The key word is gentle.

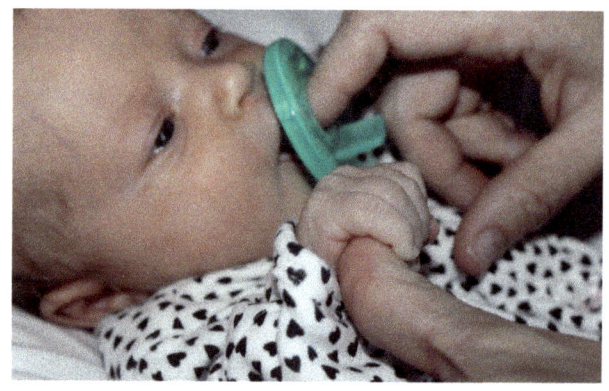

There is no need to pry your baby's fingers open when playing with them. In fact, it can cause hyperextension of their fingers, which is when a joint extends or stretches further than normal.

Your baby does not yet understand how to open their hands. When you are ready for your baby to release your finger, stroke the back of their hand until they release their grip. Another technique for opening your baby's hand is to gently bend their wrist (palm toward forearm). This technique comes in hand when your baby accidentially grasps a handful of hair. This technique helps their body to communicate to their brain that it is time to open their hands.

While you are already playing with your baby's hands, take time to rub them together.

Gently rub one hand over, under, apart, and together against the other hand in order to promote body awareness and the eventual coordination of their hands.

Rattle Things Up

In early development, your baby's main way of learning is through their hands and eyes. Stroking the back of your baby's hand to allow for the release of objects, as discussed previously, is helpful when introducing toys such as rattles. Pick a rattle that is the appropriate size for your baby. Every baby's hand size is different, and some rattle handles might be too big for your baby's little hand. If you are rattle-shopping without your baby, place each of your fingers, one at a time, in your baby's hand to see which they can most easily grasp to identify the best rattle handle size.

Once you have found the best rattle for your

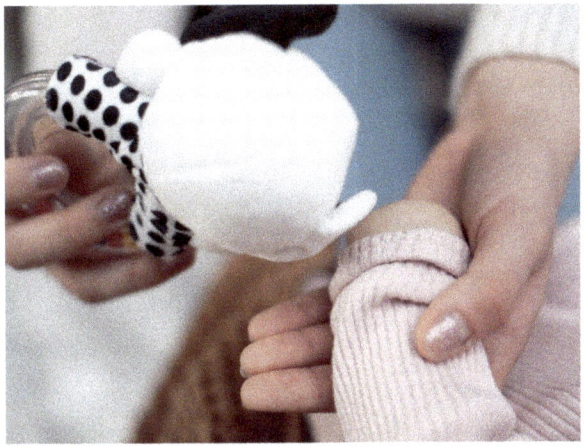

baby, dangle it for them to see and then swipe the back of their hand with the toy. Their hand will open to engage with the rattle.

Note: The ends of the rattle should be at least two inches in diameter to prevent choking. Inspect all rattles for sharp parts, strong seams, and pieces that could fall off and become a choking hazard. High-contrast rattles are best to enhance visual development during this stage. Child Choking Tube testers (used to test small objects size safety) are available online, as well as life vac kits (used to remove small objects from airway if choking).

Texture Play

Provide your baby with various textures and input to both the front and back parts of their hands, arms, back, legs, and feet throughout the day in all play positions. Bath time is an especially great time to build texture play into your baby's routine. Think of all the textures to which they are exposed during a bath: washcloths and sponges, soap, water, and tub toys.

While your baby enjoys the warmth of the water, gently splash their hands and feet up and down. Let them explore the softness of the towel. Provide more texture-enriched experience by gently massaging fragrance-free baby lotion onto their skin if they are able to tolerate it. Because your baby likely puts their hands into their mouth, avoid massaging lotion into their hands.

Gently stroking the back of your baby's hand with other safe textures, such as a fan-style paintbrush, provides a variety of sensory experiences.

Foot Press

Your baby's feet also benefit from being exposed to different textures and gentle pressure. Remove your baby's shoes, socks, and even pants. Because their legs are bare during this time, you might notice that they kick, reach, grab, and explore their legs and feet more.

Touch your baby's feet together on the bottoms and sides. By rubbing their feet together, you provide tactile stimulation. In other words, you alert their sensation of touch and bring their awareness to their feet as a part of their body. This may help to decrease any sensitivity they have to touch or varied textures.

This activity also helps your baby to develop the body awareness needed for future

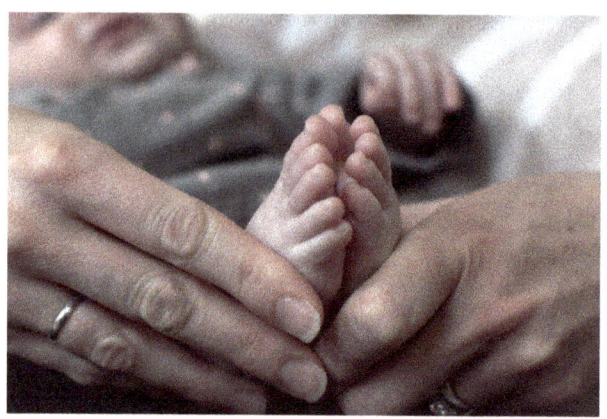

© Jennifer Bainbridge

development in bringing their hands to their feet and their feet to their mouth. It also encourages downward visual gaze, flexibility in their legs, and awareness of their midline.

An extended version of the Nutrition chapter is available with the purchase of *The Nuture Notebook for Mom and Baby* online at TheNurtureNotebook.com, at the "Bonus Extended Chapters" section, using the password BonusYBH*1.

One Month Old

Fill in the answers to reflect on the past month and to track.

How do you feel?

_____

_____

What exercises did you work on?

_____

_____

What is your baby doing now?

_____

_____

What was your baby's favorite activity this month?

_____

_____

What questions do you have for your ob-gyn and your baby's pediatrician?

_____

_____

Notes:

_____

_____

_____

_____

Two Months Old

MOMMY MOVEMENTS

Just when you think your baby is on a schedule, it changes. As you try to get back to some semblance of normalcy, you likely feel as if you have to get stuff done! Instead of enjoying moments when you felt like days blended together in the first two months, you might now feel like your time is running out and contemplating solutions for how you can do more in less time.

The truth is: The answer is actually relatively simple. Be present. Stop worrying about the to-do list, how things should look, or even potentially running around until you feel like you are going to collapse. Take your baby in your arms and look at them. Say to yourself "I am present" as you breathe in your baby's scent, and really look at their eyes, nose, fingers, and toes. No matter what, you don't get today back. So whether it is a nailed-it day or a just-get-by day, it is a good day. Practice being present in various activities throughout your day whether it is during playtime with your baby or the following addition to your postnatal recovery routine.

Postnatal Abdominal Foundation

As you learn the foundations of the abdominal and core workout, remember the importance of performing it correctly before advancing on to further core exercises. You will bring this sequence into all abdominal and core work if and when your body is ready. The foundational abdominal work will also serve as a gauge to bring recognition and awareness of your body's signals. If you cannot sustain this sequence during exercise, then pause and reassess your current needs, respecting your body until you are ready and able to move forward safely and correctly.

Now where are those abdominals? We are going to find them by breathing and feeling. There are no crunches here; in fact, you might be pleased to know they are not recommended by most pelvic floor physical therapists. The goal here is to make sure the abdominal muscles (the rectus abdominis [RA] and transversus abdominis [TA]) start to remember how they worked before you were pregnant. When your muscles stretched into a round basketball, the way they worked changed. The muscles that usually are supportive muscles, called the obliques, started to work harder and dominated some movements. This muscle pattern adjustment is required to support your core during pregnancy. However, these muscle pattern changes must return to their pre-pregnancy sequence for an optimal recovery and safe return to activity, after pregnancy. Therein lies the importance of retraining your abdominal muscle patterns.

This analogy might help: After a cast is removed from a broken leg, it is typical to continue to limp or favor your injured leg unconsciously because your body learned a new muscle pattern to move efficiently and safely during the recovery period. By bringing awareness to your new muscle pattern, you are able to retrain your body back to heel-to-toe walking or walking without a limp.

The same muscle pattern retraining concept applies to your body after delivering your baby. For this reason, there are two important factors in the recovery of your core. First, you must give your body time to heal after all of the stretching and changing. Second, you need to remind your body how it worked before pregnancy, remembering how to efficiently and safely move to set your body up for a successful recovery and wellness routine. Laying the foundation of your abdominal work is critical to prevent injury, respect your body, and work on mastery and sustainability of the deep core foundational sequence to restore your body.

Deep Core Foundational Sequence Prerequisites

First, practice the Diaphragmatic Breathing and Pelvic Floor Contraction (PFC) exercises you've learned previously and the combination of the two.

Diaphragmatic Breathing: Relax your belly muscles, relax your pelvic floor muscles, and take a deep breath in, expanding your whole ribcage. Exhale out slowly.

PFCs: As you exhale, close your vaginal and rectal openings and lightly pull up and inward toward your core.

Now remember the muscle you are able to palpate slightly above your pubic bone during pelvic floor contractions? That's your transversus abdominis (TA) waking up. The TA and the pelvic floor work together, and you want to reactivate this muscle team. Follow the quick oblique and TA muscle check-in on the next page to make sure you are correctly activating your TA.

Obliques Check-In

Place your hands on your hip points, which are the bones on either side of your belly button. Slide your fingers slightly off the bones down to the soft tissue just inside of your hip points and tighten your lower belly muscles as if you are trying to fit into a tight pair of pants. Did you feel something pop up against your fingers when you did that? Those are your obliques. Your obliques

are big helper muscles, but right now you need them to rest while you retrain your TA.

Transversus Abdominis Check-in

Keep one hand on the soft spot inside your hip point and place your other hand back above your pubic bone. Take a deep breath in and feel your belly rise and rib cage expand. Exhale, close, and lift your pelvic floor to wake up your TA muscle. If you feel a pop up near your hip point, then you are doing it incorrectly because you are using your obliques. Try again. When you feel a small movement near your pubic bone, you are doing it correctly and activating your TA muscle.

Once you have found your TA muscles, you have identified the foundational muscle groups necessary for all abdominal muscle and core strength. Your TA muscles set your pace and your core in proper alignment, so the rest of your body works in an efficient way. The downfall is that if you do not retrain your TA, you may be setting yourself up for incontinence, sacroiliac (SI) joint pain/dysfunction (like sciatica), hip pain and injuries, back pain, and the worst of all evils for some women: the never-disappearing muffin top.

So let's get to it and retrain your TA muscle.

Deep Core Foundational Sequence

Complete these exercises in either a seated position with your feet on the floor or lying down with your knees and feet bent.

Place your hand slightly above your pubic bone on your TA muscle.

Complete one set, five cycles of:

- Diaphragmatic Breathing: Relax your belly muscles, relax your pelvic floor muscles and take a deep breath in, expanding your whole ribcage. Exhale out slowly.

- PFCs: As you exhale, close vaginal and rectal openings and lightly pull up and inward toward your core.

Hold pelvic floor contraction for five seconds as you exhale. Relax for 10 seconds in between each repetition.

Complete one set, five cycles of Diaphragmatic Breathing with Pelvic Floor and TA Engagement together (contracting for five seconds) on exhale. When imagining your TA muscle, it might help to think "zip up" for zipping up tight pants.

Here are some quick tips.

- Relaxing the pelvic floor is as important as the contraction.

- Keep focusing on your TA muscles and trying to isolate them alone on your exhale, keeping your obliques quiet.

- Build exercises into your typical daily routine, such as during your baby's tummy time or right after you lay them down for a nap.

- Aim to complete five repetitions three times a day—morning, mid-day, and evening—for optimal results and to check in and reset your body throughout your day.

BABY'S DEVELOPMENT

Your baby's personality is shining through more and more each day! This month, your baby will flash that social smile, relax with your cuddles, and cry for your attention.

Motor Development

Your baby's movements are continuing to become more controlled, and they are getting stronger by the minute. When your baby is on their tummy, their elbows are under their shoulders, and they are able to prop on their forearms for short periods. This increased ability to prop themselves effectively on forearms allows them to lift their head and turn it from side to side with more ease to visually explore their environment. When turning their head to look at a toy, they may accidentally roll off their belly.

Your baby requires support to maintain sitting, but they are gaining better head control. They are able to hold their head up for progressively longer periods of time.

While lying on their back, your baby keeps

their head in midline, kicks with both legs at the same time and alternatingly, and kicks against a support surface. Their movements are starting to become more controlled and stronger in manner. Your baby is able to bring their hands to their body and mouth more easily. All of these developmental strengths help increase your baby's ability to start to reach, grasp, and hold items.

Visual Development

Your baby's visual development is strengthened as all of their motor skills are evolving because they are stronger, more controlled, and more upright, allowing them to see more of their environment.

Your baby will now be using their eyes more than ever such as making increasing amounts of eye contact with you. Practice making and maintaining their eye contact all day whenever you interact with them. Your baby can now look up and down. They are also able to converge, or bring their eyes together, to look at objects that come close to their face. Your baby will also begin to track objects and toys moving in every direction.

By the end of this month, your baby's eyes will become more coordinated as they will begin to reach out and touch objects. Your baby's color preferences might start to change also as their world is starting to become full of color. Overall, these developmental gains in vision are important for both their visual and social development.

Cognitive Development

Your baby's cognitive development works together with their visual and motor development. Their advances in visual development improve their interactions with caregivers and their abilities to explore and learn in their environment, understanding that things exist beyond what is in front of their face. You might notice improvements in areas such as foot, hand, and eye control, as well as changes in the volume of their voice and laughter.

Your baby is making substantial cognitive gains throughout this first year, and they might experience irritability during periods of cognitive growth. Fussiness is your baby's way of expressing their fears and worries. Cuddle them frequently. You cannot spoil them at this age.

Social-Emotional Development

Between now and six months old, you will start to identify what your baby's different cries mean because they won't typically cry about everything anymore. If your baby is colicky, relief may be in sight. Colicky crying often starts to decrease between now and month six. Crying may sometimes be an indication of stomach irritability, either because of gas or a potential food allergy. If your baby is excessively fussy, be sure to mention that to your baby's pediatrician and keep a food diary of what you eat if you are nursing, including your baby's response within 30 minutes to several hours after each feeding. If you are formula-feeding, take note of the base of your baby's formula, milk or soy, because your baby might have sensitivities to their formula base.

Self-Care Development

With increased awareness of their hands, your baby becomes more interested in putting them in their mouth. This hand-to-mouth engagement teaches them that objects are multidimensional and will help them with future self-feeding.

This month your baby's sucking, swallowing, and breathing become more rhythmic and coordinated during feeding.

Your baby might also be continuing to take longer naps and overall sleeping longer—four to 10 hours at a time.

> **The Moro reflex** might start to integrate between two and four months old.

Speech and Language Development

Because your baby spends more time in an upright position now, they have increasing awareness of their environment. With heightened awareness comes growing curiosity and the ability to interact with their daily surroundings, creating new opportunities to increase speech and language skills.

An easy way to embed language into your day is to continue to describe what you are doing. For example, "I am opening the refrigerator to get the milk for my coffee. Mommy looooves coffee." Use any opportunity to speak with your baby because this allows them to hear examples of suprasegmental characteristics of your typical native language, which include tone, loudness, and rate of speech, all of which add an extra layer of meaning when you are talking. It's not always what you say but how you say it. For example, emotions, sarcasm, and social cues are conveyed without words.

As your baby's language library is expanding beyond simply crying to communicate, their vowel sounds are starting to develop, such as the first emerging ee, oi, and ah sounds. In addition, you might hear back-of-the-throat consonants such as k and g.

Your baby might start to differentiate between calm and stern voices. Auditory (hearing) feedback is essential in the language acquisition process as your baby learns to talk. Your baby must hear themselves to continue making sounds or vocalizations. Control over their mouth, lips, and tongue (called articulators) and breath control coordination are stepping stones for your baby's transition from cooing to babbling to speaking words.

Developmental Play

Building playtime into your daily routine, both directly and indirectly, is an efficient, effective way to consistently embed learning experiences into your baby's day. After bath time (massage), diaper changes (foot play and tummy time), meal time (reaching for bottle), and bedtime (story time) are some of the most common routine-based times to create daily play habits.

Now that your baby's personality is shining through, you might be able to identify what their areas of interest might be and utilize baby-led activities to encourage them. As you engage and talk to your baby throughout your day, provide various positional-play opportunities, position yourself at their face level, and emphasize your words to promote eye contact and maintain their attention. What you say is still not the focus. The important elements are hearing your voice and the sounds it makes and making opportunities for personal interactions.

To help guide you with baby-led play, always observe and follow your baby's gaze. Following are various baby-led speech and language play examples.

Daily Descriptors and Routine Phrases

Describe what your baby might be seeing, such as family members, pets, and flowers or use routine phrases, such as "I'm going to catch your toes." Wait for a second to get eye contact and then grab their toes or point to an object you described. Note: Providing wait time is very important during speech and language play.

Sound, Oral Motor, and Diphthong Play

Play with sounds in such ways as kissing your baby's cheek and saying muh muh muh, making raspberries (blowing air through pursed lips), clicking your tongue (quickly moving the tip of your tongue up and down from the roof of your mouth to make a clicking sound), and experimenting with diphthongs. In this book, diphthongs are related to speech sounds and are not to be confused with diphthongs for reading print. A diphthong is two vowel sounds together making one syllable. It involves sliding from one sound to the next as seen in the examples below.

Start with the ah sound and slide to the ee sound for the development of the words hi and bye for the diphthong AI.

Start with the e sound and slide to the u sound for the development of the word you for the diphthong IU as in you.

Start with the oh sound and slide to the ee sound for the development of the words boy and toy for the diphthong OY.

Start with the ah sound and slide to the oo sound (oo pronounced as in the word two) for the development of the words how and wow for the diphthong AU.

Start with the a sound and slide to the ee sound for the development of the word hey for the diphthong EI.

Even when you are busy and unable to give your baby your undivided, face-to-face attention, it is still important to communicate and interact with them. Any and all opportunities to speak with your baby are important.

PLAY POSITIONS

Tummy Time Play Position

Airplane

Continue increasing your baby's time and frequency in this total-body workout position. Because your baby has to work harder in this position, they might get more frustrated. It is fine to continue to utilize yourself for the versatile tummy time play position, but also be sure to expose your baby to a variety of other safe surfaces. Practicing tummy time in different ways will help you to identify which forms your baby prefers and tolerates longer to promote more success.

First, make sure you are cleared by your doctor to do this activity. You might feel more

comfortable with someone sitting with you to help, depending on your healing process, as well as your comfort level as you get your baby into position, maintain their position, and get out of the position when the activity is complete. This activity helps your baby strengthen and develop the movement pattern of lifting their head and turning from side to side.

Prop your baby on their forearms with their elbows under their shoulders as in regular tummy time if they tolerate it. If your baby is uncomfortable in this position or you are unable to safely do it, then position them with their arms to the side. Remember to activate and stabilize your TA muscles and pelvic floor for your safety. Slowly move your legs slightly from side to side, back and forth, and in circles.

If moving your legs is too difficult or if you want to change it up, keep your legs stationary and sway your head to the right and left to encourage

Use every activity as an opportunity for communication enrichment. Facilitate eye contact with counting, playing music, or making up a silly song about flying up and down. You could also try story-telling, such as creating a story based on their surroundings.

your baby's ability to track while you are singing.

If your baby is beginning to make sounds, imitate the sounds back, teaching them about the back-and-forth of conversation and reinforcing the sounds.

Exercise Ball Tummy Time

You might find more success with an exercise ball because its flexible surface provides comfort for your baby, increasing their ability to tolerate tummy time. If you don't have an exercise ball, you can use a firm pillow. This activity brings your baby's visual field up higher, making eye contact and holding their attention easier. It also allows your baby to lift and turn their head from side to side more easily.

Start by securing the ball safely between your legs or in an exercise ball ring. Because it is easier to hold your baby facing away from you, place a mirror in front of them to provide them with visual feedback and see each other's facial reactions. If your baby tolerates upright positions on propped forearms, you can support them by

placing your thumb along their shoulder blade (scapula). Wrap your pointer, middle, and ring fingers around their biceps, the muscles lying between the front of the shoulder joint and elbow. Place your pinky along your baby's forearm.

Slowly move your baby side to side, forward, back, and in slow circles. Gently push down through your baby's arms, using a light pressure in the direction they are leaning. For example, if they are leaning to the right, apply pressure through that side with a slow, down/up motion, creating a gentle bounce.

If someone else is present to help, have that person read a book, move toys from side to side, or place an animated toy in front of your baby to keep their attention. Placing a noise-making toy such as an animated stuffed animal above the mirror will encourage your baby to look up. Meanwhile you can engage by singing and gently swaying side to side.

Supported Kneeling Play Position

Lap-Time Kneel

Tummy time in the first year is critical and widely discussed, but it is important to note that providing your baby with safe opportunities for a variety of play positions and movement patterns is equally important. Each play position and movement pattern strengthens different body parts, increases endurance, provides a variety of visual and sensory motor experiences, and promotes valuable environmental interactions. All of these components are necessary for optimal development.

Sit on the floor, supporting your body with a wall or piece of stable furniture behind your back if needed. Support your baby in the kneeling play position by propping their forearms on one of your legs, either to the outer side of your leg or in between your legs—whichever position is most comfortable for you. Place a toy or mirror opposite your baby to keep their attention and engagement. Place a nonslip surface under your baby's knees to help with stabilization if needed.

Back Play Position

Your baby lies on their back all night and during naps. During the day, it is very important to limit time on their back with their head pressed against a surface, whether during play or while in a seating device. After every activity completed in the back-play position, we challenge you to roll your baby into the tummy-time play position.

Rock, Swaddle, and Roll

Cross each of your baby's arms over one another and wrap them in a towel with their face exposed. While they are swaddled in the towel, rock them slowly from side to side. This gentle pressure on their back and both sides will facilitate increased body awareness, visual tracking, and midline crossing. It provides proprioceptive and vestibular feedback for future rolling. Swaddling your baby also helps them with their Moro reflex, which appears as a startle reflex with your baby flailing their arms out to the sides or crying in response to sensory stimulation. The Moro reflex is normal at birth and persists through the first two to four months but then should diminish and go away.

Making good eye contact, talking, and singing with them continues to lay the foundation for global communication. This reciprocal interaction of playing along with your baby's sounds (such as if your baby begins to coo, coo back) demonstrates the joint attention of the back and forth of conversation. Incorporating this swaddle activity into your baby's bedtime routine might calm them because it mimics the feeling they had inside the womb.

After unwrapping your baby, allow them to look at their hands, explore them, and bring them to their mouth.

Do not roll your baby onto their tummy while they are swaddled; however, you can build tummy time into this activity by placing them on their tummy after they are unwrapped.

Swing

When another adult is available, make a swing for your baby by placing them in the middle of a towel or blanket. Hold the sides of the towel or blanket at your baby's head and have the other adult hold the sides of the towel or blanket at their feet. Carefully lift the towel only slightly off the ground, swing them slightly side to side, while layering in language. Make sure that they are safe and secure in the center of the towel, not allowing them to tip so far that they might fall out. This type of slow linear motion stimulates the balance system as well as the part of the nervous system that is responsible for hearing, both of which can be calming to your baby and provoke cooing.

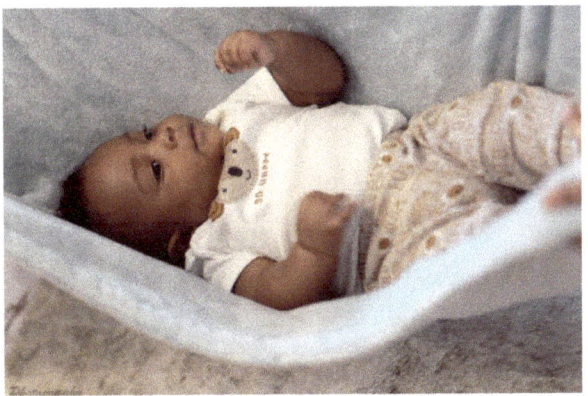

Encourage your baby to touch the blanket or towel. They need continued time to explore textures, temperatures, and sensations with their bare hands to begin to distinguish them in their brain.

High-Contrast Convergence

Visual convergence, the act of bringing their eyes inward toward their nose when an object comes close, will be stimulated during this activity. If you are practicing this in supported sitting, remember your baby is still gaining the strength to maintain upright head control, so observe signs they need a rest, for example, difficulty keeping their head up. Present a high-contrast toy quickly in front of your baby's face. Look for them to blink their eyes to adjust their visual system. Slowly move an object toward your baby's nose and back. Follow with slowly moving it from one side of your baby's face to the other and back while encouraging them to follow the toy by shaking the toy when needed or gently

tapping your baby with the toy and returning to position. Next, move slowly down toward their navel and back up, watching for your baby's eye to follow the object past the midline of their body.

I Love You Crunches

Position your baby on your lap or on an exercise ball that is safely secured between your legs, against a surface, or in an exercise ball ring. Secure your baby's feet against your chest and hold them along their sides, under their shoulders, and under their head.

Sing or talk directly to your baby to get their attention. Allow them time to inspect your face, connect with your eyes, and watch and hear words coming from your mouth. Slowly bring your baby toward your face, as if they are doing a sit-up with your support. Touch your nose to theirs or kiss their nose. Slowly lay them back down on your lap or exercise ball. Next, slowly roll your baby side to side and back and forth to

continue to promote visual tracking. Repeat this activity several times if they tolerate it.

Reaching

The goal of this activity is to encourage your baby to reach and grasp items above them while they are lying on their back. You can do this activity with a store-bought activity mat that has items dangling above the mat or any mat and toy you dangle yourself. Supervise and adjust the various moving toys attached to an activity mat so they are within your baby's reach and they can be successful.

When buying an activity mat, consider ones with high-contrast, bright colors, and bold patterns, as well as adjustable height options for hanging objects. Choose mats that promote all play positions (tummy, supported sitting, back) with engaging objects on both the mat itself and the arch.

Your baby will find pleasure in and enjoy repeating this reaching motion. When your baby reaches up, it helps engage their shoulder blades (scapulas) and strengthens their arms for continued reaching and grasp. It also encourages your baby to bring their hands to midline, promoting eye-hand coordination. When the objects move, it stimulates visual tracking.

Remember to incorporate reaching activities into your daily routines. For example, if you are bottle-feeding with either formula or pumped breast milk, prior to every feeding, hold the bottle above your baby, gently move it to get their attention, and encourage them to move their arms and reach toward it. If you are breastfeeding, promote reaching by placing your baby's hands on your breast while they are nursing.

Another time to incorporate reaching into your routines is bathtime. After squeezing the water out of your baby's washcloth, look at them, gain their eye contact, and lean in, if need be, encouraging them to reach and touch it by using gentle hand-over-hand assistance.

Shake It Up

Shake things up by placing a soft, safe wrist-based rattle on your baby and assist them with shaking their arm. Do not leave the wrist rattle on your baby when you are not actively playing with them.

The object of this activity is that your baby will make eye contact with the wrist-based rattle and begin to understand that movement has a cause and effect relationship.

Starting with a wrist rattle encourages your baby to move their arms. It will also be easier for them because it requires less motor control than holding and shaking a handheld rattle, which requires sustained isometric grasp, using extra motor skills and hand strength.

I Spy a Rattle

Once your baby has graduated to handheld rattles, lay them on their back and slowly move a soft, high-contrast rattle in different planes, such as horizontally, vertically, circular motion, closer to, and then further away from their face.

Because your baby's hand dominance is not established at this age, start with the rattle at their midline. It is important to place toys in your baby's midline to allow them to reach with their most natural hand, giving the choice of hand preference to them. When you directly hand your baby a toy, alternate sides so they have equal use on both sides.

Once your baby has made eye contact with the rattle, shake it to encourage them to reach for, touch, and grasp it. If they do not reach and grasp for the toy at that point, stroke the rattle along the back of one of their hands. This grasp release technique encourages the hand to open naturally, allowing you to offer them the rattle.

After your baby has grasped the rattle, encourage them to bring it to their mouth to

Note: Fine motor skills develop from the pinky (ulnar) side to the thumb (radial) side of the hand. Therefore, remember to start by stroking the pinky side of your baby's hand to facilitate an open hand, and eventually you will simply be able to stroke the back of the hand.

promote oral motor and sensory exploration, as they learn about the dimensional nature of objects in their environment.

As your baby becomes more independent holding a rattle, put on some music, grab a rattle for yourself, and dance, shake, rattle, and roll to your favorite song. Your baby will be more attentive and more apt to shake their rattle, too.

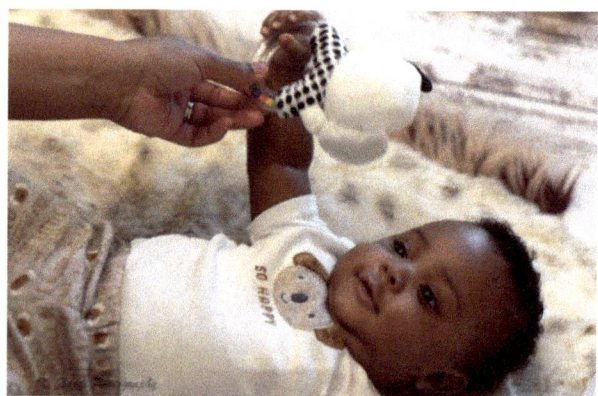

Variety of Play Positions

The following activities can be completed in various positions and incorporated into daily routines.

Blanket Peekaboo

There are many ways to play peekaboo. At this age, the goal is to visually engage your baby in activities. To play blanket peekaboo, hold a light baby blanket over either your face or gently and loosely cover your baby's face briefly to play peekaboo. Lightweight muslin blankets or infant play paper as seen in the photos are great options.

If using a lightweight muslin blanket, you can also raise the lightweight blanket up high and gently let it float down over your baby, keeping hold of one side. The gentle breeze from the blanket will stimulate your baby's touch sense as well. Make silly faces once they see your face again to maintain their attention, then repeat.

 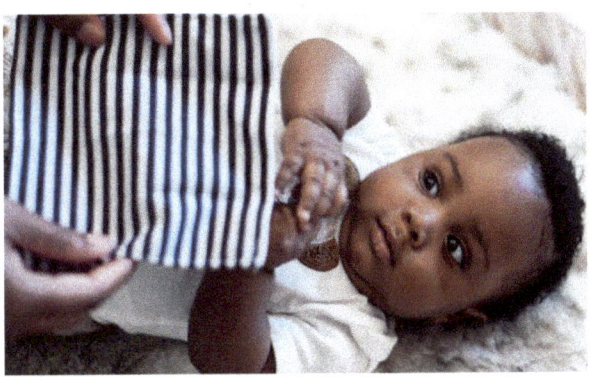

Hide-a-Toy Peekaboo

Play with a toy that makes noise in front of your baby, such as a rattle or bell. Present the toy in front of your baby. After they look at the toy, place a blanket over the toy, pull it off slowly, and say "Peekaboo."

Room Change Peekaboo

Visually engage your baby and then walk slowly around a nearby corner or crawl behind a piece of furniture so that your baby watches you disappear. Reappear slowly and re-engage your baby by talking to them.

Diaper Change Peekaboo

Incorporate peekaboo into your diaper change routine by hiding behind your baby's feet after changing their diaper, then looking up at them exclaiming "Peekaboo" as you look them in the eyes.

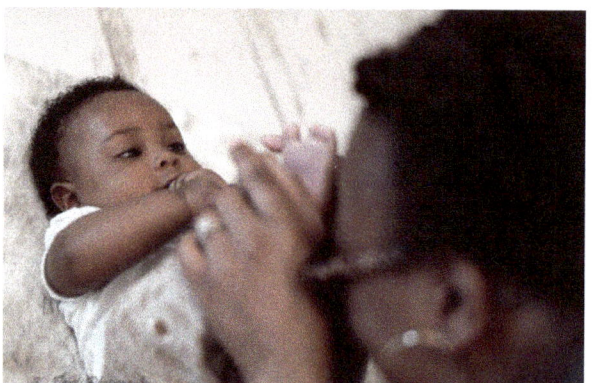 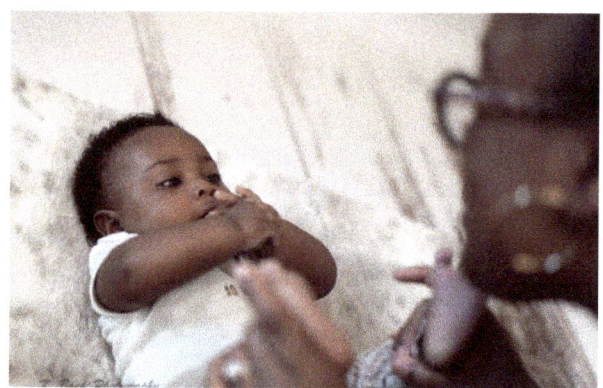

Outdoor Exploration

Although it's important to limit your baby's exposure to direct sunlight, it is also important to introduce your baby to the outdoors. Walk around outside and pick up various objects, such as leaves or flowers, show them to your baby, and name them. Follow your baby's gaze and describe what they might be seeing, such as family members, pets, or flowers.

Slow Dancing

At this age, your baby needs a combination of play and rest, with lots of snuggles in between. When they need a break, slow dancing is a calming sensorimotor activity. Bonding with your baby helps them develop confidence, feelings of safety, and the trust needed for future physical and emotional independence.

Put on your favorite soft music, support your baby's head and neck securely, and slowly dance. Use a variety of safe holding patterns, and switch it up every one to three minutes, depending on both your and your baby's comfort in each position.

While your baby is carefully secure in your arms, ask your loved one to loosely wrap their arms around you and slow dance with the both of you.

Story Time

Reading to your baby daily is and will continue to be an enriching experience. Now that your baby's eyesight is getting better, add books to your library. Choose soft, easy-to-grab books with colorful pictures, rich textures, and simple words with high repetition, rhythm, and flow, such as the That's Not My texture book series or Brown Bear, Brown Bear.

Baby Holding Positions

Belly Hold

Cradle Hold

Snuggle Hold

Football Hold

Two Months Old

Fill in the answers to reflect on the past month and to track.

How do you feel?
_____

_____

What exercises did you work on?
_____

_____

What is your baby doing now?
_____

_____

What was your baby's favorite activity this month?
_____

_____

What questions do you have for your ob-gyn and your baby's pediatrician?
_____

_____

Notes:
_____

_____

_____

_____

Three Months Old

MOMMY MOVEMENTS

The words "You are beautiful" are so easy to say to everyone else, yet might be hard for us to say to ourselves. Take a minute to think of someone in your life. Now, name what you think is beautiful about them. We bet it took you no time at all to list numerous things that you find beautiful about them, both on the inside and the outside.

Now think about yourself and name five things that you find beautiful. A minute ago, it was so easy to list five things about someone else, yet, when we turn the tables on ourselves, it may feel awkward and difficult. We challenge you to stand tall in front of a mirror and say, "I am beautiful." You are the only you in the world, and you are full of beauty and talent. Write your self-affirmations on a sticky note and put them in places you see frequently to remind yourself to stand tall and show yourself the love and kindness you show your friends and family.

Postnatal Posture

Now let's take some time to focus on strengthening your postural muscles, specifically the ones in your back required to help you stand tall. When you are feeding your baby, carrying them, or wearing them in a baby carrier, those positions mimic your third trimester pregnancy posture—except your baby is heavier now.

Therefore, it is critical to counteract all of the weight in the front, that flexed or bent-over posture, and the tension it places on your upper back and neck. Even if you don't experience pain in these places, don't skip this section. Strength and support of the back of your body is just as important as recovering the strength and support of the front of your core.

Posture Body Scan

Stand with your back against a vertical surface, such as a closed door or a wall. Your head, shoulder blades, and buttocks should be against the surface with your heels lightly brushing up against it. Position your arms at your sides, with your palms facing your body and your elbows relaxed, yet touching your sides near your lower rib cage. Your lower belly muscles will activate slightly, and thus it will help make sure you are not clenching or squeezing your butt cheeks (gluteal muscles).

Slide your shoulder blades slightly down your back a bit to create more space between your shoulders and your ears. Gently press the back of your head against the surface, looking straight ahead, making sure your chin isn't tilted up toward the ceiling nor down toward the ground. Scan your body back down again, starting back at your head, shoulders, glutes, knees, ankles, heels, and toes. This likely feels weird to you, but challenge yourself to hold this posture while you take one step away from the vertical surface, so you are standing exactly as you were—but now without support.

Does it feel unnatural, like you are leaning backward? If so, you are not alone. It is typical for this posture to feel awkward now because the adaptations your body made during pregnancy, combined with current postpartum demands, have compromised your body's ability to detect normal posture. Try the next several stretches to increase your body awareness and retrain your posture.

Ear-to-Shoulder Stretch

Sit, preferably in a hard chair, with both of your feet on the ground. Focus on sitting tall, keeping your back straight. Place your right hand under your right thigh so you are sitting on it to keep your right shoulder from rising up to meet your right ear. Now, gently tilt your head so that your left ear leans to your left shoulder. Hold this for three deep breaths. There should be no pinching on the left

side of your neck, and the right side of your neck, should feel a light stretch—a two on a scale of zero to 10, where zero is no stretch and 10 is painful. Bring your head back up, switch sides, and repeat.

Nose-to-Armpit Stretch

Sit, preferably in a hard chair, with both of your feet on the ground and your right hand under your right thigh. Turn your head slightly to the left and tuck your chin downward, bringing your nose toward your left armpit. Keep sitting up tall, spine straight, shoulders back, with no twist of your spine. All the turning toward your armpit comes from your neck only. You should feel this stretch in the back right side of your neck, toward the top of your right shoulder blade. Hold this ofr three breaths and then switch sides.

Doorway Stretch

Stand facing the corner of a room or in the opening of a doorway. Place your right hand at shoulder height on the wall, keeping your elbow bent at about 90 degrees. Step forward with your left foot, leaning your weight forward. You should feel a stretch in the muscles of your chest and maybe even slightly in your armpits. There should be no pinching or pain in your shoulders or neck. Hold for three breaths. Repeat, stepping forward with your left leg.

Backward Arm Circle Exercise

Standing tall, with your arms stretched out to either side about shoulder height, make slow backward circles with your arms, keeping your arms straight. Make these circles as big or as small as you need, keeping your lower belly engaged and shoulders away from your ears. Aim for approximately 20 circles.

Wall Angel Exercise

Stand with your back against a wall, as you did above during the Posture Body Scan. Put your arms at your sides, keeping your whole arm against the wall (from shoulder to elbow to wrist/hand). Slowly straighten your arms up over your head. Aim for five wall angels.

If you feel your arms pop off the wall or your back and shoulders arch off the wall, it is a sign of tight pectoral muscles. Do not move your arms up the wall as high next time because quality is more important than quantity. Your flexibility will increase over time. You should feel a stretch in your chest wall and some fatigue between your shoulder blades because those are the muscles working to keep your whole arm pressed against the wall as you raise your arms up and down. If these are difficult for you to do standing against a wall, start by doing them while lying on the ground.

Elbow Back Exercise

Stand with your back against the wall as previously. This time, place your hands behind your head so your elbows are bent at each side of your head, keeping your shoulders away from your ears. Activate the muscles between your shoulder blades by pressing your elbows back into the wall. Hold for five seconds or one deep breath cycle. Then relax your elbows forward and repeat the sequence five times. You should feel a stretch in your chest wall and fatigue between your shoulder blades as those postural muscles start working for you again. If these are difficult for you to do standing against a wall, start by doing them while lying on the ground.

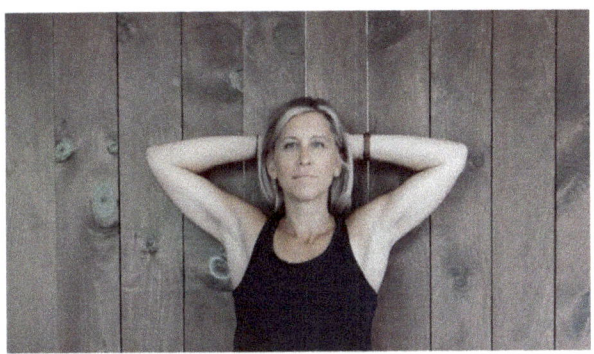

Segmental Bridge with Arm Stretch Spinal Restoration Exercise

Lie down with your knees bent, feet flat on the floor, and arms at your sides with your palms down. Take a deep breath in, and on the exhale, slowly lift your hips off the floor. Vertebrae by vertebrae, starting at the bottom of your spine (your coccyx), roll your back off the floor until you are in a bridge position. Keep the bottom of your rib cage down against the floor or mat; do not allow your rib cage to pop up and out. Hold for five seconds or one breath cycle. Then inhale, and on the exhale, slowly lower your spine, vertebrae by vertebrae, starting at mid-spine (thoracic spine), back down until your hips return to the floor.

On the next bridge, inhale, exhale, and lift vertebrae by vertebrae until you are in a bridge position. Inhale again while maintaining your bridge. On the exhale, float your arms off the floor, up over your head so that your elbows are by your ears and you are reaching to the wall behind you. Hold for five seconds or one breath cycle. Inhale, exhale, and float your arms back down to your sides. Pause for an inhale. On the exhale, slowly lower your spine, vertebrae by vertebrae, until your hips return to the floor.

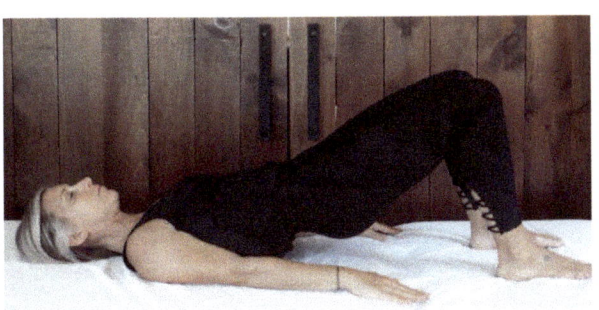
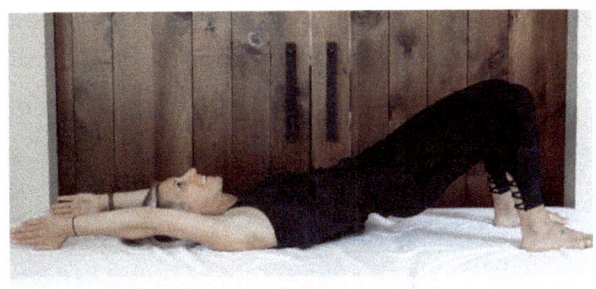

Baby's Development

Your baby starts to become more familiar with their surroundings by the day! With this new awareness, there may also be some anxiety as they start to understand that not every face they see is familiar. They might even need time to warm up to family members they don't see frequently.

Motor Development

Your baby appears more playful because they are developing improved control over their body and head in a variety of play positions to move more purposefully. Although their reaching is still inaccurate, they can bring their hands together, to their mouth, and to their body to explore and grasp lightweight toys. All this hard arm work allows them to push up through their forearms and lift their chest off the floor. However, they might not be strong enough to straighten (extend) their arms at their elbows yet while in tummy time. Seeing the world from a different view helps your baby develop head control.

While your baby is weight-bearing through their forearms in tummy time, their shoulder strength and trunk control are continuing to develop, and with a balance between their abdominal and pectoral muscles (flexors) and back and shoulder muscles (extensors), they have more head control, too. As your baby turns their head to see a toy, their weight will be shifted over the forearm that is on the same side as the toy, making it difficult for them to reach for the toy. They will slide their arm along the surface in an attempt to reach it. Lacking full stability in their shoulder might cause their arm to collapse under them when they shift their weight too far over their forearm. This abrupt roll might throw them into the startle reflex if it has not integrated yet, described earlier.

While your baby is on their back, they might roll with symmetry because their legs are often flexed with their hands at knees in exploration. Therefore, when your baby turns their head, it often elicits whole-body rolling to the same side.

Play positions are foundational to the sequence of how we move (movement patterns), and both are important for your baby's development. Now that your baby is moving more, utilize their play positions and movement patterns to their full potential. Think about what play position they are in. How are they moving? How can you help encourage play in a variety of important positions?

Visual Development

As your baby's eyes continue to develop, their vision is rapidly improving, and they are using their eyes together. Because of that, your baby now has measurable depth perception, which will impact how your baby uses their eyes in the future. Good depth perception helps us to navigate our world because we can better estimate where objects are located in space, and it can eventually help your baby with activities like sports and driving.

Your baby should continue to make eye contact with you regularly, and they should be skilled at following objects with their eyes. If you haven't already placed a crib or ceiling mobile in your baby's sight, now might be the time. Mobiles provide great visual stimulation for your baby. Keep in mind that your baby is now able to reach and grasp items, so be sure the mobile is far above your baby's reach.

Cognitive Development

Your baby loves repetition! Every time they repeat an activity, such as batting at a toy, it helps them to make connections with their environment. They will enjoy and learn from exploring their sensory world with their hands. They will explore their toys and own body more now as they enjoy reaching, touching, and grasping their own feet, toes, hands, fingers, mouth, and tongue. These spontaneous actions are becoming more intentional, and they enjoy this ability to learn more through their senses.

Your baby is starting to self-soothe in response to your voice; therefore, now is a critical time to instill a sense of security in your baby. Always use a soft voice when awakening, singing to, and playing with your baby to encourage a sense of security.

Remember, when your baby is irritable, this might be due to cognitive growth. Cuddle and be patient with them. This too shall pass.

It's exciting that these developmental skills facilitate the emergence of play.

Social-Emotional Development

Your baby demands more of your attention in other ways now. They respond to you with vocalizations when you speak with them. They will start making happy and sad vocalizations, such as grunting or whining when unhappy or cooing and laughing when happy. Your baby might enjoy short bursts of social play throughout the day balanced with periods of rest.

Your baby's growing awareness of unfamiliar people and situations makes for interesting social outings. They might respond to both unfamiliar and familiar faces in varying ways, such as apprehension, crying, shyness, or joy. Your baby will first recognize people familiar to them, which then teaches them who unfamiliar people are. This newfound understanding creates a better awareness of the role you play in their life and facilitates increased trust in you. Slowly introducing your baby to a babysitter between now and five months might be the easiest time period to avoid separation anxiety, which typically kicks in between five and eight months.

Self-Care Development

Your baby will enjoy bringing toys to their mouth to explore them, and they will learn more about their environment through this sensory

Now that your baby is bringing more items to their mouth, they are more vulnerable. More than ever, it's important to check their surroundings and follow choking safety guidelines on products. Inspect any area where you lay them down and all toys that they are playing with. Anything smaller than 1.50 inches wide presents a possible choking hazard for your baby. Small parts testers (aka child choking tube testers), with diameters of around 2.25 inches deep, will help you identify potentially dangerous objects. If you do not own one of these, consider using a two-finger width, a quarter, or a toilet paper tube as a general gauge for play safety.

hand-to-mouth play. Your baby will anticipate being fed with a bottle as they start to recognize more familiar objects.

Speech and Language Development

The "babbling" period begins now because your baby is gaining more control over their articulators (cheeks, lips, tongue, and breath support). You will hear most playful babbles when your baby is content, such as after they have eaten.

You will continue to hear vowel sounds, and your baby will begin to put two vowels together. Vowels are the framework of our language—the unsung heroes. Notice how this sentence doesn't make sense until vowels are added. Wtht vwls, wrds hv n mnng: Without vowels, words have no meaning.

Your baby will also begin to experiment with vocal volume and tones.

Language is built step by step. What begins as an arbitrary "ma" or "da" gets a big reaction from outside stimuli, such as Mom or Dad. Your baby notices this positive reaction, which increases the likelihood of them repeating that sound. Your reinforcement of sound creates meaning for your baby. The building blocks of sound expand to "Mama" (approximately age one), then "see Mama" (approximately age two), and later "I see Mama" (between two and three years of age).

Communicate while looking at your baby, this will provide audiovisual feeback, which will help them with the gradual sequence of encoding language. This reinforces the articulation of speech sounds in your native language and also establishes rules of communication needed for social cues. The interaction, in general, strengthens their skills in a variety of ways and continues to build upon that important communication base.

Developmental Play

Infants at three months are beginning to babble and are increasingly responsive to human voices. They may smile or coo in response to familiar voices. Provide a safe, well-supported seat for your baby to sit and watch you while you perform your daily activities. It might be helpful to place baby devices where you frequently complete tasks, such as a pack-n-play in your family room while you clean nearby or in your bathroom so you can shower. Always keep safety in mind and inspect the area and device daily.

Baby carriers might be another safe alternative

The rooting reflex often integrates between three and four months old.

The palmar reflex typically integrates between three and six months old.

The Spinal Galant Reflex usually integrates between three and nine months old.

for your baby. Read the carrier directions thoroughly and ensure you are wearing it properly to keep them safe. See Your Baby's Health in the chapter online for further information.

Now that your baby is babbling and more mobile, they will engage more playfully with you, such as beginning turn-taking interactions, such as vocalizing in response to being spoken to. Consider the following information now while playing with your baby: The Center on the Developing Child at Harvard University reports that neural connections are created and strengthened in your baby's brain to support development using positive and responsive baby-driven play interactions throughout your day. These baby-driven play interactions are referred to as "Serve and Return," or for the purposes of this book Ping-Pong play.

These are the steps that the researchers consider key to this successful interaction with your baby.

Step 1: Share the focus. Observe when your baby serves you their interests. They might serve you with a body response, such as moving their arms or legs, pointing, or making sounds. It is important that you share their interest by engaging with them in a supportive, encouraging way.

Step 2: Support and encourage. Support your baby with words of encouragement. Engage with your facial expression, body gestures, and movements; interact and play with them and their toys. Set up your baby for success by adapting activities, making them more difficult or easy, depending on your baby's needs, to provide realistic, attainable challenges.

Step 3: Name it. Talk to your baby about what they are seeing, doing, and feeling. Communication makes connections in your baby's brain and builds their understanding of the world around them and what they can expect from it.

Step 4: Take turns back and forth. By taking turns, your baby will learn how to socialize well with others and to develop self-control. While taking turns, wait for your baby to respond and react. By giving wait time, you foster confidence, independence, and your baby's ability to develop ideas.

Step 5: Practice endings and beginnings. When you are interacting with your baby and sharing their focus, pay attention to your baby's way of communicating when they are all done and ready to start something new. Allowing your baby to guide their play experiences gives them the opportunity to explore their world in a more enriched, meaningful way.

PLAY POSITIONS

Tummy Time Play Position

Some babies may continue to find this position challenging. Continue to provide frequent, supervised tummy time opportunities. Tummy time strengthens your baby's upper body and core muscles. It is a foundational skill needed to be able to reach several milestones, and it assists in the integration of primitive reflexes. For example, if your baby does not play in the tummy time position, they do not gain the essential strength and skills needed to learn how to roll. Building tummy time into your daily routine, such as after every diaper change, will make it easier for you to follow through with it.

Because your baby is starting to push up through their forearms while in tummy time, focus on encouraging this movement pattern. Provide a touch (tactile) cue to your baby's chest, over the muscles that span over their chest and fronts of their arms (their pectoralis muscles). This tactile cue might increase activation of the muscle, facilitating your baby's attempts to push themselves up and off their chest.

Another technique to encourage this movement is placing a toy in front of your baby and raising it vertically to gain their visual attention.

Vertical tracking and pushing up through their arms help to develop head control and strengthen your baby's tummy, back, and arms right now. In addition, it helps to balance their abdominals, pectorals, and hip flexors (flexor muscles) and trunk and hip extensors (extensor muscles).

Consistently transition your baby out of tummy time by slowly rolling them to their side, then their back, and praising them to engage them before you pick them up or when changing play positions. When rolling your baby to their side, gently bend their elbow, tucking their same side arm under them first.

Tummy Time Stretch and Reach

Slowly roll your baby from back to side and on their tummy while on a safe surface. Support your baby at their pelvis/hips during this activity; otherwise, when your baby turns their head to explore visually, they will shift their weight over their same side forearm and accidentally roll. This weight shift prevents them from being able to lift and move their arm and is the reason your baby will be more inclined to bring their mouth to a toy rather than their hand to a toy.

Place a toy in front of your baby and within their reach. Tap the toy on the floor to gain their visual attention, encouraging them to reach for the toy. Wait as long as necessary for them to attempt to reach and grasp the toy. Adjust the location of the toy closer or farther from them, depending on their ability.

Alternate sides during this activity, such as front right, front left, and front midline. Let your baby play with the toy for a while each time after they reach and grasp it. Remember that, when playing with toys, do not force your baby's hand open. Stroke the back or the pinky side of their hand to encourage them to open their hand. Forcing a baby's fingers open can cause hyperextension in their fingers as they develop.

Repeat this activity throughout your day during tummy time play. Babies have a short attention span, and their attention in a given toy might only last for a minute or two; that's typical and is no cause for concern. Observe your baby's cues and rotate to another toy once they lose interest in the current toy.

Side-Lying Play Position

Providing your baby with opportunities to play in a side-lying position encourages their shoulders and arms to be positioned forward, allowing gravity to assist the top and bottom arms to come together for hand-to-hand and hand-to-foot exploration. This will better establish body awareness, as well as development of neck and trunk righting reactions (where baby keeps head/neck aligned with their body), which will better establish their awareness of the midline of their body. Side-lying also promotes flexibility throughout your baby's body and strengthens their core, shoulders, arms, and hands.

Foot-to-Hand Play

While your baby is lying on their back, bring their hands together and to both feet. Roll them onto their side in this position, with their hands and feet together. Gently release your hands from around their hands and feet to allow them to relax. While they're still on their side, bring their hands together and to their feet again and gently release your hands. Repeat this sequence while talking to your baby and staying engaged with them. After a couple of repetitions, alternate your baby's body to the other side by rolling them onto their back first and returning to step one.

Add a wrist or ankle rattle to encourage a visual connection without the added work of grasping a rattle, to make it easy for your baby to reach for their hands and feet on their own. Dress your baby in an outfit with high-contrast patterns on their feet, which will draw their eyes to their feet for play. Or encourage your baby by using a free-standing toy, such as a colorful stacker that lights up, to hold their attention. Hand them the toy and encourage them to shake it and bring it to their mouth.

Supported Sitting Play Position

Your baby needs to experience being "wobbly" in a safe, supported environment to learn about their body in relation to the world around them. Wobbly play triggers postural adjustments, equilibrium challenges, and activation of righting reactions, which in turn enables your baby's body to form a different relationship with gravity.

Remember to read in this position, too. Books with flaps allow for further exploration and interaction, encouraging the engagement of your baby's hands during story time.

Postural Reaction Play

While in the supported sitting position, safely challenge your baby by encouraging them to shift their weight in different directions ("wobbly play") to help develop postural reactions, which help us to protect our bodies and react to the environment around us while we are mobile. Your baby develops these reactions through interaction with their gravitational environment.

Your baby is able to keep their trunk in alignment with their head and arms at midline whenever they are shifted off balance due to postural reactions. Maintenance of postural alignment and muscle tone needed for milestones such as lifting their head, rolling, sitting, crawling, creeping, standing, walking, and jumping are developed from these postural reactions as well.

Here is an example of postural reactions:

While you are playing with your baby, they lose their balance to the left side, then shift their head in the opposite direction (to the right) in attempt to regain their balance to midline, making their body "right" again. These are known as righting reactions.

Internally, your baby's body is now able to make constant slow multidirectional postural adjustments, such as weight-shifting, to maintain balance. These are called equilibrium reactions. If neither the righting reactions nor the equilibrium reactions help your baby to maintain their balance, then their protective reactions will kick in. If your baby falls to the left, their left arm reflexively responds by extending to catch themselves in the attempt to protect their body and lessen the impact of their fall.

Sit-n-Wobble

Provide your baby with opportunities to play in the seated position with your support. Because your baby is unable to sit independently yet, this position relies on your assistance. Never leave your baby unattended while in supported sitting.

Place pillows or cushions around your baby while you are supporting them or use a play nest.

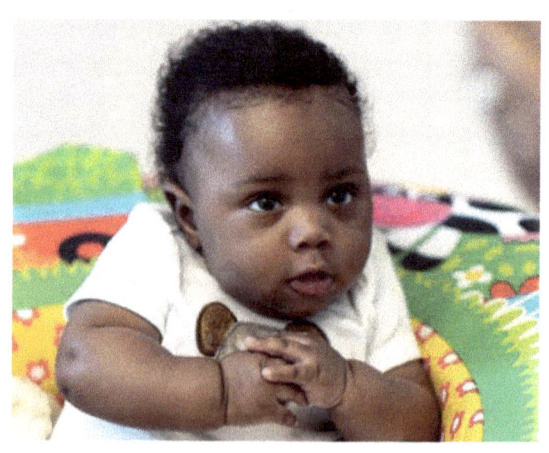

If your baby is struggling, attempt to place them in a half-ring sitting position, with one leg bent at the knee with their foot inward and against the other leg, which is straight forward.

Encourage your baby to grasp their hands independently at the midline of their body by placing a toy that they are able to grasp directly in the middle-front of them. Allow them time to process and attempt to reach and grasp. Lightly stroke the back of their hand to encourage them to let it go after you've allowed them time to hold the toy a bit. Repeat.

As this gets easier, challenge them in a variety of the following ways.

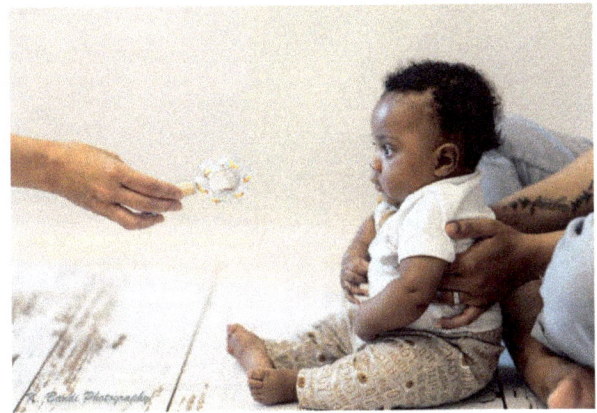

- Encourage them to reach for and grasp toys in various planes, such as lower right, upper right, lower left, and upper left.

- Place a toy under a blanket with part of it showing. Wiggle the toy to get their attention.

- Use light-up and sound-making toys. The lights and sounds might keep their attention longer. The toy might challenge their balance more due to the visual response as well. It may even encourage your baby to reach forward, eliciting a forward protective response.

- Play with moving, rolling toys, which challenge your baby by motivating them to reach for the toy.

- Incorporate reading into sitting time because your baby is likely to reach for the book.

- Play with two different high-contrast toys to provide opportunities for your baby to shift their visual gaze from one toy to another.

Your baby might start to show a preference for grasping items on the pinky side of their hand.

Seated Weight Shift

If your baby is holding their head up steadily in supported sitting, you might start the following activity with them. Sit and place your baby on your lap, holding them securely at their waist. Slightly raise one of your legs in order to shift their weight from one side of their bottom to their other side. Slowly alternate sides. This slow, reciprocal pattern provides the feeling of weight-shifting through each side of their bottom. These weight shifts are important for future stages, such as the transition from a seated position to a side-lying or tummy position.

Remember to build activities into your routine for efficiency and consistency, such as after you've read to your baby or while you are sitting and talking with someone, listening to music, or attending a sibling's extracurricular activity.

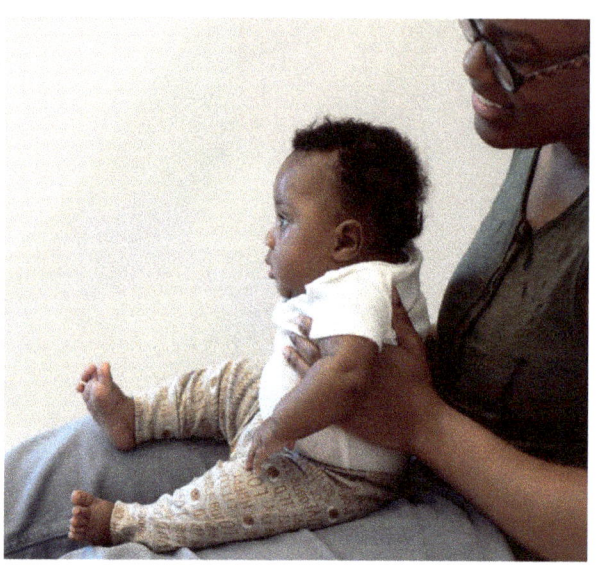

Exercise Ball

You can use an exercise ball, balance board, cushion, or even a pillow placed on top of your thighs to challenge your baby's balance during supported sitting. Start by placing your baby securely in a seated position on the ball or item of choice facing you or facing away from you with a mirror. Slowly and gently increase the weight down through one hip with your hand while holding your baby at their waist if they are strong enough, then move the ball slightly to that side. You are providing light pressure through your baby's hip and then slowly moving the ball to the same side more so than creating an actual rocking motion. Repeat this weight-bearing activity on your baby's other side as well.

Be creative with supported sitting play on the exercise ball. If your baby is facing away from you, place toys on a soft ottoman or a large box in front of them, encouraging them to lean forward to reach and grasp the toys.

Remember: Make all opportunities a good time to work on speech and language skills. Talk or sing about their body parts to facilitate increased body awareness. "Stop and Sing" songs are when you sing and then stop and wait for your little one to gain eye contact before starting to sing again. Make the song interactive by gently rocking or bouncing them on the ball. For example, sing "Row, Row, Row Your Boat" and gently rock in a forward-and-backward motion. Consistency is key. You might get sick of hearing yourself sing the same song, but your baby will pick up on this routine and identify with it.

Bubbles

Blowing bubbles is a great way to play in sitting, while incorporating visual tracking and reaching up against gravity. Using a word such as "pop" sets your baby up for simple language, whereas, singing songs frequently and over the toddler years promotes future language expansion through hearing consistent repetition. In addition, pairing actions such as raising their arms with the songs facilitates receptive language. Note: Keep bubbles away from their eyes; it might sting if one pops in them.

Bubble, Bubbles, Falling Down Song

Sing to the tune of "London Bridges":

"Bubbles, bubbles, falling down, falling down, falling down. Bubbles, bubbles, falling down. My sweet baby."

"Hold the wand and blow them out, all about, all about. Hold the wand and blow them out. My sweet baby."

"Reach your arms up. Wave around, wave them around, wave around. Reach your arms up and wave around. My sweet baby."

"Catch a bubble and watch it pop! Pop, pop, pop! Pop, pop, pop! Catch a bubble and watch it pop. My sweet baby."

Back Play Position

Because your baby is always on their back during sleep, provide limited yet enriched back play during the day, such as suspending or holding toys above them to encourage reaching. Continue to encourage lots of hand-to-hand, hand-to-mouth, hand-to-foot, and foot-to-mouth exploration.

A simple activity you can do while your baby is on their back is to make raspberries on their tummy by putting your lips together and blowing out, resulting in a vibration on their tummy. Stop, lift your head, look for their eye contact, say, "I'm going to get your tummy," then repeat the sequence.

Awakening

Place your baby in your lap facing you. Bring their hands together at midline and rub one hand on the other. This togetherness and gentle pressure help stimulate their tactile system, which is their sensation of touch. Now, grasp and hold their bare feet with their hands, encouraging them to explore their own body further. You can use your legs to gently rock your baby side to side while holding their hands together and to their feet. You can also shift one of your thighs slightly down and back up, alternating legs. Bringing your baby's hands to their feet and legs is a pre-rolling skill that develops crossing of

midline, coordination of both sides of the body (bilateral coordination), stimulates the vestibular sense, and increases their flexibility. Your baby might grasp their foot, straighten and bend their leg at their knee, or put their toes in their mouth.

Consider doing this and other activities when your baby is wearing only a diaper. By allowing your baby to explore their body when in a diaper only, you're giving them the opportunity to feel their legs and feet without any interference from clothing.

Ball Kick

Place your baby on their back. Encourage them to bat a soft ball tied to a string with their hands and kick at it with their feet. Once your baby gets the hang of it, they will repeat this motion for pleasure.

Incorporate this idea into your baby's diaper-changing routine by placing any safe noise-making item on the changing table by their feet. When your baby accidentally kicks it, they will increase the awareness that their feet are a part of them and movement can get an external response.

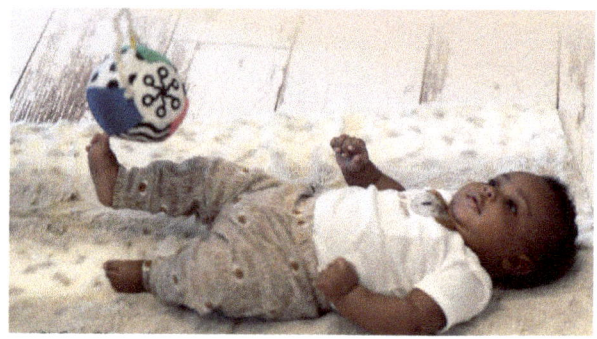

After your baby masters this activity in back position, try it in the supported sitting or side-lying play positions.

Roll Away

Now that you understand the importance of positional play, let's consider the movement pattern of rolling. This rolling activity is intended to bring your baby the awareness of their body parts and the movement that accompanies them.

Lay your baby on their back, then hold one leg at a time and gently kick it in the air.

Next, bring their feet together and rub them against one another. Touch your baby's hands to their feet and lightly roll them back and forth from side to side.

Make it a routine by pressing your baby's feet together every time you change their diaper to

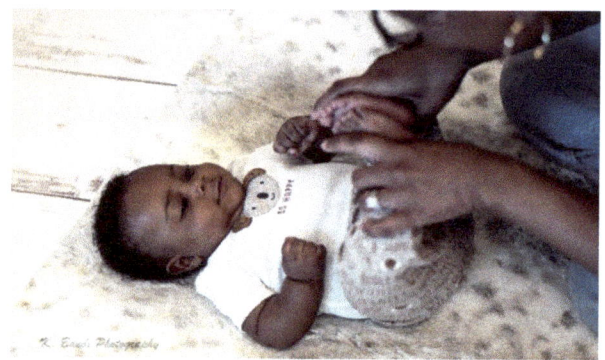

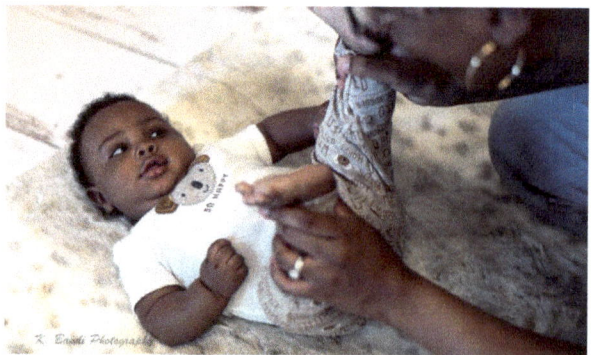

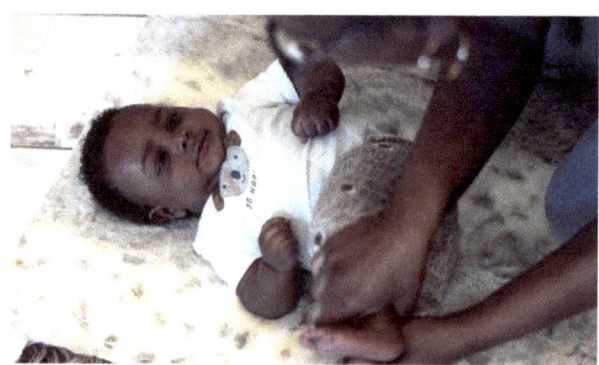

incorporate downward tracking, flexibility, and body awareness throughout the day. Note: Your baby either is starting to roll or will be rolling soon, so never leave them unattended on a sofa, a bed, or any other surface from which they might fall and get hurt.

Morning Stretches

This stretching activity promotes range of motion and works on crossing the midline. Lay your baby on their back. Gently stretch your baby's opposite arm and leg. Do not force this. Then bring their opposite arm and leg together. Repeat this pose, alternating sides. Count with each hand-to-foot touch.

Incorporate this stretching activity into your baby's bath time routine by gently holding up one body part at a time. Look at your baby and gain eye contact, leaning in if need be, and then label the body part, such as "foot," saying something such as, "I'm going to catch your toes, wash, wash, wash. I'm going to catch your nose, wash, wash, wash." During this time, use hand-over-hand motion to touch their hand to their foot and label the different body parts you are washing throughout.

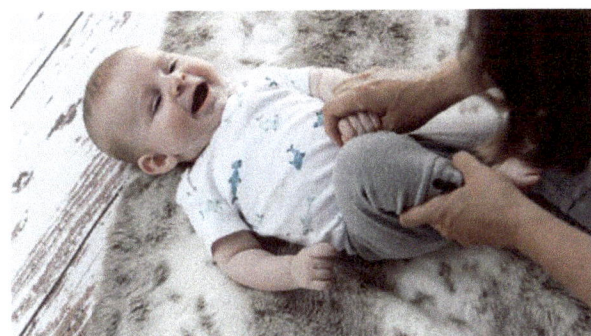

Foot Roll

Providing input through your baby's hands and feet in general will help to promote self-awareness and the sensation of future heel-to-toe walking. In a seated position, lay your baby in front of you and between your legs. Use the palm of your

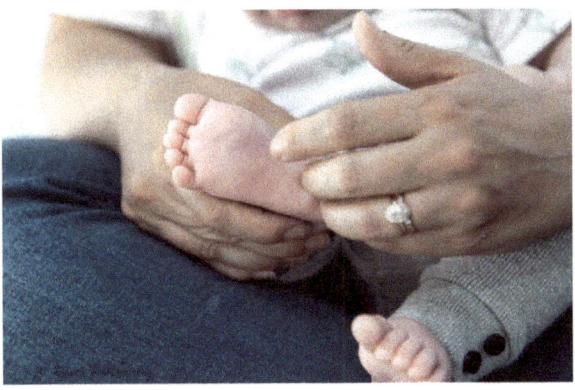

> **Be sensitive** to your baby's response to this activity. Your baby might prefer certain textures over others.

hand, a small textured ball, or a balled-up sock and gently roll it from their heel to their toes three to five times on each foot. Roll it on their hands as well to provide input through their hands.

Track This Way

Hold a toy that either makes noise or is high-contrast in both hands, approximately 10 inches away from your baby throughout this activity. Slowly move each toy in the following sequences to promote depth perception and tracking.

- Make an arch slowly from the left side of the ear up and over to the right side of the ear.

- Make another slow arch from the top of their head down to their belly button.

- Make another slow arch on a diagonal from top left to their right hand and then top right to their left hand.

- Move the two toys apart and back together as well.

- Encourage your baby to follow the toys visually and reach for one.

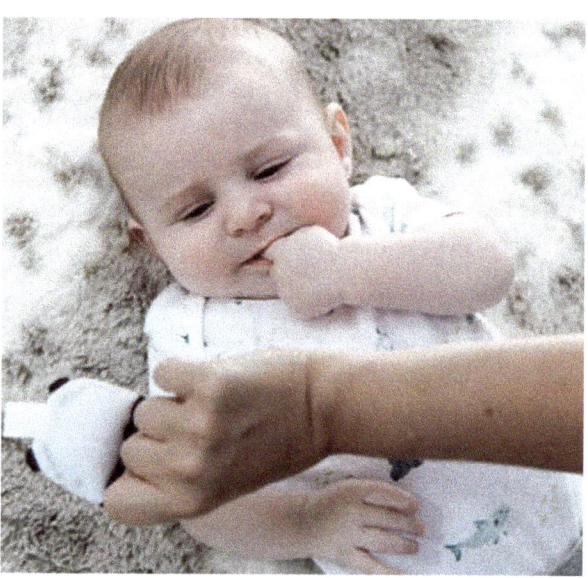

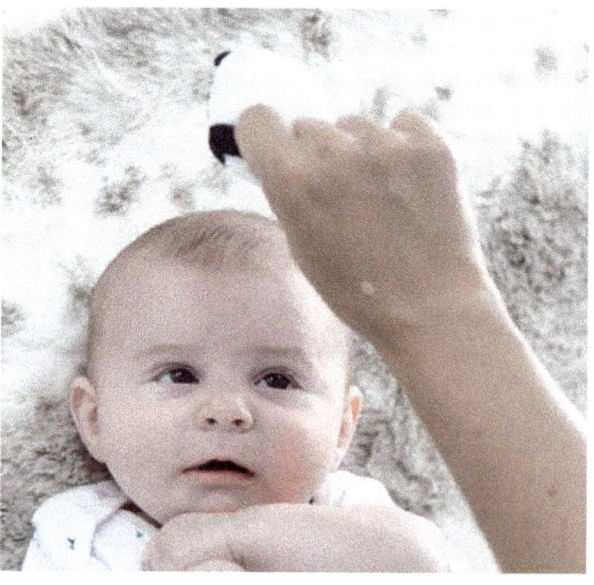

Texture Play

Your baby's sensory system plays an important role in their learning and development. Encourage your baby to explore textured objects with their mouth, hands, and feet. Safe, supervised texture play is a nice pre-solid-food activity that provides your baby with sensations similar to having their gums and teeth brushed.

Provide a variety of baby-safe sensory mouthing toys composed of a variety of surfaces: smooth, bumpy, soft, cool, and warm. Vibrating baby-safe toys are also beneficial, alerting or awakening their sensory system. Gently and slowly move the toy or a baby toothbrush over their gums, their cheeks, and the tip of their tongue. Engage with them by talking or singing.

If you are using a baby toothbrush for this activity, consider singing the alphabet slowly and pronouncing each letter clearly. As your baby gets older, this song may resonate with them and facilitate good oral health cleansing duration. Once you hand the toothbrush over to them to explore with your supervision, sing the alphabet again while they are "brushing."

Three Months Old

Fill in the answers to reflect on the past month and to track.

How do you feel?

_____

_____

What exercises did you work on?

_____

_____

What is your baby doing now?

_____

_____

What was your baby's favorite activity this month?

_____

_____

What questions do you have for your ob-gyn and your baby's pediatrician?

_____

_____

Notes:

_____

_____

_____

_____

The Nuture Notebook for Mom and Baby

Four Months Old

MOMMY MOVEMENTS

You are probably starting to feel a bit more like yourself, but there might be days you feel like you are just not going to make it through. You are not just juggling your baby's needs and figuring them out but also balancing other life demands. Sometimes it seems as though every piece of you is challenged—your mind, spirit, body, and even your faith in yourself.

You are so much stronger than you think. You have the power within to stand tall and strong. During moments when you doubt yourself as a parent, career-driven person, home manager, spouse, friend, or sibling, you might feel like you can't take on one more thing. Know that you have the strength within you, whether that means the strength to say no to an opportunity or to move forward with it. Close your eyes. Take a deep diaphragmatic breath. Look into your own eyes in a mirror, assume your power stance, and remind yourself, "I am stronger than I think." You've got this!

POSTNATAL PELVIC STABILITY

It's time to restore stability in your pelvis and rebalance the muscles around your core foundation (pelvic girdle) to find that power stance again.

These positions are designed with both orthopedic progression and the positions in which our body performs daily activities (typical functional positions) in mind. For example, the exercises in phase two are not only to mimic picking up toys but also to prepare your body for planks or push-ups.

Pelvic Girdle Stabilization

Girdles: They can be your best friend or your worst enemy, depending on how you look at them. They might not be worn as much anymore, (thank you, Spanx!), but the goal of them remains desirable—to keep your core supported (okay, and maybe even a little sucked in). Here's the good news: If you do this right and address the muscles in your core and surrounding your pelvis, your internal girdle is activated, and you don't need that crazy restrictive undergarment.

When you picture a girdle, two things come to mind, right? It surrounds your whole torso (front, back, and sides), and it zips (or clasps or laces) up the middle. In fact, the verb girdle means "to encircle." This definition makes perfect sense when it comes to looking at the pelvic girdle, whose bones create the circle from which this internal girdle rises. It's the base of the canister that creates your core. It surrounds the base of your torso (front, back, and sides), and it comes together, stabilizes up the middle, and is the foundation for your inner girdle to "zip up."

The pelvis is securely attached to your spine by a web of ligaments before puberty, allowing your pelvis to become a stable base of support for your spine and legs to move on and an anchor for all the muscles that attach to it. This connection enables optimal functioning of your muscles. However, at times during the menstrual cycle, and then to an extreme during pregnancy, hormones start to cause that web to stretch more freely, allowing the pelvis to shift and thus permitting passage of your baby. The ability of your pelvis to open is critical during labor, but it needs to be a secure, stable base for movement otherwise. So let's start by zipping your muscles up in a balanced way so they can remember how to safely work together efficiently and effectively.

Note: It is important that you complete these exercises in the correct sequence, which enables your body to maintain deep stabilizer muscles in a static position before progressing to holding these muscles during movement, particularly functional movements. If you cannot sustain these isometric exercises, which are exercises that do not produce visible movements of muscles and joints, your body is not able to move forward safely and correctly to more difficult exercises yet.

The Nuture Notebook for Mom and Baby

Pelvic Girdle Isometrics

As a reminder, five main muscle groups surround the pelvic girdle to provide muscular stability and work the front, back, sides, top, and bottom of the pelvic girdle. The pelvic girdle isometrics (PGI) below will help you to identify each muscle and learn how to activate each one individually. Once you've mastered individual activation, you will be ready to progress to pelvic girdle stabilization (PGS), which is the ability to turn on all of these muscles together.

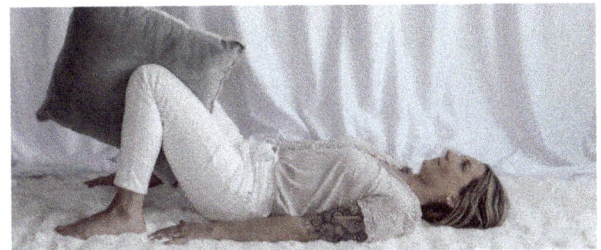

Grab a pillow and lie on your back on the floor with your knees bent.

Start with review of your pelvic floor (PF) and lower abdominals. Contract and relax your PF two to three times. Then contract your lower abdominals. (Zip up from your pubic bone up toward your belly button. Think of your belly button moving upward. Remember, don't activate your obliques.) Hold for two to three seconds, relax your lower abdominals, and repeat two to three times.

Next, place the pillow between your thighs/knees and lightly squeeze the pillow just enough to feel your inner thigh muscles turn on but not so hard that your knees would bang together if the pillow was removed. Hold for two to three seconds, relax, and repeat two to three times.

Next turn on the gluteal muscles that are close to the spot where those big dimples are in your side seat. Think about rotating your sit bones toward each other. Hold for two to three seconds, relax, and repeat two to three times.

Last, keep your elbows straight at your sides and try to squeeze your arms to your body, using the muscles in your armpit as if you are squeezing a lemon between your arms and armpits. Hold for two to three seconds, relax, and repeat two to three times.

Pelvic Girdle Stabilization

You have just found and woken up the five muscle groups that surround your pelvis! Now it's time to turn them all on one by one in a more fluid sequence, so that they learn how to work together. Although it might not feel as if you are completing a hard workout, the Pelvic Girdle Isometrics (PGI) that follow activate the five main pelvic girdle muscle groups, and mastery is required for continued successful exercising. Whether you want to return to running, barre class, yoga, or CrossFit, these PGI exercises lay the foundation for all future movements, big and small. Still lying on your back, with a pillow between your knees/thighs, pull your PF up and in.

Inhale, and as you exhale, hold and maintain your PF contraction, while simultaneously following this sequence: Zip up your lower abdominals. Squeeze the pillow lightly between your knees/shins.

Turn on the sides of your glutes/dimples Squeeze your arms to your sides, using your armpit muscles/your lemons.

Hold all of these contractions together for five seconds, while maintaining your breath.

If you feel as if you lost one of the muscle groups, don't worry, just turn it back on again. Relax your muscles, then repeat three to five times.

Pelvic Girdle Stabilization with Bridge

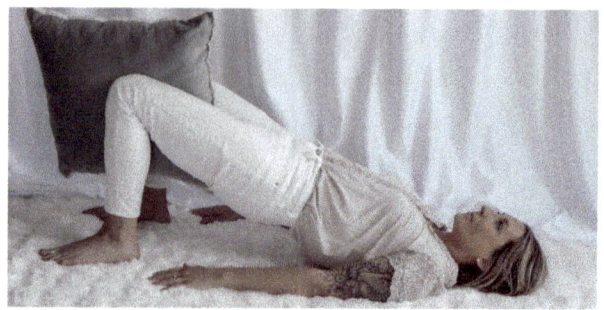

Grab a pillow and lie on your back with your knees bent. Inhale, and on your exhale, pull your PF in, hold, and zip up your lower abdominals. Hold there and squeeze a pillow between your knees/shins. Hold there, and turn on your side seat/glute muscles (dimples). Hold there and pretend to squeeze a lemon between your arms/armpits. Moving forward, the activation of all these muscles together will be referred to as PGI. Then continue to maintain the position you have worked yourself into and tilt your pelvis, or bridge hips up to the ceiling. Hold for five seconds or two to three breaths and maintain your isometrics as you lower your hips back down. Relax your muscles and then repeat five times.

Wall Slide/Squat

Stand against a wall with your feet approximately six to 10 inches forward. Turn on your PGI (see above). Hold this position and on your next exhale slide down the wall into a squat. Hold the squat position, maintaining stabilization of your isometrics for five seconds or two to three breaths. As you slide back up, continue to maintain stabilization of your PGI. Relax your muscles and then repeat five times.

It is common to hold your breath during workouts. However, breathing is the number one priority throughout any exercise, so it is important to maintain your breath cycles. Movement always occurs on the exhale.

BABY'S DEVELOPMENT

These first several months probably have come and gone so quickly! Your baby recognizes your face and voice now and craves all your love and attention. Gently snuggle your baby in, wrap their arms around your neck, kiss their cheeks, and quietly talk to them. Moments like this will be imprinted in your memory and in theirs. Keep repeating this, and eventually they will initiate putting their arms around your neck and giving you a kiss on your cheek.

Motor Development

With increased control comes increased mobility. Your baby gets an abdominal workout as they bring their hands to their feet and even in their mouth. Your baby will roll to their side with symmetry, then they might straighten their bottom leg while keeping their top leg bent to allow them to roll onto their tummy. When rolling from their side to their tummy, they can momentarily lift their head off the surface to clear their arm. While playing in side-lying position for longer periods of time, they are building neck strength and will rest their head on a surface, learning skills such as reaching across their body to play with toys.

While your baby is on their tummy, they might now be able to push up through their hands with their elbows extended. Alternating between this position and a pivot position (resembles a swimming pattern) of both arms pulled back and legs lifted off the surface is common.

As your baby gains strength in their trunk and shoulders, they can shift their weight onto their opposite forearm, allowing them to unweight the arm closest to a toy and reach for it. If they shift their weight too far over their forearm, their shoulder might collapse, causing your baby to roll away from the toy they are reaching for.

Your baby might be able to prop on their hands briefly with arms extended in front of themselves to maintain a supported sitting position. They can reach out, grasp your fingers, and assist when pulled up to sitting.

Your baby's grasp reflex has moved beyond the reflexive response, and they now have more volitional control now (the reflex has integrated, meaning it is no longer present), and their hands are open and relaxed most of the time. They will begin to progress toward reaching for objects with both arms and hold them in the palms of their hands.

Visual Development

Your baby's eyesight is continuing to develop, allowing them to explore and interact with the world around them with greater accuracy. They should be coordinating their eyes together at all times. As their depth perception continues to improve, they will use this ability to touch and grasp objects with more precision, in all positions of support—on their tummy, back, and sitting—to explore the world around them.

You might notice that your baby is able to see smaller objects. Your baby begins to fixate on and follow objects that are farther away from them,

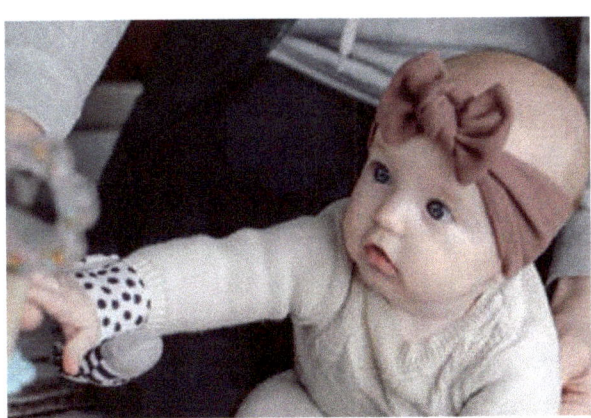

such as a person or object across the room. They can also locate where objects are in their space (proximity).

Cognitive Development

Your baby's rapidly developing brain and scope of vision helps them locate an object that is only partially in view. When interested in continuing with an activity, they will let you know with vocalizations or excited movements. Identification of tactile body awareness is evidenced in your baby's visual reaction of localizing the site of touch.

Remember: When your baby is irritable, it might be due to their developing cognition.

Social-Emotional Development

Your social butterfly continues to make a variety of different sounds, smiles frequently, giggles, and recognize more people. This is the month where you reap the rewards of all your hard work when your baby beings to smile back at you with gratitude. Your baby is making more eye contact with other people when they talk to them, even more so than objects they play with. They are

smiling and laughing during play and might get upset if you stop playing with them.

It's fun to watch the emergence of play skills and imitation. For example, when you shake a rattle, they might shake one in response.

If your baby gets frustrated, try to introduce new activities and praise them. You might see their frustration turn to motivation with this positive reinforcement. As your baby's nervous system develops, their hands start to find purpose, and you will notice spontaneous yet more controlled movements instead of reflex-driven reactions.

Self-Care Development

Your baby needs their sleep so they have lots of energy for all their socializing. You might notice that they begin to sleep 10 to 12 hours at night and occasionally wake up once or twice. If your baby wakes in the middle of the night, do your best to encourage self-soothing, such as sucking on their own hand. Avoid playing with them in the middle of the night. You do not want to reinforce a waking pattern.

This month, if you are bottle-feeding, you might notice your baby patting their bottle and later even putting their hands on their bottle while you are feeding them.

Between four to six months of age, the tongue thrust (tongue extrusion) reflex will disappear. Although this reflex is important during the first months of life because it helps your baby latch onto a nipple and protects them from aspirating or choking, inhibition is equally critical because various tongue movements are necessary to safely manipulate solid baby foods when introduced.

Speech and Language Development

Babbling should be more and more apparent with each passing week, and you will hear a variety of sounds from your baby. Your baby chuckles and babbles when they are alone. They make nonspeech sounds, such as growling. It is important to respond with your native language speech sounds. While it is tempting to smile and growl back, you don't want to reinforce noises such as growling as communication.

You can make exaggerated faces, such as sticking out your tongue, raising your eyebrows, or opening your mouth wide, to encourage your baby to mimic you. Sing songs with facial expressions because babies are drawn toward music and exaggerated facial expressions.

You will start to hear your baby using consonant chains, such as ba-ba-ba, which is called reduplicative or canonical babbling. They may start to repeat simple vowel sounds back to you or laugh during peekaboo, and they play with their lips and tongue by blowing saliva bubbles.

Try not to compare your baby to other babies. We know, it's so hard not to! Even though there is a developmental framework, all babies have different strengths and needs. If you notice your baby is babbling a lot but not sitting up, remember it is normal for your baby to decrease their practice in some skills while they are focusing on gaining another skill.

One research study posits that infants begin to shift their attention from an individual's eyes to their mouth between four and eight months of age. This shift allows them to process audiovisual cues (listening to words while seeing them being produced by the mouth), and it also helps your baby witness social cues. Research suggests that the

The Landau reflex appears between four and five months of age. This reflex is important for postural development, helps integrate motor actions to decrease clumsiness, helps with emotional regulation, and supports visual perception.

The Tonic Labrinthine reflex might start to integrate between four months and three and a half years old.

The Moro reflex often integrates between two and four months old. Some signs of retention might be hypersensitivity, vestibular problems such as motion sickness, oculomotor and visual perceptual problems, allergies, lowered immunity, poor stamina, and poor adaptability.

The rooting reflex is often integrated by the end of the fourth month. Breast-fed babies might retain this reflex up to eight months. Some signs of retention might be a tongue tie, thumb sucking, oral hypersensitivity, poor swallowing, eating, chewing, and speech and articulation problems.

emergence of speech sound is directly correlated to your baby's environment. Therefore, continue to give a rich linguistic environment of unscripted dialogue to your baby all day long during unstructured time. Tell them you love them, retell a story about you or their grandma, recite the lyrics to your favorite song—all to reinforce speech patterns, as well as to increase audiovisual and social cues.

On the other hand, during structured play, reduce your baby's "linguistic load" by keeping it simple and providing lots of repetition. Examples of simple, repetitive speech are embedded throughout the play positions section.

Developmental Play

Your baby is more active now, and you are utilizing various play positions and observing your baby's movement patterns. Previously changing your baby's positions was important for skin integrity and to maintain symmetrical head shape. Now positions and patterns impact development differently. Your baby's play positions and movement patterns help to enrich their development for future movement and ability, enabling them to learn about their body in relation to their environment.

While engaging your baby in the play routine you have established, remember to use baby-guided-play, which is also known as serve and return play interaction or Ping-Pong play, because your baby serves you their interest and you return with positive, supportive feedback.

PLAY POSITIONS
Tummy Time Play Position

Tummy time continues to develop back, neck, shoulder, and arm strength throughout the first year. It simply looks different each month. During tummy time play this month, your baby will be primarily in forearm weight bearing, pushing up through their hands with their arms extended.

Encourage your baby to be propped on bent forearms for tummy time. Utilize yourself, a mirror, or a book during tummy time to facilitate vertical scanning. Be creative and give your baby new visual experiences, opportunities to feel different textures, different movement experiences,

and overall an abundance of sensory-enriched exposure. An example of being creative with this position is laying your baby over a stuffed animal and having a tea party. Consider blowing bubbles ("ooooooh bubbles") or racing cars ("vrrroooom, vrrroooom car") in front of them while they are propped on their forearms or pushing up into extended arms during tummy time.

Forearm weight bearing during tummy time is important for the development of head control, as your baby learns to balance between their abdominal and pectoral muscles (flexors) and back and shoulder muscles (extensors) so they can initiate lifting their chest off the floor.

Push-Ups

Sit on the floor with your back supported so that you are comfortable and able to safely support your baby. Place an exercise ball or stack of pillows securely in between your legs.

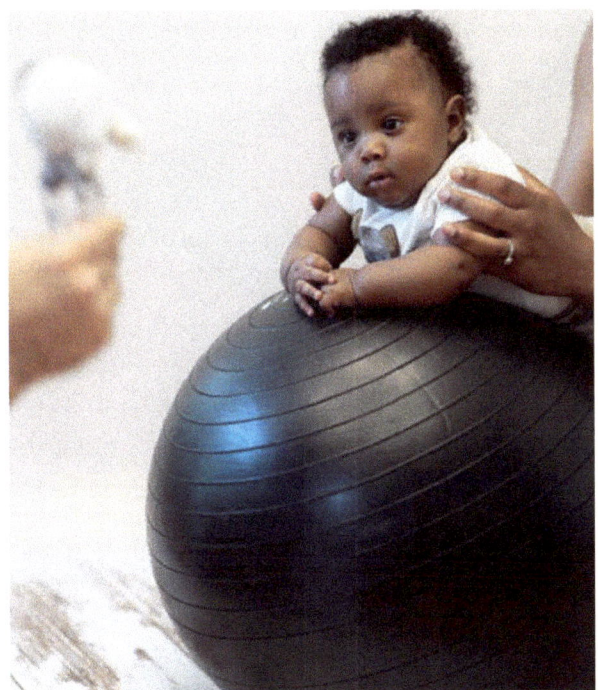

Place your baby lying on their tummy on the ball or pillows, facing away from you. Place your fingers over your baby's chest (pectoralis muscles) with your thumb around their shoulders. This touch (tactile) cue gives their muscles the awareness that they need to extend their arms up, activating their chest muscles. Control must be activated at your baby's chest/shoulder (proximally) and then down through their arms and hands (distally), enabling them to push up.

When you gently decrease the amount of pressure and support you are giving your baby through their chest, you will signal your baby's body to bend their arms and return down to forearms. Gently encourage and practice the transition between being propped on their forearms and pushing up to straight arms by providing your baby with frequent opportunities throughout the day to play in this tummy time position.

As your baby progresses, try rocking the ball forward and backward and side to side. This allows your baby to activate their core muscles in different planes of movement to further work on stability.

If you have someone helping you, they can dangle a toy over your baby's head to encourage this movement. Otherwise, place toys on something higher, such as an ottoman, in front of the ball. If you don't have a ball or someone else to help, you can also complete this activity on the floor.

Side-Lying Play Position

Side-lying continues to be an important position to play and explore in this month. Side-lying play helps your baby activate their extensors and flexors equally, providing the balance needed to develop neck and trunk righting reactions against gravity so they are able to maintain their balance when sitting. If your baby's extensors are stronger than their flexors, they will arch backward (side to back).

If your baby's flexors are stronger than their extensors, they will curl in forward side-lying. Both of these scenarios inhibit your baby from rolling.

Carrying your baby in the side-lying position, facing them out and away from you, which is often referred to as a football hold, is a simple way to incorporate the side-lying position into your daily routine.

Eye-Spy Rolling

When done consistently, singing or using the same phrase each time you roll your baby during play helps to prepare them for transitional movements (the ability to get into and out of the sitting, quadruped, kneeling, and standing positions). For example, gently rock your baby on their side while singing "There were 10 in the bed, and the little one said," pause, "Roll over, roll over," then roll your baby over.

Place your baby on their back in front of a mirror with a toy in between. Bring their hands together and then to their feet. Next roll them onto their side. While you roll them into the side-lying position, gently apply pressure through their shoulder and hip. Encourage your baby to search for the toy by shaking it or activating a light-up or sound component to gain their attention. Allow them time to look at it, reach for it, and play with it. Place it back down between your baby and the mirror, then roll your baby into tummy time.

Make this activity more challenging by placing the toy under a small blanket partially exposed. Encourage your baby to locate the object in partial view. Help them to slowly pull the blanket off with hand-over-hand assistance, placing your hand on top of your baby's and gently guiding their movement. Allow your baby time to play with the toy before placing the toy back down between your baby and the mirror under the small blanket. Roll your baby into the tummy time position and allow them to explore again.

Next roll your baby onto their other side and repeat this play activity. Bend down so that you are in their line of vision, enabling them to make eye contact with you at times, which allows you to watch for fatigue or frustration so you know when to stop the activity.

The Nuture Notebook for Mom and Baby

When your baby has mastered side-lying play, work on propping them up on one elbow with your support. This propped side-lying position, which is a prerequisite for rolling, might be over your arm or over a pillow such as a Boppy with your support. This position helps strengthen your baby's neck too.

Remember to alternate sides during play in the side-lying position, encouraging midline play with your baby's hands to feet and hands and feet to mouth.

Supported Sitting Play Position

As each month progresses, your baby is becoming stronger and more functional in the supported sitting play position. Your baby is still unable to sit without support; however, playing with them in the supported sitting position and allowing wobbly play continues to be important.

Hand Push and Press

Sit with an exercise ball or stack of pillows between your legs. Place your baby in between you and the ball or pillows. They can be either in the supported sitting or supported standing positions. Gently push their open, flat hands through the exercise ball. Enhance your play by communication, through singing or counting.

Sit and Lean

Sit on the floor with your back supported in a comfortable position. Position your baby either facing you seated with a Boppy pillow or between your legs. Encourage your baby to lean forward on their hands while playing with toys. This position strengthens their back and tummy, which is critical for future strength and posture. You can encourage this forward movement by placing toys in front of them and making exaggerated expressions while you speak. Over time, slowly move the toy away from your baby so they keep leaning further forward toward it.

Mirror, Mirror on the Wall

Place your baby safely and supported on the ground in front of a mirror. Turn off the lights and quietly talk or sing a song to your baby to comfort them. After a minute or when the song is done, turn the lights back on. Watch your baby enjoy seeing themselves in the mirror, then disappear, only to return again.

Add more excitement to mirror play by gathering your baby's favorite stuffed animals and silly accessories, such as hats, sunglasses, reading glasses, scarves, gloves, or any safe, colorful, fun things you have lying around. Use these items to tell your baby a story in the mirror or set a book to the side for you to act out with their stuffed animals. Incorporate your baby and their body parts into the story. For example, touch their favorite stuffed animal's nose and say something such as, "A bee landed on Penelope's nose!" in your story. "Where is your nose?" Point to your baby's nose. This position allows them to look up and see your lips moving to speak or read while they are also looking at the book.

Sit-Reach-Touch

While your baby is in the supported sitting position, gently brush a toy across the back of their hand. Hold the object at the middle of their body and encourage and wait for your baby to bring both of their hands together to play with the toy. Allow your baby to hold it, play with it, and purposefully release it. Provide your baby with opportunities to play with a variety of toy shapes and textures.

Working on visual tracking while you are playing with various toys for your baby to grasp and play with continues to be important. Utilizing toys that you can roll might encourage your baby to follow, touch, and grasp for them while maintaining their interest.

Curious George

Your baby is showing more interest in smaller items; therefore, another great activity to perform in supported sitting is to place a safe, small object, such as a Cheerios or puff, in a sealed, clear container for your baby to reach for, shake, and examine.

Pat-a-Pattern

While sitting, encourage your baby to lean forward on their hands by playing a game of pat-a-pattern. Model a patting pattern with your own hand, such as pat, pat, pat or pat, pat, clap. Hold your baby's hands hand-over-hand and repeat that pattern with their hands. Allow for wait time and observe if your baby shows any interest. Repeat.

Supported Sitting Peekaboo

While in supported sitting, move a toy around to gain you baby's attention and observe where they are looking. Once you know your baby is engaged, put a blanket over the toy and wait. Watch your baby look at the blanket. Ask, "Where could it be?" Pull the blanket off and say, "There it is!"

Back Play Position

Remember to limit daytime back play to when your baby needs a break from tummy time, side-lying, and supported sitting positions.

Finger Puppets

Laying your baby on their back allows you to be hands-free to engage your baby visually in activities such as using finger puppets. Put on a finger puppet and use a light touch to stroke your baby's arm or leg.

This month, continue to encourage your baby to turn to look at the spot where you touched them as well as track the movement of the finger puppet by moving it slowly in all planes, including far right, up and down to midline, to far left up and down. Also place the finger puppet in your baby's central vision in midline and move it toward their nose and back.

Babble On

When your baby is happy and content, start by massaging their cheeks, lips, and mouth to increase sensation. Try these massages.

Cheek circles: Take your thumb and pointer fingers, flanked on both cheeks, and gently make the "fishy face" in a circular motion, five times. You can add funny words like "fishy face."

Lip tracing: Trace the top and bottom of your baby's lips, similar to the motion of putting on lip balm. Do this five times.

Nose-to-chin tracing: Use your fingers to trace down your baby's nose, drag your finger down over their top lip, bottom lip, and chin.

You can even try to open and close your baby's jaw by gently pushing up on their chin at the end. Repeat five times.

Lastly, make sure your baby can see your face and babble with them, concentrating on sounds B/M. You can start saying "bababababa" or "mamamama." While concentrating on these two sounds, slowly trace your index and middle finger over your baby's top and bottom lips and gently try to open and close their lips five times.

Don't force anything. This should be fun. If your baby isn't having it, stop and try again at another time.

Baby Burrito

This interactive activity is similar to a towel wrap; however, now you are incorporating the rolling in after your baby is unwrapped. Place your baby on the floor, on top of their favorite blanket. You can pretend to add ingredients to your "baby burrito" or sing a simple song such as, "Don't be blue! I love you. Snuggle (state your baby's name and hand them their favorite stuffed animal). Wrap you both with love (wrap each side around your baby, always making sure their face is out). Roll you, hug you, and sprinkle you with kisses from head to toes" (roll, hug, and kiss your baby and repeat as many times as they like). This deep "squeeze" feeds your baby's sensory system and is very calming for infants, as well as slow rolling, which feeds their balance system.

End by unwrapping your baby, gently rolling them from side to side and then onto their tummy.

Baby Wants to Take a Walk

Your baby should be lying on their back at this age for this interactive story; however, this activity can be carried through the next several years and done standing.

Begin by saying, "Baby wanted to take a walk." (Say your baby's name or two-syllable nickname instead of just saying baby). "Step, step, steppity, step" (walk your baby's feet). "Step, step, steppity, step."

And on their walk, they saw MR. BEAR. "Hello, MR. BEAR." "Hello," he said.

"How are you, MR. BEAR?" "I'm well," he said. "Would you like to take a walk?" "I'd love to take a walk." "So stomp, stomp, stompity, stomp" (stomp your baby's feet). "Stomp, stomp, stompity, stomp."

And on their walk, they saw SLY FOX. "Hello, SLY FOX." "Hello," he said. "How are you, SLY FOX?" "I'm fine," he said, "Would you like to take a walk?" "I'd love to take a walk." "So tip toe, tip toe, tip toe, tip toe" (tap the balls of baby's feet at the base of their toes). "Tip toe, tip toe, tip toe, tip toe."

And on their walk, they saw LITTLE BIRD. "Hello, LITTLE BIRD." "Hello," she said. "How are you, LITTLE BIRD?" "I'm wonderful," she said. "Would you like to take a walk?" "I'd love to take a walk." So flap, flap, flappity, flap" (flap your baby's arms). Flap, flap, flappity, flap."

And on their walk, they saw HAPPY

HARE. "Hello, HAPPY HARE." "Hello," she said. "How are you, HAPPY HARE?" "I'm happy," she said. "Would you like to take a walk?" "I'd love to take a walk." So hop, hop, hoppity, hop" (hold your baby's feet together and hop them up/down). "Hop, hop, hoppity, hop."

And on their walk, they saw SHY FAWN. "Hello, SHY FAWN." "Hello," she said. "How are you, SHY FAWN?" "I'm magnificent," she said. "Would you like to take a walk?" "I'd love to take a walk." "Trot, trot, trot, trot, trot" (Trot your baby's feet). "Trot, trot, trot, trot, trot."

And on their walk, they saw TINY FROG. "Hello TINY FROG." "Hello," he said. "How are you, TINY FROG?" "Fantastic," he said. "Would you like to take a walk?" And he said... (dramatic pause) "Ribbit, ribbit"... (dramatic pause) AND JUMPED INTO THE POND. THE END. (Gently roll your baby onto their tummy when you say he jumped into the pond.)

Note: This is a grow-with-me interactive story because you can use this story through kindergarten simply by varying it, depending on your child's age. Though it will be familiar to your child from birth on, you can expand on it, making development of motor skills and social skills fun and easy as your child is ready for each next step.

Responding to Voices

This activity is intended to facilitate visual and auditory tracking and response, which are important for receptive language skills and social communication.

Try this after eating or when baby is alert and content. Place your baby on their back. Make sure your baby can see you. Stand in your baby's line of sight, off to the right and not directly in front of them. Make noises such as clicking your tongue, stomping, and clapping while calling your baby's name. Continue to do this until they look at you. Once they look at you, reward them with something that makes them happy. Now move to a different spot and repeat this exercise. Eventually you can fade the noises and just say your baby's name.

Want to make things harder? Move behind your baby, make noises while saying their name, and see if they try to look. The most challenging is to leave the room, make noises and say their name, and see if they look for you.

Four Months Old

Fill in the answers to reflect on the past month and to track.

How do you feel?

_____

_____

What exercises did you work on?

_____

_____

What is your baby doing now?

_____

_____

What was your baby's favorite activity this month?

_____

_____

What questions do you have for your ob-gyn and your baby's pediatrician?

_____

_____

Notes:

_____

_____

_____

_____

The Nuture Notebook for Mom and Baby

Five Months Old

MOMMY MOVEMENTS

It's time to free yourself from everything holding you back from being the parent that you were meant to be—the expectations you or society is placing on you and what you think you should be doing. It's time to focus on what feels right to you. Free yourself from any negative thinking, anxiety, and peer pressure. Free yourself from social media perfections, self-imposed pressures, and self-doubt.

Clear your mind, open your heart, love fully, and enjoy your baby. When negative thoughts creep in, stand tall, open your chest, take a deep breath and tell yourself, "I am free" as you shift your thoughts to the positive, smile, and feel the weight melt off your shoulders. Take another deep breath. Bring the quiet moments of just you and your baby into your focus, then carry on and focus on your recovery.

Postnatal Core Progressions

Your muscles, skin, fascia, and connective tissue went through a lot in almost 10 months of pregnancy. They were stretched, pulled, and kicked and are (somewhat) trying to shrink back again. Your mind and body have developed a new neuromotor pattern, changing the way they worked since pregnancy. Because the muscular foundation of your midline (rectus abdominus (RA), aka your "six pack" and linea alba, the thick white line of fascia that runs through your belly button and bisects your "six pack") has stretched and cannot harvest the force needed to work for your body, other muscles—such as your side abdominal muscles (obliques) used for twisting—have to help. Your obliques typically become the primary stabilizer for your core during pregnancy, so most women become oblique dominant—a pattern that remains even after you have your baby. You have to wake up your RA and the linea alba and retrain them to take the wheel to set your core again postpartum.

Core organization, which means defining the order in which your muscles turn on and how they work together, is necessary first. Then you can progress to working on core strength. It sounds complicated, but it's not. It is critical to regaining any semblance of your pre-pregnancy belly.

Abdominal Activation and Sequencing

Once you've mastered the core activation and foundation sequence in a slow, sedentary manner, adding movement through your trunk and legs will make it more difficult to maintain both your breathing and the engagement and stabilization of your pelvic girdle. Remember, when weaker parts get challenged, dominant patterns take over. Reverting to a comfortable pattern is typical but needs to be corrected. Keep your core-setting basics in mind as you transition to core-stabilizing exercises and do not rush through any exercise series. If you do exercises incorrectly or utilize the wrong sequence of core engagement, you might make your midline more vulnerable to injury, such as diastasis recti (aka abdominal separation).

First, perform one set, five cycles of

A Note on Progressive Challenges: Do not rush through any exercise series, no matter how simple they may seem. If you do exercises incorrectly or utilize the wrong sequence of core engagement, you may make your midline more vulnerable to injuries. Once you've mastered an initial exercise, Progressive Challenges are different movements that are added to a previously acquired exercise to challenge you farther. The ability to be comfortable and sustain core setting throughout an entire exercise may indicate that your body is ready to add one Progressive Challenge.

Diaphragmatic Breathing with Pelvic Floor Contractions (see page 14) and transversus abdominis engagement (TA) together (contracting for five seconds) on exhale. When imagining your TA muscle, it might help to think zip-up, for zipping up tight pants. When your body is ready, you might progress through the following either sitting with your feet on the floor or lying down with your knees bent.

Visit our website for more women's health information, including the progressions and further information.

Progression Challenge One: Pelvic Tilt

Inhale, exhale, and pull in your PF, zip up your lower-belly, and tilt your pelvis back, focusing on the spot directly above the midline of your pelvic bones (your pubic symphysis, the spot where both sides of your pelvis meet). Use that spot (this is your PF and your TA working together) to bring your pubic bone toward your belly button. Make sure you are not driving this movement by squeezing your glutes or rounding your shoulders/upper abdominals. Hold this position for five seconds, relax, and repeat the entire sequence five times.

Progression Challenge Two: Leg March

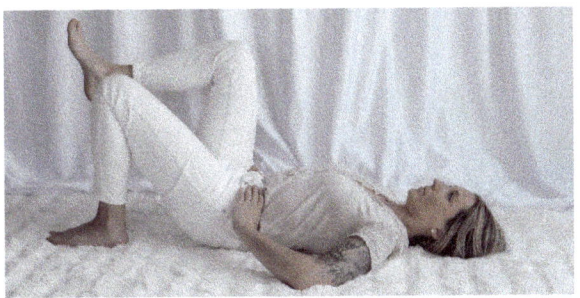

Inhale, exhale, and pull in your PF, zip up your lower belly, and lift your left knee up, as if you are marching. Again, focus on the spot directly above your pubic symphysis. Use that spot (this is your PF and your TA working together) to start this movement. Hold this position for five seconds, release your left knee down, and repeat using your right knee. Repeat the entire sequence five times per side, alternating your legs throughout. Keep your pelvis level while marching by holding your PF and lower abdominals.

Progression Challenge Three: Leg Extension

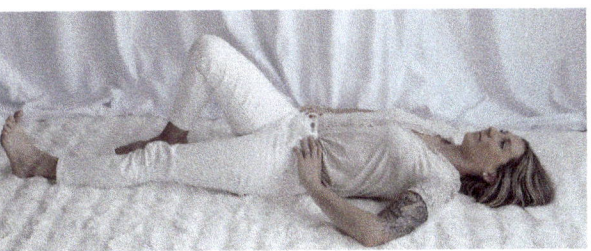

Inhale, exhale, and pull in your PF, zip up your lower belly, and tap (straighten) your right leg out in front of you, sliding your heel along the ground. Inhale and on the exhale, still using your PF and TA, start bending your knee and sliding your heel back toward your bottom as you return back to start. Reset your body, your breath, and your pelvic floor and TA. Repeat using your left leg. Repeat the entire sequence five times per side, alternating your legs throughout. Your pelvis should remain level while performing these leg extensions.

Progression Challenge Four: Hip Opener

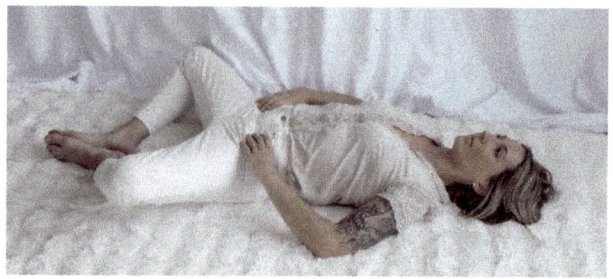

Inhale, exhale, and pull in your PF, zip up your lower belly, and while keeping your knees bent, open your right hip by releasing your knee to the side, while keeping your feet in place. Inhale and on the exhale, still maintaining your pelvic floor and TA activation, bring your knee back up to the starting position. Reset and breathe. Repeat using your left knee. Repeat the entire sequence five times per side, alternating your legs throughout. Your pelvis should remain level while performing these hip openers.

BABY'S DEVELOPMENT

Your routines are set, and hopefully sleep is more bountiful. One thing about babies is that as soon as you find your groove, they throw a wrench in the works. Don't despair. Parenthood might feel hard at times. Remember you are doing an amazing job, and it is always important to celebrate the little victories.

Motor Development

Around this time and moving forward, babies' motor skills tend to vary greatly due to a variety of factors, including temperament, motivation to explore, and strength.

Your baby is becoming more active this month, interacting with toys and their environment. Your baby continues to roll from their back to their side with symmetry of hands to feet. Once in the side-lying position, they are able to dissociate (bend one leg and straighten the other) their legs, straightening the bottom one and then righting their trunk and pushing up through their bottom forearm while rolling over to their tummy.

Your baby is able to shift their weight around and will begin to pivot in a circle to move around their environment and reach for toys. They will push up through their hands with their elbows extended, but they might return to the position with their shoulders retracted and arms up.

With a wide base of support, typically in a Boppy or play nest or with their legs out in front in a circle, your baby is able to sit momentarily while leaning forward on their hands and keeping their head upright. They do still need your support and close supervision in this position. By the end of this month, you might start to see your baby sitting independently and using their hands to play with a toy. You might observe protective extension forward, which is when your baby puts their arms and hands forward and downward when they are moved into a face-down position, as if they are trying to protect or brace themselves from falling.

While your baby is lying on their back, they might start to lift their head up when you are putting on their shirt or taking it off. Your baby can lift their bottom off the ground while on their back, pushing their feet into the floor, which looks like a bridge. They are also lifting more of their trunk off the floor when on their tummy, bearing more weight through their hands and enabling their shoulders, arms, and hands to get stronger. This strengthening of the legs, arms, and core muscles helps prepare your baby for crawling and transitioning between positions in the future.

While in a supported standing position, your baby is able to support almost their entire body weight through their legs. They might also like bouncing in this position or while on their knees.

Your baby's fine motor skills are going to start to explode. Pick up your art supplies because your baby enjoys observing you create artwork and will grab a marker or pencil if it's within reach. Paint, color, draw, and scribble in front of your baby; they will love watching you!

Your baby might also be able to release a toy and pick it back up purposefully, as well as reach for a toy with one hand, hold it, and transfer it from one hand to the other. Babies at this age enjoy tapping toys, and they attempt to grasp small objects. Be aware of your baby's surroundings now that they are more mobile and show an interest in smaller objects.

The Moro reflex is typically inhibited by now. Therefore, you will not see your baby's startle reflex anymore.

Note: Now that your baby is rolling and prior to them sitting independently, lower their crib mattress for their safety. Be sure crib mobiles are out of reach.

Visual Development

We have some exciting news! Your baby's color vision has developed enough that they are now able to see most colors as well as an adult.

As your baby's binocular vision continues to develop, their eyes will stay aligned. Your baby's depth perception will rapidly improve over the next two months now that they are using their eyes together. These gains in depth perception and hand-eye coordination facilitate the exploration of the world through their eyes and hands. Depth perception and hand-eye coordination are key to your baby's ability to navigate their world and determine where things are in space. Your baby will also be able to anticipate the direction, path, and movement (trajectory) of a slowly moving object. Their visual acuity is now improving as their eyes develop and is approximately 20/120 to 20/100. An adult is able to see only five to six times better than your baby at this time.

Cognitive Development

Your baby distinguishes between friendly and angry voices, as well as showing an overall interest in the sounds of objects. They enjoy hearing you vary your tone of voice and talk silly. When your baby wants to restart an activity, they might indicate this by touching a toy or your hand. As their abilities progress, so might their frustration due to the growing knowledge of challenges presented to them, such as a toy being difficult to reach.

Last month, your baby might have been focused on their hands and tongue as they explored them and gained the awareness that they are a part of them. Now your baby will be focusing primarily on their feet and bringing them to their mouth.

Remember, when your baby is irritable, they might be going through another cognitive leap.

Social-Emotional Development

Your baby shows some new areas of interest, such as exploring and analyzing your facial features. They might start to touch and grab your face, particularly your nose or chin because they are easier to grasp.

Your baby may smile at themselves in a mirror when they get a glimpse of themselves. They also might analyze their own facial features.

Another important part of your baby's social development is their growing awareness of who strangers are and their boundaries in regards to them. Over the next couple of months, your baby might start to become truly fearful of people whom they consider unfamiliar. Because they might cry if acquaintances attempt to handle them, this is not the time in their development to leave them with anyone unfamiliar, such as a new childcare provider.

Encourage caregivers to speak with you directly rather than to your baby. Allow your baby to make the initial move toward them when they are ready. Meanwhile hold your baby and remain calm because they will be able to sense whether you are comfortable or not. Pay attention to your baby's cues, such as reaching up for you or clinging to you if they feel uncomfortable around someone. Be sure to respond to your baby's needs for reassurance.

Self-Care Development

Your baby is continuing to learn how to move their tongue to prepare them with the oral-motor skills required to move food in their mouth prior to swallowing. Your baby may be cleared by their pediatrician this month to begin eating solid foods. Every baby and parent are different, so talk to your baby's pediatrician to obtain specific information about your baby's readiness for this developmental stage. You must also do what you feel comfortable with as you introduce solids.

Consider registering for a CPR class specifically for pediatrics before starting solids with your baby.

Continue to encourage your baby to start holding their bottle or your breast when drinking and explore different textured toys with their mouth.

Speech and Language Development

As your baby grows, their communication is evolving. Communication starts as a random cry and turns into a deliberate cry, eventually evolving into sounds and babbling. Emerging is also your baby's ability to recognize their name by turning their head or looking up. Your baby may even chuckle and babble when they are alone and may respond to increased attention or excitement when hearing familiar voices.

It is important to note that not all communication is verbal. At this stage, it is actually more frequently non-verbal. For example, when your baby reaches for something, they are communicating. The subtleties are there, and taking a step back and observing will provide you with an abundance of information. Your baby continues to attempt to copy your facial expressions, such as grinning and frowning. You can make exaggerated faces, such as sticking out your tongue, raising your eyebrows, or opening your mouth wide, to encourage your baby to mimic you. Sing songs with facial expressions because babies are drawn toward music and exaggerated facial expressions

Sometimes we like to jump in and facilitate activities to a fault. Remember serve and return or Ping-Pong play. Observe the serve, which is what your baby is looking at, and in return give them your full attention, communicate with a simple statement, take the item of interest, and create a game with it. For example, if you observe your baby staring at a ball, pick up the ball, hold it up, say "ball," roll the ball, and state "roll ball." If your baby is still attending, throw the ball up in the air and say "up." Your baby hasn't attached meaning to words quite yet. You are teaching them. The action of labeling items teaches your baby that sounds are assigned specific meanings. What is important is that your baby is engaged in the activity. Once they lose their attention to the object, move on. Your baby will attend to and learn from you best when they are already engaged.

Makes sense, right? When you are already paying attention to something, that something is more likely to keep your attention. Advertisers make millions on this idea. You will be better able to gather information and support your baby by observing and enhancing, rather than controlling.

It is an amazingly magical experience seeing everything new through your baby's eyes.

At this time, your baby begins to vocalize to music and people, as well as to communicate their emotions in ways other than simply crying and laughing. They show you that they understand their name by looking at you, and they continue to babble, combining both vowels and consonants, such as "bababa" or "dadada."

Developmental Play

Your baby might exhibit frustration this month due to their growing knowledge of themselves and objects around them, in comparison to their abilities. Remain patient and calm.

Precrawling Play Positions

As you've noticed throughout this book, your baby doesn't need an abundance of toys. What your baby does need is a lot of enriched sensory experiences in a variety of play positions while utilizing movement patterns. The quality of your baby's movements is significant in their development.

For your baby to feel secure in their motor abilities, there must be a constant interaction between stability and mobility within their body. Transition between various positions during play will help promote this interaction and provide important sensory experiences needed for motor learning.

Tummy Time Play Position

Tummy Rock

While in tummy time, your baby is now able to lift their head well and look around. This development enables them to interact more with you and their environment. When you sing and rock side to side, do it with more enthusiasm. Your baby's improved upper body, neck, and head control allows you to focus on the weight-shift through each of their arms, one at a time as you rock further to each side. They can lie with their legs straight back or bent with feet planted against your thighs, providing pressure through their feet and legs.

Safe Table Time

If your baby often straightens and arches their back, with their legs extended as well (an extension pattern), this position might be helpful. Note: Reflux might cause your baby to go into an extension pattern frequently to relieve discomfort they may be feeling. Concerns about reflux should be discussed with your baby's pediatrician.

Start by placing your baby's chest and tummy on a surface, such as a pillow or folded-up blanket, that allows you to safely support them at their torso while also allowing their legs to dangle from their hips down. This position lets gravity work with your baby's legs, relaxing them toward the ground. Furthermore, it breaks up the extension pattern so your baby's efforts might go toward bearing weight through their forearms to play. While your baby is in this position, place a toy with which they can engage in front of them.

Circular Pivoting

Circular pivoting is a precursor to crawling because your baby is learning to weight-shift over their shoulders and hands laterally while moving.

Place your baby in the tummy time position on a safe surface, such as on the floor or a tummy time mat. Place a toy to the side of your baby and tap it to encourage them to pivot on their tummy toward the toy and reach. As they get closer to the toy, continue to move the toy, encouraging them to continue to turn in a circle. Read your baby's cues, praise them, and allow them to play with the toy before they get frustrated.

Quadruped Rock

Playing on hands and knees (the quadruped position) is an important pre-crawling position required to strengthen your baby's arms and legs. If your baby is able to maintain this position with your support, place them on their hands and knees with their hips and knees both bent at a 90-degree angle. Hold them around their torso and gently rock them back and forth, left and right. This rocking pattern, the shifting of weight back and forth between each of their sides or forward and backward, primes their muscles and joints for future crawling.

Repetitive movements like rocking help to distribute weight through muscles and joints, which

encourage the next level of control in their body. Your baby must also have lateral balance to maintain an upright position and stand. If your baby is not able to maintain this position with your support, no worries. You can try again next month.

Ball Balance

Place your baby on a small, slightly deflated ball, small bolster, round stuffed animal, or pillow. Encourage your baby to put weight on the ball through their flat hands and bent knees. Provide very gentle and slow bounces into the ball while rocking your baby forward and backward.

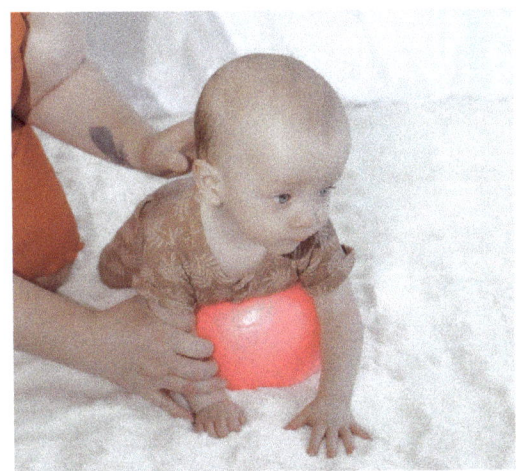

Supported Sitting Play Position

The side-lying position continues to be a great play position. However, now that your baby is moving more, they might not stay in this position long. Side-lying is a transition position so your baby will likely roll onto their back or tummy instead, as well as prefer sitting upright.

Supported sitting continues to be an important play position because wobbly play is needed to stimulate your baby's balance (vestibular) system. You can do many things in this position, enabling your baby to see the world more easily. At this point, you need to be more cautious about seating devices, such as a baby swing, because your baby is able to pull themselves forward, creating a risk of falling out.

Sit and Reach, Gradually Decreasing Level of Support

Sit on the floor. Place your baby in between your legs. Place a toy in front of them to play with. Focus on working toward providing less postural support to your baby. If your baby is stable and safe, maintaining an upright trunk posture while using their hands to play, gradually move your support from their torso/trunk to their hips/thighs. Provide cues to keep your baby upright only as necessary for balance. Encouraging wobbly play challenges your baby's muscles and teaches them to support themselves, enabling play with both hands.

Push the toy down to the side and encourage your baby to reach their hand out to the side and weight-bear through it to balance themselves while playing.

Weight-Shift Wiggles

Sit on the floor. Place your baby between your legs in a supported sitting position. Encourage weight shifting through one side by placing a toy slightly to the side and front of them within stretchable reach. Shake the toy to get your baby's visual attention if needed while verbally encouraging them to lean, reach, and grasp the toy. Remember to switch sides so they get practice on both sides.

If your baby is having difficulty with this exercise, place a pool noodle or rolled-up towel under one of their thighs and over the

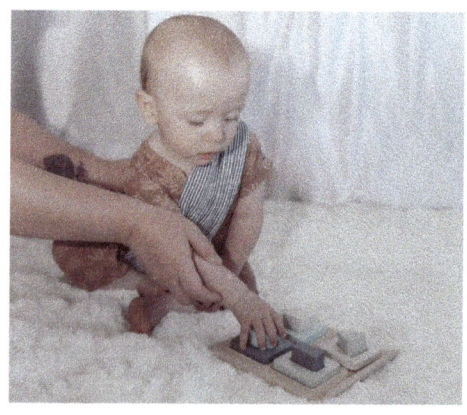

other. Use the noodle to manipulate their weight shifting through each side.

Ball Weight Shift

Kneel with your baby between your legs. Place a ball in front of your baby, then encourage them to hold on to it. Gently shift their weight from side to side in a rocking fashion while they hold onto the ball.

Next place the ball by your baby's right side with their arm over it. Roll them slightly against and up the ball and back down to provide a gentle stretching input through their side. Elongating the weight-bearing side is needed to move from side-lying up through their arm. It is also important for your baby to develop elongation through each side of their trunk/torso for future symmetrical transitional movements. Switch sides.

Point and Touch

Reading with your baby from birth through their young life is one of the most important things you can do for them. This month while reading to your baby, point to pictures, encourage them to touch the pictures, say simple words like "bee," and make simple sounds like "buzz." You don't need to read a new book each night. In fact, repeating books will build familiarity with vocabulary and increase the likelihood your baby will repeat sounds.

Although your baby will not be able to turn pages independently for several more months, you might notice that they attempt to reach for the book and turn them. You can facilitate these attempts by lifting a page slightly but not fully turning it. Wiggle the page back and forth to get your baby's attention. Hold their forearm and gently turn the page using hand-over-hand, placing your hand on your baby's hand and helping them turn the page.

Textured books are fun at this age. Introduce your baby to various textures by rubbing their fingers or the palm of their hand along the different textures. Exposure to textures on the hands directly translates into tolerance for different food textures in the mouth, so get adventurous.

Side to Side, Forward, and Back

Sit on the floor with your legs around an exercise ball or stack of pillows. Place your baby on top of the ball or pillows, facing toward you or away from you or to the side, holding them around their torso.

Gently move your baby with the ball side to side and forward to backward three to five times while singing or counting to them. After your baby is comfortable, quickly yet gently shift your baby to one side to work on activating protective extension reactions, which are important to keep them safe while transitioning between positions and help protect them if they fall.

Complete the same steps one to three. Encourage the same side arm to extend out (e.g. shift to left, extend out left arm). Repeat this a couple times on each side.

Next, quickly yet gently shift your baby forward, encouraging their hands straight forward and eventually flat on the ball. You might motivate them forward by placing a mirror in front of your baby and saying "peeka" for them to anticipate movement and then "boo" as you move them toward the mirror.

Interactive Nursery Rhymes

Incorporate movement into your favorite nursery rhyme. For example, hold a plastic ring and "steer" the bus while singing "The Wheels on the Bus." Shift your baby's weight through each side of their bottom by tilting them slightly to each side.

If your baby is more stable, you can place them on one of your thighs with their legs on either side and act out the song further perhaps by raising your leg up and down with them as you "steer" and sing the verse "The people on the bus go up and down, up and down, up and down." Shift their weight from side to side by gently swaying them to verses such as "The wipers on the bus go swish, swish, swish, swish, swish, swish."

You can change your positioning for this activity in a variety of ways, for example by having them sit on your stomach or facing you with your legs around them. Doing this interactive nursery rhyme play in a variety of positions will change their visual perspective and challenge their balance differently.

Meet the Artist

Your baby might start to show interest in watching you draw. As an effective prewriting skill, this activity facilitates tracking and visual attention. As a bonus, it might even be relaxing for you.

Position your baby in the supported sitting play position between your legs or draw on a dry erase board, Magna Doodle, or paper. Use a writing device with contrasting colors, such as a white dry erase board with black or red dry erase marker, being careful that your baby doesn't put the marker in their mouth. Using all areas of the board or paper, draw vertical lines, horizontal lines, crosses, circles, or whatever captures your baby's attention. You can encourage your baby to explore with pudding or whipped cream on a sheet pan, in the bathtub, or on their feeding tray.

Mirror Drawing

While your baby is sitting up and observing themselves in a mirror, use a dry erase marker, washable crayon, or window crayon to draw a hat on their head, a butterfly above them, or any other creative item. Sing a song or say a phrase about what you are drawing.

What's in the Box?

There are many ways you can play this activity with your baby. You can purchase a specific toy or simply use a tissue box or wipes box with a wide soft opening. If using a tissue box, remove the clear plastic around the opening, throwing it away immediately so your baby doesn't play with it. In addition, make sure the opening is not sharp and that your baby doesn't put the box in their mouth.

Place your baby in the supported sitting play position. Sit in front of or behind them, with a mirror in front of them so you are able to see their engagement. Place items such as scarves, small soft toys, baby paper or edible puffs in the box for your baby to pull out.

To expand on the activity, if you use a scarf, throw it up in the air so they can watch it fall down. Gently move the scarf back and forth and up and down over their face and body.

Make a story with the soft toys you are using.

For example, farm animals can be scattered in front of your baby, and the box can turn into the barn for a bedtime story in which you are the farmer bringing the animals into the barn one by one for the night.

Flashlight Tag

Grab a flashlight and watch your baby giggle during this fun visual tracking activity. Sit with your baby between your legs. Turn out the lights. Shine the flashlight on the left side of a blank wall. Slowly move the flashlight from left to right and top to bottom, following the natural reading pattern for future learning. Turn off the flashlight in between to return to the top left and repeat.

You can also turn the flashlight on and off, moving it to different areas on the wall for an eye-spy-the-light game.

You can repeat this activity when your baby is older to work on learning the start and sequence of letters and numbers.

Bilateral Hand Play

Encourage the integration of both sides of your baby's body through hand togetherness play. Use two colorful toys of different textures and practice this hand togetherness play in multiple positions. Start by holding your baby's hands in your hands and rubbing or clapping their hands together to increase their body awareness. Next, put one toy on either side of your baby's body within their reach. Encourage your baby to reach for and pick up one toy in each hand. Eventually this bilateral hand play will lead to banging two toys together, which is a prerequisite for clapping.

Ball Sit-to-Stand

Ball sit-to-stands are a great way to start to work on the transitional movement patterns involved in sit-to-stand and stand-to-sit. Sit with a small, slightly deflated ball, stack of pillows, or bolster between your legs. Alternately, you can just use your leg. Place your baby on top of the object or your leg in a seated position, holding them around their torso. As they get more stable in this position, you can hold them at their hips. Encourage movements between sitting and standing to forward movements to the floor while you allow your baby to play their favorite activity.

Supported Standing Play Position

As your baby continues to develop, they will be able to support more and more weight through their legs and feet (lower extremities). However, your baby still requires your continued support, so hold them around their trunk (rib cage), while encouraging them to stand to give them a new view on the world.

The supported standing position helps your baby strengthen their legs and to explore the sense of touch in a different gravitational plane, down through their legs and feet.

Providing your baby with opportunities to explore different textures through their feet, such as grass or other safe surfaces, will help them to learn about and tolerate these textures over time.

Caution: Test any surface that might be hot, like a sidewalk, with your hand before placing your baby's bare feet on it.

Standing Shift

Now that your baby is bearing almost all their weight through their legs, you could start to encourage more play in the supported standing position.

Sit on the floor and support your baby around their torso or hips, depending on their ability level, while they are standing. It will be helpful to have either a surface, such as an ottoman or sturdy box, slightly below your baby's elbow level with toys on it or another person in front of your baby or a mirror and interact with them through songs or stories.

Start to decrease the amount of support you are providing your baby in this position as they become more stable from their torso to their hips. While in this position, encourage weight bearing equally through both legs.

Next, encourage weight bearing through one leg at a time by gently shifting them side to side at the hips through each leg. Use the position side to side of toys to motivate your baby to weight shift and move.

Incorporate different safe textures, such as baby-safe play paper, foam mat, or a towel, for your baby to stand on during either of these activities. If it makes a noise, that's even better.

You can also incorporate the short sitting position (with your baby's thighs on a surface such as your lap, with their feet on the floor), on your leg, up to stand, and then back down to sitting at a low support surface.

Similar to the quadruped position, this position might be worked on if your baby is maintaining almost full weight through their legs in supported standing, but, if not, no worries. You can try again next month.

Back Play Position

Your baby will play less on their back now because sitting and quadruped are the primary play positions. However, when your baby is on their back, continue to encourage play such as feet to mouth.

Baby Bridges

Bridges is a developmental skill your baby is learning that will promote them taking an active part in their diaper changes. Hold their feet down with your hands, tap the sides of their hips with your index fingers, and say "up/down" to practice the up and down movements of lifting/ resting their hips during diaper changes, making it easier for you to remove and replace their diapers. If your baby has difficulty, roll a moving toy over and under them to engage and hold their attention during this activity.

Rolling Movement Patterns

Here are a couple of ways to encourage rolling movement patterns. The basis for motor learning stems from allowing your baby to have the sensory experience of activating a new position.

Encourage, yet wait for, your baby to initiate these new experiences to help them to make the connections.

Cross and Roll

Start by playing with your baby's legs and feet while they are flat on their back. Next lift the leg that is opposite from the way you want them to roll and cross it over their body. Wait to see if your baby tucks their bottom arm under and pushes up and over to the tummy time position. Another way to strengthen your baby's positional transitions is to place a toy on the side to which you want your baby to roll. Encourage your baby to look at the toy by using one that makes noise or lights up. Once they turn their head, engage their shoulder blade, then their arm to reach and roll toward the toy.

Photo Book

Filling a small, floppy photo book with family photos creates a wonderful activity for your baby to engage in while riding in the car. Dedicate each page to one of your baby's family members and close friends. When you read to your baby, page through, point to, and label each person, such as "Mama" and "Dada." Include a picture of your baby as well! They will love to see themselves in a picture. At the end of the book, have a family picture.

Five Months Old

Fill in the answers to reflect on the past month and to track.

How do you feel?

_____

_____

What exercises did you work on?

_____

_____

What is your baby doing now?

_____

_____

What was your baby's favorite activity this month?

_____

_____

What questions do you have for your ob-gyn and your baby's pediatrician?

_____

_____

Notes:

_____

_____

_____

_____

Six Months Old

MOMMY MOVEMENTS

How is this for a thought: "It is a fact of neurology that the brain cannot be in a state of appreciation and a state of fear at the same time. The two states may alternate, but they are mutually exclusive," wrote Dan Baker, PhD, in his book *What Happy People Know*. Here's the beauty: We can make a conscious choice about which emotion is taking over in a given situation.

Now let's replace fear with similar words: anger, frustration, displeasure. Similarly, we get to choose if we want these emotions to take us over or if we want to focus on emotions like joy, happiness, and love. One way to make this shift is to practice gratitude.

Practicing gratitude on the difficult days is more challenging but most impactful. Therefore, when starting to practice gratitude, whether it be in a journal or spoken, begin during your good days to make future daily consistency easier. The goal is to practice daily so it's less challenging to shift your attitude and your focus from negative to positive when the circumstances are not so light.

The blessings you express can be big or little, serious or silly. Consider beginning each statement in the present tense. Here are two examples to get you started.

"I am grateful that my body is on the road to recovery."

"I am grateful for change."

Postnatal Pelvic Girdle Stabilization Progressions

We cannot change nor move forward until we push ourselves out of our comfort zones. However, remember to listen to and honor what your body is telling you. As we turn our focus to the progressions of the core stabilization in more challenging positions and addressing your body's functional stability and mobility using whole-body movements, listen to and honor what your body is telling you.

When you attempt any progression or challenge, remember the following.

Breathing: If you find yourself holding your breath, breathe! If you find that maintaining your breath is too hard, this exercise progression might be too challenging. Go back to the previous one, reset, and try again. You might have to practice and train at the previous level a little more so that the new level is challenging, but not so much that you cannot breathe through it.

Maintaining your pelvic girdle isometrics (PGI): If you feel like you are losing your pelvic floor engagement, or you can't engage those muscles under your armpits while progressing through, the exercises might be too hard, the resistance might be too much, or you might be moving too quickly. Make small adjustments to the exercise to see if that helps you hold those isometrics. If you can't, return to the prior level and train your body until it is ready to try the new challenge.

Backing up does not mean failure. Sometimes you might try a progression and nail it immediately, but the very next day that progression might be more challenging. That is normal. Hormones, energy level, mood, and other physical demands that you have placed on your body throughout any given day, such as baby wearing and running extra errands, all play a role in what your body can handle.

Pelvic Girdle Stabilization (PGS) Progressions

It's time to use the pelvic girdle stability exercises as your foundation and progress forward by challenging your body to mimic more functional activities, such as bending and lifting, cleaning, and exercising.

Start each exercise by completing five repetitions of your pelvic girdle stabilization exercises on page 86 to activate your PGI. When you are able to consistently maintain pelvic girdle stabilization, you are ready to add the progression challenges that follow.

Progression Challenge One: In Quadruped

Start on your hands and knees (quadruped) with your PGI maintained. This is a great precursor to planks and pushups. Continue to maintain and stabilize everything pressing into your toes as if you are going to lift your knees up. If you feel like you are able to maintain and stabilize everything at this point, exhale and lift your knees up from the surface, just an inch. Breathe. Hold for five seconds and lower back down. Repeat this sequence five times.

Progression Challenge Two: Leg Extensions with Sliders

Now, it's time to stabilize your core and engage your spinal extensors and flexors in different planes, starting with your upper body and lower body separately and then combining them. This combination is powerful because it integrates how we actually use our body during almost any functional activity. You are strengthening your body and also training your body to work in the most efficient way it can all day long.

Your PGI continue to be your building block. Using a pair of exercise sliders, a small towel, or furniture mover sliders under your feet during this progression is optimal for controlled movement, balance, and resistance. Lie on your back with your knees bent in the Core Foundation position and your feet on sliders.

While maintaining PGI, inhale, and on the exhale extend your right leg straight down and out on the slider, then return to the starting position with your knees bent. Alternate your legs, repeating this sequence five times per leg.

Progression Challenge Three: Leg and Arm Combination Phase One

While maintaining PGS, inhale and on the exhale, extend your right leg straight down and out on the slider and raise your left arm overhead. Bring your right leg and left arm back to the starting position with your knees bent and arms at your sides. Alternate your leg and arm, always using the opposite arm and leg, and repeat for five repetitions on each side.

Progression Challenge Four: Leg and Arm Combination Phase Two

While maintaining PGI, inhale and on the exhale extend your right leg straight down and out on the slider. Then slide your right leg out to the side, back to the middle, then return to the starting position with your bent knees. Alternate your legs, repeating this sequence five times per leg.

Progression Challenge Five: Leg and Arm Combination Phase Three

While maintaining PGI, inhale and on the exhale extend your right leg straight down and out on the slider and raise your left arm overhead. Slide your right leg out to the side and reach your left arm out to the left side. Bring your right leg back to midline and your left arm back to straight overhead, then return to the starting position with your knees bent and arms at your side.

Alternate your leg and arm, always using the opposite arm and leg, and repeat for five repetitions on each side.

Pelvic Girdle Stabilization with Bridge Progressions

The starting position for each of the progression challenges that follow is Pelvic Girdle Stabilization with Bridge. Always start by setting your PGI. When you are able to consistently maintain pelvic girdle stabilization with bridge, you are ready to add the progression challenges the follow.

Remember: Activity happens on the exhale!

Progression Challenge One: Pelvic Girdle Stabilization with Bridge (PGS) Leg Extensions

While maintaining PGS with bridge, inhale and on the exhale, extend your right leg straight forward on the slider and then return your leg back to start. Alternate your legs, repeating five times per leg.

Progression Challenge Two: PGS with Bridge Leg and Arm Combination Phase One

While maintaining PGS with bridge, inhale and on the exhale, extend your right leg straight forward on the slider and lift your left arm overhead. Return back to the starting position. Lower back down to Core Foundation and reset your PGI. Alternate your legs, repeating five times per leg. As you get stronger and are able to hold your PGI between reps, you can challenge yourself further by staying in your PGS with bridge pose throughout all of your repetitions.

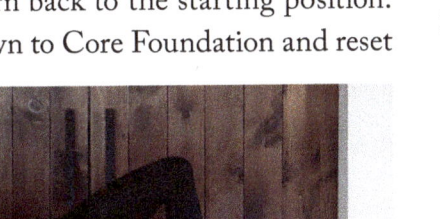

Progression Challenge Three: PGS with Bridge Leg and Arm Combination Phase Two

While maintaining PGS with bridge, inhale and on the exhale, extend your right leg straight forward on the slider and lift your left arm overhead. Slide your right leg out to the right side while reaching your left arm out to the left side. Return to midline, then back to the starting position. Lowering back down to Core Foundation and reset your PGI. Repeat this sequence five times per leg and opposite arm. As you get stronger and are able to hold your PGI between reps, you can challenge yourself further by staying in your PGS with bridge pose throughout all of your repetitions.

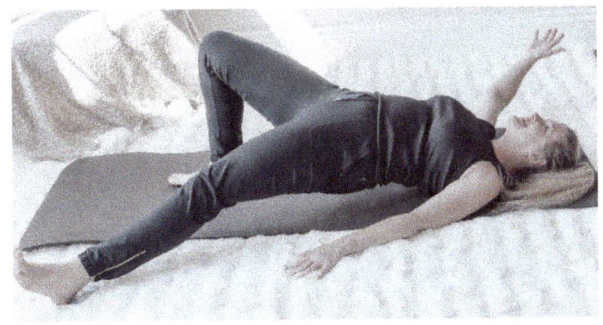

BABY'S DEVELOPMENT

Letting your baby explore through their senses is an essential part of nervous system development. We have to enjoy what we experience through our hands, eyes, mouth, nose, and skin to feel safe and comfortable in our environment. Sensory experiences create enriched learning environments and impact our well-being throughout the rest of our lives. Stay calm and let your baby get messy.

Motor Development

Your baby is eager to explore and move toward toys. They will roll from their back to their tummy easily and frequently, not playing on their back for long. Your baby can pivot in a circle on their tummy with their arms extended. They are able to shift their weight from their tummy toward side-lying and prop themselves up on their forearm, allowing their top arm to be free to play with toys.

Your baby might even begin to get up into quadruped themselves by pushing onto their hands and knees. To do this, they might shift their weight toward the side, flex their top leg, then shift their weight over the flexed leg while pushing up through their hands.

Your baby might belly crawl or commando crawl before quadruped crawling or might go right to quadruped crawling. If your baby is getting up into quadruped, they will begin to shift their weight back over one hip to transition to sitting.

This month, your baby will bring their head forward and flex their elbows to assist you when they are pulled to sit. Your baby might sit independently with upright posture and might even be able to turn their head to look around without falling.

Your baby is beginning to transition from sitting to quadruped or back down to their tummy. They will rotate their trunk, shifting their weight forward over their hip, then tucking their leg under to lower themselves to their hands and knees or to the floor.

In the sitting position, balance reactions are present anteriorly, allowing them to put their hands out to stop themselves from falling forward, and balance reactions are emerging laterally, allowing them to start to put their hand out to the side in an attempt to prevent themselves from falling to the side. Your baby will not yet have posterior balance reactions, and they might fall backward if they get displaced too far.

Your baby might begin to transition from hands and knees or sitting up to tall kneeling (two knees on the floor with hips extended) at a sturdy support

Balance (equilibrium) reactions are postural reflexes that occur subconsciously when your baby's center of gravity is displaced forward, backward, or side to side to restore your baby's upright balance.

Quadruped is the foundation to the crawling movement pattern, but your baby is not likely to be strong enough nor coordinated enough to crawl yet.

surface. Once in kneeling, they will begin to press down through their hands and extend their legs, pushing up to stand over both feet simultaneously. As this transition matures, your baby will achieve half kneel (one knee on the floor with hip extended and one foot on the floor) to transition to stand over one foot. Your baby can stand at a sturdy support surface with close supervision.

Regarding fine motor abilities, your baby is beginning to isolate wrist movements, which is an important prewriting skill. This means your baby is starting to move their hand in more directions without the need for entire arm movements.

Remember: There will be a wide range of abilities. This range is influenced by your baby's individual strength and motor proficiency and by their temperament and desire to move and explore.

Visual Development

As your baby continues to grow, their eyes are now able to follow objects that are farther away from them. Your baby should notice you from across the room, look at objects outside through a window, and reach for objects they are interested in. They enjoy looking at themselves in a mirror and might even reach for and touch their reflection, laugh, or make faces at themselves.

Between six and 12 months of age, it is time for your baby's first eye examination. The American Optometric Association's Infant-SEE program provides a free examination to all babies between six and 12 months of age. During a comprehensive eye examination, your baby's eye doctor will check their visual acuity, the pressure in their eyes, and the health of the front of their eyes. In addition, they will dilate your baby's eyes to check the health of their retina and optic nerve and determine whether your baby needs eyeglasses (prescriptive care).

Your baby's eye (ocular) health is very important to many aspects of their future. If they need a strong prescription, the sooner this need is

The symmetric tonic neck reflex (STNR) aka the crawling reflex appears between six and nine months old and facilitates flexor tone for proper development. This reflex is another reason why tummy time is important and is foundational for crawling, helps fire both sides of brain hemispheres, reinforces bilateral coordination, and improves binocular vision and hearing.

The asymmetric tonic neck reflex (ATNR) typically integrates this month. Some signs of retention might be poor visual motor skills, hand-eye coordination, tracking, and balance and difficulty crossing midline.

The palmar reflex is typically integrated by the end of the sixth month. Some signs of retention might be poor manual dexterity, visual coordination and posture, tactile and proprioception difficulties, and decreased prewriting/writing skills.

identified and corrected, the better the outcome for their vision. Other issues, such as eye turns, also have better outcomes when they are identified early in a child's life.

Cognitive Development

Because your baby is becoming more attentive, they might play for two to three minutes with a single toy. This increase in attention span and engagement in activities makes playtime and reading more fun. Use colorful, textured books to maintain your baby's attention and encourage continued interaction through touching and turning the pages.

Pause for your baby to touch the book, then turn the page which encourages social engagement.

Social-Emotional Development

Your baby is starting to understand that they are a separate entity from you, their family, and their environment. With this new understanding of their dependence on their caregivers, their affection, love of others, and self-confidence begins to evolve. Meanwhile, this growing knowledge of their separate self also triggers the onset of separation anxiety. They might become fearful of familiar situations they previously were fine with, such as having their hair washed or hearing a vacuum cleaner.

Your baby might start cooperating in games. They enjoy activities that involve their body, which will help increase their awareness of self. Help your baby to comprehend that each of their actions, such as crying, creates a reaction by responding to their needs.

All ths increased mobility allows your baby to see the world in a new way, and they will love it. Now that your baby is exploring in a seated upright position, they prefer to view the world upright as adults do. This excitement creates a new challenge for you when keeping your baby on their back. Of course, you don't want your baby on their back often, but sometimes it's a necessary position, such as diaper changes. Using an easily washable toy or learning to change your baby while you are holding them upright will be helpful for you during this new little power struggle. A baby-safe mirror next to their changing station might keep them occupied while you change their diaper. You can also try singing a short song to your baby during diaper changes. By repeating the same short song and ending the activity when the song ends, your baby will begin to understand and anticipate timing of activities and learn what to expect.

Self-Care Development

Mealtime decisions, whether it be to breast-feed or bottle-feed or when to start solids, always need to be made within your comfort zone and specific to your baby. You certainly can't go from using a bottle daily to just handing your baby a cup and expect them to make the transition overnight. However, if your baby is cleared by their pediatrician, you might start slowly offering them breast-milk or formula from a sippy cup or cup that you are holding and controlling. It is not always necessary to transition from a bottle to a sippy cup to a traditional cup. Every baby develops at a different pace. Also consider your comfort and confidence during activities.

A sign that your baby might be ready for a baby cup that you hold and control is if they are able to hold objects in their hand and bring them to their mouth, showing that they can judge how quickly they move their arm and wrist to bring objects to their mouth. If your baby appears ready to start drinking from an open cup in the next couple months, see cup exploration in the 10 Months Old chapter.

In the meantime, one way for your baby to

practice using a baby cup is to offer them an empty, open cup on their tray at the end of a meal. By offering them an empty cup to explore, you are giving them opportunities to practice manipulating a cup with graded control in a safe way and creating less mess. Or, incorporate a cup into bath time, filling it with fresh water from the faucet and allowing your baby to explore bringing it to their mouth. This way, if your baby spills, no mess is made. As your baby learns to grade and refine their movements of bringing an empty cup to their mouth and back down, they enhance their motor planning skills.

If your baby is eating solids, having a drink available helps them swallow their food in between bites.

Speech and Language Development

Research argues that both nurture and nature develop speech and language skills. Adults are the facilitators that provide enriched experiences to enhance skills, but the skills were inherently there already.

First, it is essential to understand that language has many facets, and the emergence of language is not just contained within speaking. Consider the importance of the following skills acquired before your baby communicates using words (prelinguistic skills): receptive language (your baby's ability to understand what you are saying), gestures, eye contact, imitation of actions and social interactions, and joint attention. In other words, these are the skills acquired *before* your baby communicates using words.

As your baby grows, so do their social (pragmatic) skills. Joint attention is a very important indicator of emerging language and one of the first social activities to mimic future conversations. What is joint attention? This pragmatic skill is when your baby is looking at or attending to the same thing you are in a shared experience, shifting their attention from you to an object (jointly) and reciprocating similar emotions or facial expressions, such as excitement over a toy.

Encouraging your baby to look at you during play times will aid in the development of joint attention. This can be as simple as putting your face in front of theirs and showing them a toy or when your baby babbles, babbling back.

Once your baby is engaged, you have joint attention and can support their language experiences further by playing with different sounds to show your baby their voice has power and can gain your attention. For example, if you hear your baby babble "mamamam," say "mamamam" back and add a "mamam moo moo." Expanding (scaffolding) on your baby's language allows them to hear changes and eventually imitate those changes.

This is why nursery rhymes are so popular among little ones. They provide repetition, which encourages imitation. "Old MacDonald" is especially relevant because it provides imitation of simple consonant vowel combinations (farm animal sounds) and language expansion (farm animal names, categorizing) at the same time.

This month, your baby is starting to babble using front-of-the-mouth sounds, such as m, p, t, d, and n, waving with your assistance, and using simple gestures to communicate, such as holding up their arms when they want to be held. Research suggests that you can now begin to expose your baby to sign language and that babies who use sign language have better language skills (although the jury is still out) when they are three to four-years old. Additional benefits are reduced frustration, increased joint attention, providing a bridge to words, and giving your baby extra motor practice. Refer to the

Simple Baby Sign Language section on page 132 on how to introduce sign language to your baby in an appropriate developmental sequence.

The takeaway is that prelinguistic skills are fundamental in the acquisition of language. Therefore, do not focus only on vocalizations at this stage; rather, enhance prelinguistic and joint communication skills to increase your baby's overall communication repertoire.

Developmental Play

With each month, your baby's attention to tasks grows, as they play with a toy for two to three minutes now. Bilateral integration and maturation of fine motor skills continues as well; thus it's important to facilitate use of both sides of your baby's body by consciously varying the sides to which you offer toys.

Movement Pattern Play

This month, reinforcing play through movement patterns takes precedence over play positions because your baby is motivated by movement. You might feel as if you are a human jungle gym, and your baby might be more difficult to hold onto due to their ever-changing exploration of movement.

Some of the movement patterns you will see this month and want to reinforce are crossing midline, circular pivoting, transitioning into and out of sitting, and transitioning into and out of kneeling. These important transitional movement patterns are significant precrawling skills.

PLAY POSITIONS
Quadruped Play Positions

Toy Roll

Once your baby is stronger and is maintaining quadruped position with less support, you can encourage them to play with a toy.

Position yourself behind your baby, supporting them at their torso/trunk and allowing their feet to rest up against your knees or on a stable surface, such as your legs or a foam climbing cube. This positioning will provide your baby with the ability to push off with their feet, enabling them to rock in the quadruped position and receive input through multiple surfaces and joints. Roll a toy back and forth in front of your baby and encourage them to reach for the toy with one hand. Don't forget to position the toy on the other side of the body as well so your baby uses both of their hands. One arm will be the functional one for play, and their

other arm will help them to maintain stability. Alternating their arm and hand use will balance the functionality and stability of both arms and hands.

While playing in quadruped, work on transitioning your baby from their hands and knees to their hands with one hip and leg tucked forward while the other leg is behind them.

One Leg Forward

Similar to how you encouraged the functionality and stability of each of your baby's arms and hands individually previously, you will do the same with your baby's legs. Position yourself behind your baby with one of your baby's feet against you. For example, if you are kneeling, their foot will be against your knee. Bring your baby's other leg forward. Support them at their hip and chest while gently rocking them back and forth.

Kneeling Play Position

Now that your baby is transitioning from their tummy to quadruped, they will want to explore further. You might see them try to transition from sitting to kneeling or from quadruped to kneeling and then up to stand.

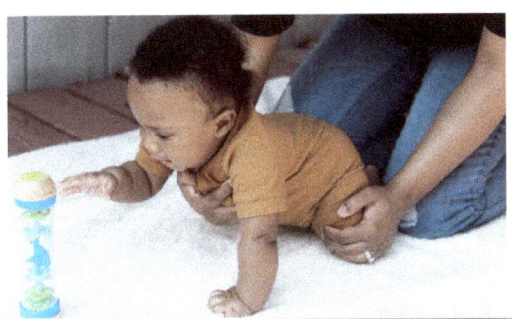

Half-Kneel Play

This activity encourages your baby to transition from sitting to kneeling. Position your baby on a slight diagonal at a surface that is chest height, such as a diaper box with a blanket over it, bottom step, or sofa with the cushion removed. Encourage your baby to reach up for toys and help them rotate over the hip closest to the toy to push up onto both knees, allowing them to play in the kneeling position.

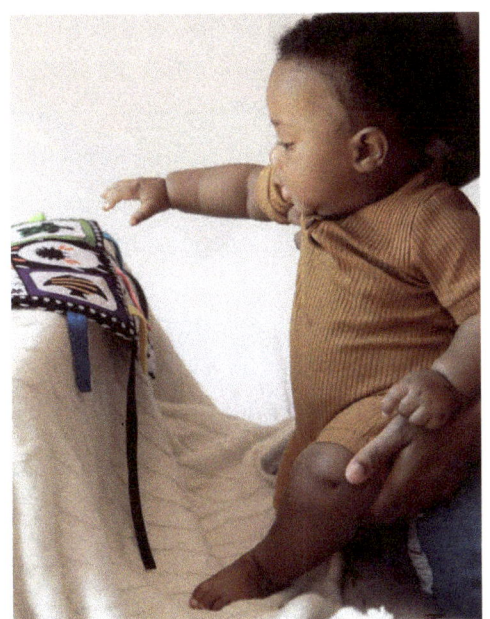

As you practice this play position, over the next days or weeks, your baby will become more stable, and you can challenge them by bringing one leg forward and putting their foot flat on the floor. If you notice that your baby begins to push up through their planted foot or tries to pull up with their arms in an attempt to stand, you can help them with this transition.

Continue to be positioned behind your baby, supporting them at their torso. Because they are still not standing stably, they need your support for their safety. When your baby is in the standing play position, encourage them to bear their weight through one stable arm and play with their other arm. Remember: One arm is the functional arm, and the other the stable arm.

To challenge your baby, move the toy farther back on the box, step, or couch and encourage them to stand and reach for it. Move the toy to different parts of the surface to encourage them to gently shift their weight in different directions.

Sitting Play Positions

Wobbly play continues to be important. It challenges your baby's balance, helping to develop it further.

Sit-n-Wobble

Observe your baby's stability in the sitting play position to help you determine how you need to support them. If they still need a lot of support, sit behind them. If they do not need as much support, sit in front of them with your legs wrapped around them. Always consider how you can place objects during play to challenge them. For example, think about how you can challenge their sitting balance. Place toys to their sides, in front of them, and above them so they will need to reach for the toys. Promoting reaching across the midline of your baby's body with toys is a great way to work on the right and left sides of the brain.

When you place toys off to your baby's side, encourage weight shifting through one side of their bottom with weight bearing through one hand across the midline of their body. This position eventually allows your baby to reach across their body with the opposite arm.

The following activities are great developmental activities to play with your baby while you are sitting and engaging with them. Always start each activity by modeling it for your baby. In other words, show them how to do it first.

Remember: You can also use the hand-over-hand technique by placing your hand on your baby's hand to help them to complete the activity.

Pull, Stack, Drop, Activate Toy Exposure

All of these developmental activities are simple cause-and-effect games to help your baby understand that every action creates a reaction. For example, when your baby shakes a toy, it lights up. Or if they turn a small bucket over, the items inside spill out. Your baby learns to open their hand and let go of a toy so it falls to the ground.

With assistance, they move their hands out while holding a pull-apart toy, such as large pop beads or magnetic blocks to pull them apart.

While you are playing with your baby, use simple words, such as "pop," "up," "look," "down," or "wow."

Hello Body Activities

Help your baby to understand they are their own entity more with the following activities.

Mirror, Mirror on the Wall

Who is the cutest baby of all? Your baby, of course! Mirror play is fun this month as you might see your baby lean forward toward their reflection and give themselves a big smooch.

Incorporate mirror play throughout the day. For example, if you are out shopping, stop at a mirror and talk to your baby. When you are in your bathroom with them after a bath or diaper change, hold your baby in front of the mirror, talk, and sing to them. Use this time to draw your baby's attention to your body parts and theirs, such as eyes, nose, and mouth.

Clapping

Over the past several months, you have been increasing your baby's body awareness through holding, touching, and rubbing their hands together, bringing attention to the midline of their body, and exploration of both sides of their body. Now by encouraging your baby to mimic clapping, you will further increase their body awareness and also their coordination and their ability to integrate both their arms and their hands with more independence.

Position your baby in front of you supported by pillows or a Boppy if they are able to sit with little support. If they are not able to sit with little support, then they are not ready for this activity. Save it for next month. First model what you want your baby to do. For example, clap your hands while singing a song or counting rhythmically. Then hold your baby's hands in yours and open and close their arms, making an exaggerated clap while singing or counting rhythmically. This use of the hand-over-hand technique encourages a movement pattern. Then let go of your baby's hands. Again, clap your hands while singing or counting and allow your baby wait time to see if they mimic you.

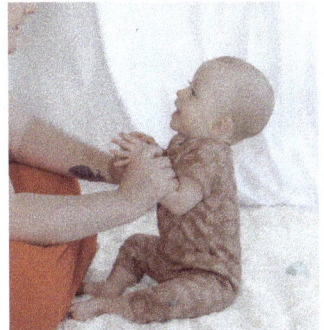
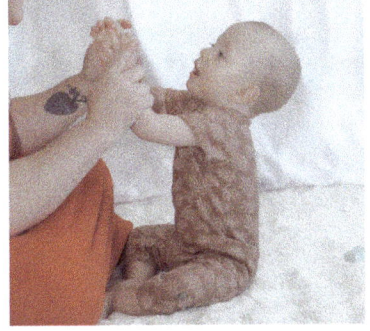
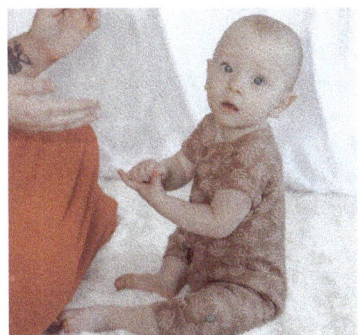

Modeling Simple Baby Sign Language

Baby signing is the use of sign language specific to your baby's native language. These modifications simplify sign language, making it baby friendly, with the goal of opening up communication between you and your baby.

Although there is some controversy as to whether baby signing will increase language skills, in this book, we introduce only simple, functional baby signs to promote communication prior to verbalization. These signs are not intended to be used for the hearing impaired. If your baby is hearing impaired, they should be treated and monitored by an audiologist.

Typically, the motoric control needed for simple sign language does not occur until your baby is eight to nine months old. However, at this age, it is appropriate for you to start modeling sign language for them. It is important to be aware of the skills needed before your baby can actually utilize sign language. Think about when you were required to have pre-algebra as a prerequisite to algebra one; this requirement is the same idea.

An article published by the American Speech-Language-Hearing Association suggested that signs with dominant O-hand and C-hand shapes are easiest, such as more, drink and eat. However, some signs, specifically "more" are more prone to being overused and misused due to the simplicity of the movements. Caregivers might also unintentionally reinforce the use of these signs by responding positively whenever the infant produces them, leading to their frequent repetition. Gesture overgeneralization can occur when infants apply their limited repertoire of signs to a wide range of contexts. For example, a child might use the sign "more" to request additional food and also for toys or drinks, even if it is not contextually correct.

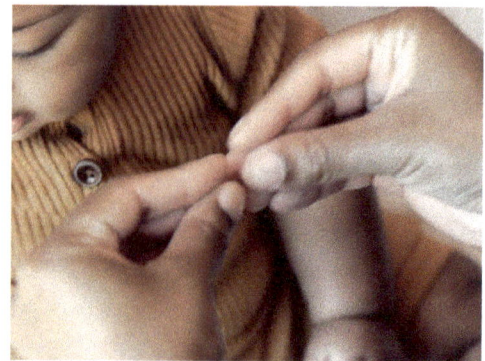

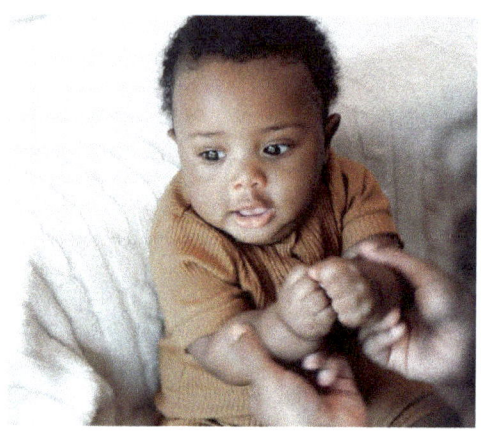

Here are some prerequisites before your baby can begin to sign.

- Uses communicative intent, which is the ability to employ gestures, facial expressions, or sounds with the intention of delivering a message. For example, your baby reaches for an object and pushes it away or whines with intention.

- Shares social experiences with you through eye contact and joint attention.

- Understands the symbolic nature of non-verbal communication that for every action, there is a reaction. For example, your baby understands nonverbal gestures, such as an outstretched hand indicating that you would like them to hand you their bottle.

- Emerging receptive language—the ability to understand what you are saying. Test receptive language by asking "Where is Dada?"

and observe if your baby looks around for Dada.

- Able to imitate basic motor movement, such as clapping or waving. Signs do not have to be precise to be understood, but the motor capability must be present.

Modeling one or two frequently used, functional, simple words through sign language will increase your baby's likelihood of utilizing sign language when motorically appropriate, in an attempt to communicate before they are able to verbalize their needs. Because food is an effective motivator, some basic words to consider starting with are more, eat, drink, and all done because those simple hand shapes will help your baby articulate their wants and needs.

Here are some tips for signing with your baby.

- Signing during functional routines and activities, such as reading and feeding provides contextual support for signing.
- Signing should be interactive; therefore, avoid using flashcards and DVDs.

- Modeling a sign while saying the word out loud reinforces the word.
- Signing combined with parentese (overemphasizing motor movements by adjusting their rate, size, duration, and frequency) makes communication interactive and will hold your baby's interest longer.

Keep in mind that baby signing should not be referred to as language because without the morphology, pragmatics, and syntax, signs from your native sign language are simply signs, not sign language.

Also, motor skills mature over time; therefore, baby signing approximations should be accepted and perfection should not be expected. For example, when your baby is first learning a sign, gross approximations are acceptable; however, as your baby develops, so will their motor skills, making signs more exact and refined.

Your baby will most likely drop baby signs by themselves once they are able to express themselves verbally.

Bath Time Play

Your baby will become more independent every day. Building play into their daily routines helps you and is rich in sensory exploration.

Your baby needs to be able to sit independently in the bathtub for this activity. Consider putting a swim diaper on your baby if they are going to be in the bath for an extended time.

Allow your baby to explore small cups and encourage them to pour water between cups to promote bilateral hand coordination and cause-and-effect play. (But don't allow your baby to drink the bathwater!)

Using hand-over-hand techniques facilitates

your baby to scoop and dump water. To build in extra sensory input, use hand-over-hand to dump water on the opposite hand or arm. Remember to practice with both hands, alternating.

Bath time is also great for messy food play because it's fun for your baby and easier for you to clean up. When you take your baby to the bath, bring along some food and utensils, such as yogurt and a spoon and some water-safe toys. In the bath, allow your baby to experiment with dipping the spoon or toys into the cup of yogurt.

When you give your baby soft foods in the tub, such as yogurt or pureed fruit, place them on a toy or utensil to encourage your baby to mouth the object and allow them to explore taste and smell.

When feeding your baby, talk to them about the food you are presenting, by saying, "This is applesauce." Encourage your baby to smell each food safely before eating it. Describe the smell and taste. "It smells like apples. It tastes sweet."

Hand-to-mouth exploration during mealtime increases speech sounds in terms of how your baby feels their articulators (tongue, mouth, lips, alveolar ridge, hard palate, and gums for babies and teeth for kids and adults) move within their mouth.

Another benefit to bath play is the horizontal and vertical surfaces of the tub sides offer great ways for your baby to begin to isolate their wrist movements. Allow your baby to "paint" with their hands by placing pudding or brightly colored pureed foods, such as blueberries, on the sides of the tub. Watch your baby explore how creative they can be with their hands. Playing with both hands and moving their wrists help your baby begin to isolate important hand movements, which later develop their handwriting skills.

When your baby is done playing with the food in the bath, simply turn on the water and wash the mess away.

Peekaboo Pull-Off

This month when playing peekaboo, your baby will engage by starting to pull a light blanket off an object. Cover a favorite stringed toy with a blanket and uncover it when your baby is watching. Hold the blanket between you and your baby and drop it on the toy. Give your baby time to find the toy.

Incorporate this game into your daily routine when your baby is a captive audience, such as during dressing, bathing, and diaper changes. Playfully explore your baby's understanding of cause and effect by placing a shirt, light blanket, light towel, or even their feet in front of their face so they can try to remove the object. If you are placing something light over them for the game, hold it in between you and them. Drop it swiftly, exclaiming "Peekaboo!" Repeat this several times, allowing a slight pause to wait to see if your baby pulls the blanket or towel away themselves. If your baby does not remove it themselves, you can encourage it with the hand-over-hand technique.

Back Play Position

As discussed earlier, you don't want to have your baby on their back all the time nor will they want to be. They are now even more interested in all the world has to offer. However, when your baby is on their back, encourage them to continue to play with their feet and hands with toys.

Six Months Old

Fill in the answers to reflect on the past month and to track.

How do you feel? _____

_____

What exercises did you work on? _____

_____

What is your baby doing now? _____

_____

What was your baby's favorite activity this month? _____

_____

What questions do you have for your ob-gyn and your baby's pediatrician?

_____

Notes: _____

_____

_____

_____

Seven Months Old

MOMMY MOVEMENTS

When you first held your beautiful baby in your arms, how often did you think, "Oh, my goodness, they are just so perfect!" But as these last few months have progressed, how often have you thought, "Once we get past this stage, will things get better?" The truth is there is no perfection in parenting. Yes, there are many perfect moments, but they are fleeting. And the truth is that the imperfections within the journey are actually so much more beautiful.

Imperfection yields hope and goals, the ability to do over, the ability to make changes, the ability for second (and third and fourth) chances, and the ability for flexibility and for originality. No two parenting journeys, postpartum experiences, or baby milestones are alike. So this month, we focus on progress, not perfection. In each imperfect moment, tell yourself, "I am making progress."

Postnatal Gluteal Strengthening

It's important to focus on progress over perfection as you move forward to focus on pelvic stabilization and gluteal engagement.

Wall Squat Progressions and Single-Leg Stance Progressions

You have worked hard at laying the foundation for your core strategies and stability. You have been setting the stage for your pelvis to be the balanced starting point of safe movement for the rest of your body. Now you are ready to work on the largest muscles of the body: the muscles that will protect your back and quite literally propel you through life—your gluteal muscles (glutes). Instead of doing a whole new set of exercises to try to fit into those not-so-extra moments of your busy life, you are going to simply build on the program you have already started. Review Wall Slide/Squat in the Four Months Old Chapter if needed prior to completing the following progressions.

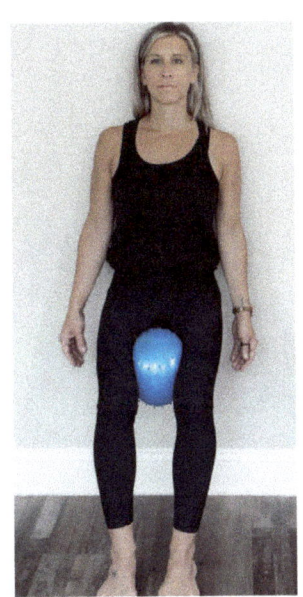

Progression Challenge One: Wall Squat with a Hold

Maintain your wall squat for increased time, holding for a slow five-second count or two deep-breath cycles while down in the squat position. Repeat this sequence five times.

Progression Challenge Two: Wall Squat with Block

Place a yoga block, small step stool, or thick book under your right foot to complete your wall squat. While squatting, you will feel slightly more pressure and focus in your left gluteal muscle group as you push through your left leg to push back up because the yoga block should be taking about 25 percent of the weight out of your right leg. It's important to hold those isometrics both on the way down into the squat and then back up. Alternate which foot you place on the yoga block and repeat five times per foot.

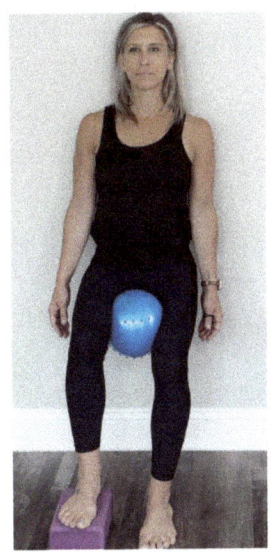

Progression Challenge Three: Wall Squat with Block, Alternating Foot

Repeat the last challenge, but this time hold for a slow five-second count or two deep-breath cycles while you are down in the squat position with the yoga block under your right foot.

Return to standing. Repeat five times. Then switch feet so the other foot is on the yoga block/step stool and repeat five times.

A Reminder about Breathing and PGS: Your ability to maintain your breath pattern and sustain your PGS is your guide. If you feel as if you are holding your breath or losing any of the five stabilizers of your PGI, then it is wise to back up. For example, don't go as deep into your squat if you lose the PF engagement. Or don't add weight if you can't keep "squeezing the lemons." This doesn't mean you can't eventually advance to these progressions; it just means that your body is not ready yet. Modify the exercise, practice more here, and then try again as you feel more control within the modification.

Single-Leg Stance Progression

The following series of exercises focuses on the muscles that support you in standing and walking all day long. A bonus is that they help shape your backside with a little lift and a lot of strength!

Standing Stability Pose

The starting position for this series if the Standing Stability Pose. Stand with your arms at your sides and activate your pelvic girdle isometrics (PGI), referring back to the Four Months Old Chapter if needed, then progress through the exercises that follow.

Progression One: Standing Stability Pose with Forward Bend

Start in Standing Stability Pose and hold and maintain your PGI. Inhale and on the exhale, lean forward like you are going to touch your toes, keeping focus on the engagement of your side-seat/gluteal muscles. Still holding your PGI (with that special focus on your gluteal muscles), on the exhale slowly lift your body back up to Standing Stability Pose. You should feel like your butt muscles are doing all of the work.

Progression Two: Standing Stability Pose Bend with Yoga Block

Start in Standing Stability Pose with forward bend, but this time place your left leg on a yoga block, small step stool, or thick book. As you bend, you will feel more engagement of your left gluteal muscles because the block will take about 25 percent of your weight out of your right leg.

Progression Three: Standing Stability Pose to Single-Leg Stance

Start in Standing Stability Pose with your left leg on a yoga block, small step stool, or thick book. This time, instead of bending forward, continue to engage your isometrics, with special focus on your left gluteal muscles. Hold your PGI and gradually attempt to lift your left leg off the yoga block, if even just an inch. Hold for five seconds, then slowly lower your leg back to the block, while still engaging your isometrics. Once your leg is back on the block, relax. Repeat this sequence five times, alternating sides.

The goal is to lift your leg to hip height. Higher than that is not necessary.

Progression Four: Standing Stability Pose to Forward Tilt

Start in the Standing Stability Pose with a forward bend and your PGIs engaged. Hold this position as you bring your right leg behind you, so that just your toes touch the ground.

Hold all of your isometrics and on the exhale begin to hinge forward at your hips while gently lifting your right leg off the ground if possible. Keep your shoulders to your toes in a straight line, only tilting your torso forward as much as you can lift your right leg off the ground. Hold this position for five seconds, then return to Standing Stability Pose. Once you return to Standing Stability Pose, you can relax your stabilizing isometrics. Repeat this sequence five times, alternating sides.

Progression Five: Standing Stability Pose with Trunk Rotation

For these next two exercises, we recommend using a resistance band, preferably anchored on a hook or around your door as pictured. If you do not have access to a resistance band, you can perform these movements without one.

Anchor your band on a hook around a door. Start in Standing Stability Pose with your body facing perpendicular to your resistance band anchor/door. Step away from the anchor/door so that the resistance band has a slight stretch on it. Hold the band with your hands clasped together at your chest. Engage your PGI, with particular focus on your glute/dimples. Hold your isometrics and on the exhale rotate just your trunk/upper body (from your waist up) away from the door. Your pelvis and legs should not move. Maintain your PGI as you return your trunk to Standing Stability Pose. Repeat this sequence five times on each side.

Progression Six: Single-Leg Stance with Trunk Rotation

With your resistance band anchored onto a door, stand in Standing Stability Pose with your body facing perpendicular to your resistance band/door with your right side closest to the door. Step away from the anchor/door so that the band slightly stretches. Hold the band with your hands clasped together at your chest. Engage your PGI, with particular focus on your gluteal muscles. Lift your right leg so that your foot is raised anywhere from an inch up to hip height but no higher.

If this exercise is too difficult, you can place your right foot on a yoga block, small step stool, or thick book to take about 25 percent of your weight off of your right leg rather than lifting it.

With increased focus on the gluteal muscles in your left leg on the exhale, rotate just your trunk/upper body from your waist up away from the door. Your pelvis and legs should not move. Return your trunk to the Standing Stability Pose. Repeat five times on that side, then turn and repeat on your left side.

If needed, place your raised foot back down on the ground and reset between each repetition. As you progress through this series, you may be able to repeat five rotations without resetting between each one.

Progression Seven: Standing Stability Pose with Step Up

Stand behind a step in your house (or a stepper) in Standing Stability Pose, engaging and maintaining your PGI throughout. Stand on your left leg and tap your right toes on the step, with focus on your left gluteal muscles. Return to Standing Stability Pose and repeat this sequence using your left. Reset by returning to Standing Stability Pose and repeat five times per side.

Progression Challenge One

Repeat the Standing Stability Pose tapping sequence; however, instead of tapping your toes on the step, step fully up onto the step then back down. Repeat five times per side.

Progression Challenge Two

Repeat the Standing Stability Pose step-up sequence above, stepping on the step with your right foot. Then, while maintaining your PGI, "float" your left hip up as if you are marching. Make sure you are not overusing your thigh muscles or hiking your hip to lift your leg. Repeat five times per side.

BABY'S DEVELOPMENT

This month watch in amazement as your baby's hands and fingers start becoming more functional with a raking grasp. Note: your baby might become frustrated if they get food stuck in their palm and don't have the fine motor skills yet to get it off.

Motor Development

If you put your baby in a stroller when you are out, they might fuss because they don't want to be constrained anymore. Simply holding on to your baby is a workout now because they twirl, climb, and tilt their head and body constantly. Can you blame them? They are learning that their body can move, and they want to explore!

Your baby is very interested in exploring their environment by trying to commando crawl on their tummy or up on their hands and knees, then beginning to pull to kneel, and possibly to stand. They can get into a variety of sitting positions, including ring sitting, half-ring sitting, long sitting, and side sitting. Your baby will shift their weight to transition through rotation diagonally over each hip to reach for toys. They might transition up into sitting over each hip from the quadruped position or push up from side-lying. As your baby practices crawling, they will begin to move their opposite arm and leg at the same time (a reciprocal pattern).

If your baby is transitioning to stand, although their arms are still doing most of the work, their

Ring sitting allows for the rotation of your baby's torso and side sitting, which are needed to help your baby maintain their balance and reach for objects.

Side sitting

Ring sitting

Long sitting

Half-ring sitting

legs are becoming more active. When trying to sit back down from standing, your baby will begin to squat, but they might fall part of the way down due to lack of control.

At this stage, your baby might coordinate their eyes and hands with more precision. Reaching has become more accurate, and your baby is able to turn their wrist while playing with toys. Your baby will use a raking movement with their fingers only to retrieve smaller items. They will grasp single, small items with their thumb, index, and middle fingers. They might even start to isolate their index finger and thumb to grasp, which is called a pincer grasp.

Visual Development

Your baby's eyes are continuing to develop, and this is important for their exploration of the world around them. Improving hand-eye coordination allows your baby to grab objects that they are interested in and to explore those objects. Tracking and scanning allow your baby to follow interesting objects that are both close and far away from them.

Take your baby outside and watch to see if they view and follow objects that are both close, such as a flower, and far away, such as a bird. As your baby's hand-eye coordination improves and they become more mobile, they will change their position with ease to reach for items that they want. Hand-eye coordination and eye tracking are foundational skills for your baby's visual and motor development.

Cognitive Development

Your baby might now be able to detect the source of sounds that are not in their sight. They might also begin to imitate and respond with simple, familiar gestures, such as waving bye-bye, or react to simple commands like holding their arms above their head when you say, "So big!"

Remember: When your baby is irritable, it might be due to cognitive development.

Social-Emotional Development

Your baby now demonstrates their likes and dislikes toward specific people, toys, and places.

You might notice that your baby only wants to be taken care of by you, the primary caregiver, the parent they are with most. They might continue to or start feeling anxious about situations with which they were previously fine. So you may not want to pass your baby too quickly to someone with whom they are not familiar, even if you are comfortable with that person. The developing awareness of their environment and abilities causes these feelings. They are positive indicators of their cognitive growth; this phase is normal. Respect your baby's boundaries and facilitate positive relationships and situations slowly and at your baby's comfort level.

Teach gentle touch. With all these new social-emotional changes in combination with increased motor control, your baby might test the heaviness and force of their new abilities. They might pull your hair or the dog's fur, swipe, or hit. Take each new challenge as an opportunity to teach them about "gentle." Babies don't understand this concept yet, so you can teach them by saying "gentle" while stroking their hand gently and then holding their hand and stroking your hand or their other hand gently. Even if they are not testing out their force, this suggestion is still a great sensory activity. You might see these seemingly aggressive actions resurface in the toddler years.

Self-Care Development

Your baby has spent months practicing and learning to bring objects to their mouth, which is an essential prerequisite to self-feeding. As these oral motor skills develop, you might notice that your baby is drooling less, except when they are teething. They can better manage the secretions in their mouth.

Exploring toys with their mouth will also promote their oral motor skills for language development. Bringing texture to their mouth early can help to minimize food aversions as they advance to a solid food diet.

Mealtime is an excellent time to advance the dexterity of your baby's little fingers. Once your baby's pediatrician gives you clearance, and after your baby is sitting independently and maintaining their own balance (which helps to keep their airway open), provide easily dissolvable foods, such as melt-away snacks and puffs, for your baby to pick up and put in their mouth.

Your baby's curiosity now gets the best of them as they start to understand that objects don't vanish into thin air, and they will pursue finding them to delight themselves in independent play. Your baby's intention in play is more active, and they will reach farther to obtain objects. Encourage their tenacity by teaching them interactive skills, such as waving bye-bye and baby signing to request their bottle.

Speech and Language Development

This month, your baby's receptive language grows each and every day. They might be able to look toward a familiar object or person when named, such as "bottle" or "Mama."

Keep labeling familiar people because repetition of words helps your baby with comprehension and retention of information. Expand their language by making associations to common objects, such as, "Look! They have blue shoes on just like you!" Socially, prelinguistic skills continue to emerge such as purposefully seeking attention, requesting (either nonverbally or by babbling), rejecting (pushing items away or verbally protesting), and acknowledging the presence of familiar people.

While completing an activity, you are concentrating on increasing the likelihood that your baby will say a word through modeling and repetition. Currently, your baby's sounds are simple; therefore, simplifying your words is appropriate during activities.

For example, during baby Airplanes, saying "weeeeeee" might be enough! The word "weeeee" is actually two sounds "w" and "e." /W/ is a lip-rounding sound, and /E/ is an open-mouth sound. When your baby repeats the word/sound together, they are strengthening their oral motor abilities to eventually string many sounds together.

Intonation is developing at this age, and your baby will babble in melodic patterns as if they are babbling sentences. Continue to add sounds to the end of your baby's babbling to promote and increase the complexity of their vocalizations.

Right now, your baby puts everything in their mouth. While you might think it is gross and it might sometimes pose a hazard, your baby uses their mouth to get information from the outside world. Mouthing objects also strengthens their oral muscles, calms your baby, and helps to desensitize your baby's mouth, which enables toleration of a variety of textures when they eat solid foods.

Developmental Play

Now that your baby is on the move more and more, you want to baby-proof your house.

Movement patterns continue to develop rapidly. Tummy time is still important, but it looks different because it might have transitioned into pre-crawling activities, such as pivoting on their belly to obtain a toy, pushing themselves forward off of a support surface, rocking on their hands and knees, or army/commando crawling and possibly even crawling, at this point. Every baby develops at their own pace. Remember: Your role is to encourage the next step in development wherever your baby's might be. You can always go back a chapter, continuing to work on the same activities until your baby has mastered them, or move ahead if they are cruising along quicker.

It is very important to differentiate between your daily language expansion where you convey your day and play activities where you simplify language in play. This means that during specific play activities, you want to keep things simple, short, and repetitive.

PLAY POSITIONS

Sitting Play Position

Continue wobbly play to strengthen your baby's back and tummy muscles, improve balance, and activate their protective reactions. Now that your baby is sitting more upright, they might enjoy the outdoors even more. The more your baby sees and takes in, the more they learn. Taking your baby outside and to new environments gives them different things to watch and visually track. However, have fun with the following activities when you are inside with your baby.

The "Gentle" Song

Sing this song to the tune of the "Clean Up" song during each step of the following activity.

"Gentle, gentle. Everybody, everywhere. Gentle, gentle. It's time to be gentle with our hands."

Gently stroke your baby's face with your fingers apart from their ear to their chin while singing.

Make sure they are seated safely in front of you on the floor. Take one of their hands and gently stroke their face with their hand and gently stroke their face with your hand at the same time while singing.

Gently stroke their hand from wrist to fingertips and each finger one at a time while singing the song.

Gently take both of their hands on your face, stroking from your ears to your chin while singing the song.

Asking Activity

You can continue to expand your baby's receptive language skills with this simple activity. Offer two items. For example, hold up a ball and a block and ask, "Do you want the ball?" (gently shake the ball) or "Do you want the block?" (gently shake the block). Watch your baby's gaze, then based on which item they are looking at say, "Oh! You want the _____. Here it is!"

You can also do this activity with food.

Baby Fun Fall

As you did last month, work with your baby on their sitting balance by continuing to encourage them to reach for toys in all areas either on an exercise ball or on the floor. Gently shift them left, right, back, and forward. Hold them at their torso for support, lowering your hands to their hips or thighs as they get stronger and need less support.

For an interactive poem you can do the following activity: Sit on the floor. Secure an exercise ball between your legs. Place your baby seated on top of the ball. Sing the song below to the tune of "Humpty Dumpty" to work on core strength and sitting balance. While singing the song and holding your baby securely, gently tilt your baby to the side as if they are "falling to the side." Use "happy baby," "little baby," or an individual nickname for your baby.

"Happy baby sat on a ball. Happy baby had a great fall." (Tilt your baby to the side for a pretend fall.) "All of my kisses and all of my hugs. Help to make baby feel happy again." (Kiss and hug your baby.)

Catch That Ball

Your baby is too young to have a ball toss with you. They do enjoy reaching and catching toys, though, and both activities are great for their visual motor skills.

Use a toy on a ribbon or string. Sit your baby in a play nest or in between your legs in front of a mirror. Place pillows around them or remain close by if they are sitting independently now. Encourage your baby to reach and catch the toy by slowly moving it toward them, away from them, and side to side.

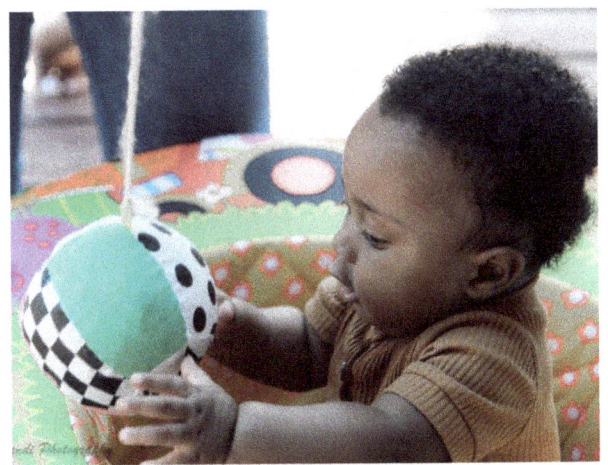

Note: Whether storebought or homemade, never leave your baby with toys unattended. Ribbons, strings, cords longer than 7 inches are considered unsafe.

Tug of War

Place your baby's favorite lovey or toy in front of them, moving it in different positions around them, such as in front, to their right, and to their left). Then hold the item in front of your baby at arm's-length away, moving and playing with it, to encourage them to reach for it with a straight elbow. When your baby grabs the item, make a big deal out of it saying, "Well done! You have your stuffed animal." Then give the item gentle tugs to encourage your baby to tug back. Praise them when they do by saying, "You are so strong!" Excitement is contagious with your baby.

You can give your baby a choice of two items, one preferred and the other one less preferred. Offering choices promotes decision making, giving your baby a sense of control of their environment.

Hide-and-Seek Box

Seat your baby safely and place a box with a toy inside in front of them. Open the box so your baby sees the toy, then close the box, describing what you are doing in simple terms, such as, "Look pig. Oink, Oink. Where did the pig go?"

Facial Expression Games

This month, it's fun for your baby to try to imitate you. They might start to wave bye-bye and hold their arms above their head. Encourage this imitation play through gestures and exaggerated emotions. Ask your baby, "How big are you?" then hold your hands up in the air and say, "So big!"

You can now encourage direction following by pairing actions with simple commands. For example, when you ask, "Do you want to get up?" assist your baby in raising their arms. After repeating the verbal prompt "up" and helping your baby raise their arms, slowly phase out your physical help and simply ask "up?" Repeat this process until your baby learns to raise their arms when you say "up." Overall, work on imitating gestures and emotions as well as following simple commands. The skill of mastering facial expressions enhances your baby's social skills as they develop.

Sit or stand with your baby in front of a mirror and make different facial expressions. Allow for wait time in between to see how your baby reacts to you in response to your emotions.

Introducing a book of facial expressions, either homemade or bought, might be fun for your baby, too.

You can do this same idea through peekaboo by placing a light blanket over your face, slowly pulling it off, and revealing a different facial expression each time.

Want to change it up? Place a light blanket over your face or your baby's face and wiggle it, encouraging your baby to pull it off. Each time the blanket is removed, make and describe a different animal sound, such as, "The cow says moo."

Pat-a-Pattern

Aside from continuing to work on clapping with your baby, promote the expansion of imitation skills by adding variety. Pat and clap a pattern with your hands such as "pat, pat, clap" or start nursery rhymes such as "Pat-a-Cake" or make up one of your own. Using movements of rubbing their hands over and under each other clapping, and patting are all great ways to engage their hands in the sense of touch and pressure. Your baby will enjoy watching it, and you can encourage them with hand-over-hand to complete the same pattern.

You can use a favorite musical toy, two music sticks, or a metronome to create a repetitive beat to work on "patting a pattern." If a family member has a favorite hobby involving a repetitive pattern, such as dancing to a beat or dribbling a basketball, engage your baby with that.

Sock Puppets

Use a homemade or storebought puppet, make simple sounds for your baby to repeat, and use silly intonation to attract your baby's attention. For example, give your baby a kiss with the sock puppet, emphasize the "muuuuwahh," kiss your baby on their stomach, or pretend to eat their toes. Keep it simple. If your baby laughs, repeat the movement to keep the engagement going. Make sure to use wait time and notice what they are looking at. After you say "muuuuwahh," wait up to three seconds before trying again. Give them a chance to process the information.

Using puppets with different themes, such as farm animals, is a great addition to this activity. Tell a simple story or sing a song such as "Old MacDonald Had a Farm" with animal sounds and names.

Finger Play

With rapidly developing gross motor skills, strength, balance, and hand proficiency, your baby will start to show more interest in fine motor activities. They will likely use a raking movement to grab items. Their fingers will be spread apart and open, like a garden rake, raking toward an object, then bending all of their fingers to try to pick it up.

If your baby has good sitting balance and their pediatrician approved advancing their diet to puffs, you could place some on their feeding tray and watch them rake away. Encourage them to grasp the puffs themselves and attempt to feed themselves. Placing a lightly colored puff on a dark plate will enhance visual contrast, helping your baby to see it more easily.

With the advancement of their fine motor skills, your baby will start to isolate and use their thumb, index, and middle finger in what is called a three-jaw chuck grasp. Their pinky side will eventually become more stable, allowing for more functionality and flexibility of their thumb, index, and middle fingers.

Your baby's interest will grow toward smaller objects such as tags, ribbons on toys, shoestrings, and drawstrings on your outfits. Encourage this more-precise grasp by presenting safe, smaller items such as a dissolvable puff to them with your index finger and thumb, modeling finger isolation, always with supervision and active involvement from you. Your baby will inevitably work to isolate and use their index finger and thumb or index, middle, and thumb to pick up the toy when you hand it to them that way.

Finger-Play Songs

Music enhances language and vocabulary skills. Consider singing finger-play songs slower than usual to allow your baby to hear all the words and see the finger movements. Keep it simple, find a few songs you like, and repeat them often to make it more likely that your baby will eventually sing and finger play along.

Increase your baby's joint attention and social skills by singing a familiar song, stop for a couple seconds, wait for your baby to look at you, and then start again.

"The Itsy-Bitsy Spider" is one of the many great finger-play songs you can use. Your baby will not yet be able to touch their index finger to their thumb and rotate their wrist and forearm to participate, but they will still love to watch you.

You can even make up your own words and movements, such as this silly version.

"The teeny, tiny birdy flew up into the tree." (Open and close your fingers like a bird chirping while raising your arms up.)

"Swoosh went the wind and knocked the birdy out." (Sway your hands around, then down.)

"Up stood the bird while chirping 'Tweet,

tweet, tweet.'" (Move your hands back up.)

"Then the teeny, tiny birdy flew up in the tree again. (Open and close your fingers like a bird chirping while raising your arms up again.)

Your baby will thrive on routines, so consider embedding finger play songs into mealtime, bathtime, or bedtime. Get your baby's eye contact and make the songs fun.

Get Dressed

Struggling with dressing your baby these days? You're not alone; most parents are! Your little one is learning more and more about their body. They want to explore their body and see what it can do!

Incorporate a structured poem or song, such as "Head, Shoulders, Knees, and Toes" to make dressing fun for your baby, while teaching them about body awareness. Seat your baby safely with you and in front of a mirror if possible to increase your baby's body awareness further. In lieu of the verse "eyes, and ears, and mouth, and nose," you say, "put your shirt on over your head" or "pull your pants up to your hips," while helping them don their shirt and pants.

Toy Transfers

Getting your baby dressed is the perfect daily routine in which to embed toy transfers. Right before changing your baby's top, hand them a toy. Put one arm through the shirt sleeve of the arm without the toy, say switch, use the hand-over-hand technique to help them to transfer the toy to their other hand, then put the opposite arm through the sleeve.

Your baby might get frustrated at first. But with practice, they will get it, and you won't even need to cue them. It's not a bad thing to allow your baby to get frustrated. Encourage them to persevere.

Bath Time Play

Bath time continues to be a great sensory environment to explore toys (watering cans or old plastic spice containers with holes) and textures (foam letters or blocks) and to participate in messy play (pureed food on a vertical baby surface). Your baby should have mastered sitting balance to complete these activities. Caution: Never leave your baby unattended in water.

Talk about the colors and textures of the toys. Show your baby how to turn toys, such as a watering can or empty plastic spice jar, upside down, allowing water to sprinkle out, by rotating your forearm.

You can continue to support your baby's future prewriting skills during bath time by placing pureed food on the tub walls, vertical dry-erase board, or other baby-safe object. Use fingers isolated or in unison to make marks in the pureed food.

Quadruped Play Position

Consider the surface that you are playing on with your baby. An anti-slip surface, such as a cushioned rubber mat, provides resistance and safety and might make your baby feel more successful.

As your baby becomes more stable playing in quadruped, you can challenge them on different surfaces that are not anti-slip to provide less and less resistance.

Quadruped Sit and Return

While your baby is on their hands and knees playing, encourage them to move between quadruped and sitting. You can guide your baby through this transition by helping them to tuck one leg under their body to move to a sitting position.

Encourage your baby to reach and play with toys positioned at eye level when in quadruped. This position promotes weight bearing through one arm at a time and weight shifting forward, which are needed to complete these transitions.

Quadruped on Ball

Choose a small, slightly deflated ball that allows your baby's hands to relax flat on the floor. Place your baby's tummy on the ball with their hands flat on the floor. Gently rock the ball forward to stimulate a protective extension response yet continue to provide gentle weight bearing through their hands and strengthen their arms. Guide your baby on the ball by supporting them at their hips and gently shifting their weight forward, back, and side to side.

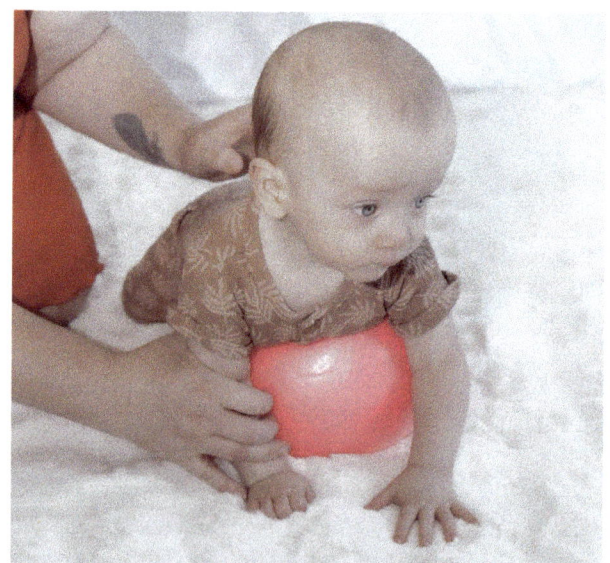

Standing Play Position

Your baby can now pull up to stand when you hold their hands, typically pushing up through both legs equally because it is easier. As your baby masters pulling up to stand, they should transition through half-kneel. You can encourage half-kneeling by helping them place one foot on the floor before transitioning to stand. Provide opportunities to play at a surface that is slightly above their shoulder height while they are sitting to encourage them to transition to kneeling, such as an upside-down diaper box placed against a wall or sturdy piece of furniture or a couch with the cushion removed.

Facilitate half-kneeling by using your leg as a guide. Place your baby in a sitting position over your leg with one foot on either side. Next, rotate their body toward a supported surface or a partner so that they are now in half-kneeling over your leg. Gently rock your baby forward and backward while here a couple times and then shift their weight forward over their planted foot to help them transition to stand.

Crawling

Some people debate whether crawling is a crucial milestone. However, let's consider why crawling is an important skill to encourage. Crawling overall strengthens your baby, develops binocular vision, increases hand-eye coordination, and encourages cross communication between both sides of the brain.

Reach and Move

This activity will work toward initiating crawling forward. Place your baby in front of you on their hands and knees. Place a toy in front of them. While giving them enough support to maintain quadruped, gently rock them back and forth. Bring one leg under their body and encourage them to reach out for the toy.

Seven Months Old

Fill in the answers to reflect on the past month and to track.

How do you feel?

_____

_____

What exercises did you work on?

_____

_____

What is your baby doing now?

_____

_____

What was your baby's favorite activity this month?

_____

_____

What questions do you have for your ob-gyn and your baby's pediatrician?

_____

_____

Notes:

_____

_____

_____

Eight Months Old

MOMMY MOVEMENTS

Making promises and setting goals is easy. Following through to completion of those goals, however, is challenging.

You would do anything for your baby: protect, love, fight for, stand up for, support, and nurture them. Your actions on your baby's behalf now and throughout their life will likely prove that. When we are consistent in what we say we will do for them and what we actually do for them, we create trust that we will follow through on our word. Your baby learns that they don't have to ask you to follow through because your words become enough.

Now, turn the tables. When is the last time you promised yourself something, then actually followed through? Actions can either support your words or oppose them. When your actions support what you say, even to yourself, then you are proving that the promises you are making are authentic. Fostering trust in yourself establishes the foundation needed to believe in yourself, the goals you are setting, and your ability to achieve them.

Sometimes, although we really want to achieve a goal, the magnitude of change becomes overwhelming, which can make it easier to give up than to follow through. As you move forward with the core stabilization progressions, break your goals down into smaller action steps to make following through feel more manageable as you move closer to achieving your ultimate goal. And each time you take a moment to work on these goals, proudly remind yourself, "I am following through."

Postnatal Core Stabilization Progressions

To help you start setting small goals, remember that your ability to maintain your breathing pattern and to sustain your pelvic girdle isometrics is your guide for these progressions, so start with these small maintenance steps. If you are holding your breath or losing any of the five stabilizers, it is wise to back up the exercise.

For example, if you lose the pelvic floor engagement, don't go as deep into your squat. You can still advance to these progressions. Your body is not ready quite yet. Modify the exercise, practice a bit more, then try again when you feel more control within the modification.

Prior to advancing, review the Breathing, Pelvic Girdle, and Standing Stability Pose on page 138.

Standing Stability Squat

Start in Standing Stability Pose with your arms at your sides and your pelvic girdle isometrics (PGI) engaged while maintaining your breath, with your feet about hip-width apart. Engage and maintain your PGI throughout this sequence. Bend your knees and bring your backside down to a squat, as if you are sitting in a chair. Keep your knees over your ankles; do not let them slide forward in front of your feet. Return to Standing Stability Pose.

Progression Challenge One: Standing Stability Squat with Hold

Remember: small steps. When you feel ready, challenge yourself by holding your squat for a count of five seconds before transitioning back to stand. Keep breathing while you maintain your PGI!

Progression Challenge Two: Standing Stability Squat with Weight

Replicate the Standing Stability Squat exercise while holding two- or three-pound handheld weights at your sides.

Progression Challenge Three: Standing Stability Squat with Block

Place your left foot on a yoga block, small step stool, or large book, shifting your weight onto your right foot when completing the standing stability squat. Keep your pelvis as neutral as possible, enabling your right gluteal muscle/leg to work to return you to Standing Stability Pose. Repeat five times on both sides.

Progression Challenge Four: Standing Stability Squat with Block, Alternating Feet

Place your left foot on a yoga block, small step stool, or thick book, shift your weight onto your right foot, and lift your left foot off of the block. Squat down through your right leg only while keeping your pelvis as neutral as possible. Return to stand, place your left foot back on the block, then return to Standing Stability Pose. Repeat five times on both sides.

Standing Stability Pose with Reverse Lunge

Start in a Standing Stability Pose and progress through Standing Stability Squat. Engage and maintain your PGI throughout this sequence. Shift your weight onto your left leg, stepping back with your right leg, lightly bending your back knee into a lunge. Even out your gluteal/side-seat muscles, trying to keep your pelvis in neutral. Hold for one full breath cycle, return to Standing Stability Pose, and repeat five times on each side.

Progression Challenge One: Standing Stability with Reverse Lunge Repeater

Once in Standing Stability Reverse Lunge Pose, perform five lunge-repeaters before stepping back into Standing Stability Pose. Repeat five times on each side.

Progression Challenge Two: Standing Stability with Reverse Lunge Alternating Repeater

Once in Standing Stability Reverse Lunge Pose, perform five lunge-repeaters before stepping back into Standing Stability Pose. Repeat five times on each side, alternating sides between each repetition.

Progression Challenge Three: Standing Stability Reverse Lunge with Weights

During the Standing Stability Reverse Lunge movement, hold light hand weights by your sides. Repeat five times on each side, alternating sides between each repetition.

BABY'S DEVELOPMENT

As your baby begins to master their ability to move about their environment, they become more independent and focus on higher level thinking skills. For example, they consider one of two choices, then purposefully respond and engage, and believe it or not they can voluntarily whimper just for attention.

Motor Development

If you haven't started running after your little mover yet, now you might find your pace quickening. Your baby is now commando crawling or crawling on hands and knees to get toys and is very motivated to pull up to stand at furniture and to cruise. Your baby will actively shift their weight in sitting to transition between long sitting, side sitting, and then onto their hands and knees. Your baby might move into w-sitting.

While it is typical for your baby to obtain this position, it should not be the only sitting position they use. W-sitting does not require as much activation of the trunk muscles and blocks weight shifts through rotation. If your baby begins to use w-sitting frequently, transition them out of the position by shifting their hip up and over their foot and onto the floor.

Your baby is able to shift their weight back over one hip to get to sitting instead of shifting their weight straight back from crawling to a w-sitting position. They are refining their crawling pattern, using a reciprocal pattern with their arms and legs and increasing their speed. They are transitioning from a crawling position to a kneeling and half-kneeling position at a support surface or with a tall toy while playing. You will also notice that they transition from half-kneel to a standing position during play. Provide them with a safe and stable surface to hold onto.

Your baby is starting to lower themselves to the floor but will also fall to sitting when they become engaged with a toy and rotate or reach too far. When they are standing at furniture, they might begin to take steps while holding on. You will notice them taking sideways (lateral) steps to move along a surface and turning their body and unweighting one hand to reach.

Your baby will also show interest in climbing, so be ready because they might enjoy practicing climbing up the stairs and onto lower surfaces such as a child-sized chair. Your baby climbs up the stairs by transitioning to stand at the first step, advancing their knees one at a time to the next step, then transitioning to stand again.

Your baby is beginning to walk when you hold their hands. They are most stable when you hold their hands above shoulder height so they can use their shoulder blades to help stabilize their trunk.

Your baby continues to develop their smaller muscle groups as they transition from raking objects with their whole hand to refining their grasp. To isolate their pointer finger and thumb using an inferior pincer grasp, they work toward using the side of their pointer finger and the pad of their thumb with more accuracy.

Now your baby is also able to grasp an object in each hand and bang them together. They might even reach for a third without releasing either of the other two objects.

Visual Development

Your baby's eye color has been changing since they were born, but they will most likely remain the color that they are at this time. Most babies' eyes reach their final color around nine months of age.

Now that your baby is crawling, they are using their hands and eyes together more than ever. They are able to see an object across the room, and they might even be able to move themselves to that object. They are using their hand-eye coordination to grasp toys or other objects that they want. As their cognitive development continues, they begin to understand more about objects and object permanence. They might also recognize an object even if they only see part of it and might be able to find a partially hidden object.

The knowledge that an object exists even when it cannot be seen (object permanence) develops dramatically during the first year of life. Around eight months of age, a baby can recognize an object even if they can only see part of it. As they continue to develop, they will be aware of objects (or people) even if they are not within their sight.

Cognitive Development

This month, your baby might show signs that they are learning to connect people and objects with words and labels. They begin to model skills such as clapping and dancing along to music. They are beginning to understand the concept of having two sides of their body that coordinate together. Your baby might be able to problem solve, for example, by retrieving a toy that has obstacles in the way. Your baby will also show increasing attention (two to three minute) to pictures this month, so story time will become more fun.

Social-Emotional Development

Your baby will continue to learn the previously discussed areas of their social-emotional skills. Your baby becomes clingier, only preferring to be with you or whomever they are primarily with, to meet their needs.

Self-Care Development

You've probably noticed your baby biting on everything in sight, including you. Over the next months, you will see an increase in your baby's coordination of chewing movements. Initially, your baby will make an up and down munching pattern, which once mastered will evolve into a rotary chew to effectively grind food. Continue to encourage further exploration of simple, soft, chopped, or mashed textures, such as applesauce or mashed potatoes, allowing small lumps. You can enhance these crunching and rotary chew patterns by placing small spoonfuls to the sides of your baby's mouth, on the biting surfaces of their gums.

Speech and Language Development

Each and every day presents limitless possibilities to expand on your baby's communication center. Research shows that the more words your baby hears, the larger their future vocabulary will be.

Continue to expose your baby to language by narrating your day, sharing observations, and making connections. For example, say, "Looks like rain today! Do you see the dark clouds in the sky?" (while pointing to the clouds) or "Woah! Do you smell the dog? I think he was rolling in the dirt again." (while holding your nose and pointing at the dog).

Your baby is beginning to understand words, and by using nonverbal communication strategies such as pointing and holding your nose, you are adding an extra layer of information for them. Your baby might become more responsive to your speech and your actions. They might begin to look toward an object in response to simple requests, such as, "Where is the bottle?" or to look for family members when they are named. You might also hear some turn-taking and respond with babbling to being spoken to.

Receptively, your baby shows understanding by using appropriate gestures, for example lifting their foot when you say, "Let's put on your shoe. Can I have your foot?" Your baby stops playing when they hear their name called, indicating they have heard you. Teach your baby body parts, such as nose, eyes, head, and ears, and watch them eagerly identify them.

Expressively, your baby combines gestures with vocalizations to show interest in objects. Your baby might imitate consonant-vowel sounds you model and also independently simplify their babbles to one sound, such as ga. They begin to attempt to emulate the sentences you say (echolalia).

Remember the difference between language expansion in regards to narrating your day (convey your day) versus targeting simple language during activities (simplify with play). Keep your language simple and concise to help expand your baby's vocabulary. When your baby picks up a ball, simply say "ball." This will increase the likelihood of your baby attaching meaning to the round object being the "ball."

Developmental Play

Allow your baby to have opportunities to learn through unstructured exploration rather than facilitating and directing every activity. Create a safe environment in which you sit back, observe, and comment on what your baby is doing, such as, "Wow, that block fits in the shoe too!" With your baby's growing independence, they might gravitate toward non-toy items, such as ripping a paper towel to pieces while exploring. This is why supervision is critical. Remember, activities do not always need to be done a certain way because your baby learns through trial and error.

Research shows that allowing unstructured play time can boost creativity, executive functioning skills (mental skills such as self-control and working memory), and problem-solving ability.

PLAY POSITIONS

Sitting Play Position

If you are able to get your baby to sit with you for short spurts of time, here are some activities that are beneficial for their development.

Apart Together

Your baby enjoys pulling things apart. As always, supervise your baby during play to decrease the likelihood of your baby placing smaller or torn items into their mouth. Because your baby is developing the movement pattern of apart and together, in combination with their developing fine motor skills, you might find them tearing apart things they are able to. Several toys on the market facilitate the apart and together movement as well, such as bristle blocks and pretend food.

Story Time

Remember to read, read, and read some more to your baby! Repetition is key. Enhance your baby's experience by continuing to read sensory play books that they can touch and explore. Consider a book that has small holes and raised items in it so that they can start to point, put their fingers through, or trace along to engage and encourage isolation of their index finger.

You can add a layer of receptive language practice by asking your baby to identify items on a page. Remember, language learning is never a quiz or game show. Ask the question, "Do you see the sun?" Wait for a second to see what your baby will do and then give them the answer, "There is the sun!" Incorporating the same books into your routine will increase the likelihood your baby will start to point at familiar objects. Practice makes perfect!

Don't feel as if you need to buy an entire library for your house. You can borrow books at a library, which will allow you lots of variety, plus the library might even have an age-appropriate story time you could bring your baby to.

Up and Down

Your baby is not able to stack blocks yet, but they certainly enjoy banging them together and knocking them down! Collect several blocks or baby-friendly stackable items, such as tissue boxes or plastic food containers. Sit down with your baby and stack one block or object on top of another counting, "One, two." Hand your baby one block and hold out another to see if they will reach and grab it. Allow them to explore the blocks, knock them down, bang them together, and pick them up. If they have two in their hands, give them another to see what they will do with the blocks. An alternative activity is to use nesting cups that your baby can stack or turn upside down and nest in one another, teaching them about shapes and sizes in all dimensions.

The Rhythm in Me

Continue to encourage songs such as "If You're Happy and You Know It" that encourage your baby to clap their hands. First model clapping for your baby so they see how you do it. Next, hold your hands over your baby's hands to produce a clap.

Encourage your baby to clap, dance, and bounce to music by physically assisting your baby motor plan through it or by modeling these actions for them. While using the hand-over-hand technique, bounce up and down or bang two objects together in coordination with a metronome or beat to help teach your baby tempo.

Body Awareness

Focus on facial recognition, language expansion, and body identification. Point to your nose and say "nose," then point to your baby's nose while saying "nose." Involve a sibling or even a well-mannered pet, "Where is sissy's nose?" and then point.

Caution: Be careful with eyes as your baby doesn't understand pressure and speed just yet. Because they are still learning this concept, using peekaboo hands is helpful for practicing eye awareness. Peekaboo hands is using open hands, palm over eyes as if your baby is playing peekaboo rather than encouraging them to point at their eyes.

Baby Signs

It is important to be aware of the skills needed before your baby can motorically utilize signs. See page 132 for the list that provides what to look for when considering your baby's ability to reciprocally engage in learning the signs you've modeled over the past couple months.

When teaching a sign, always say the word out loud while simultaneously using the sign to reinforce the target word. Start with one or two functional signs, such as more, eat, or milk, to help your baby request what they want and need. Use what motivates your baby, such as food, bubbles, or motion activities. Tell your baby what you are signing, simultaneously model the sign, then use the hand-over-hand technique to guide their attempt.

Once your baby initiates a sign, remember that it doesn't have to be precise. As long as the intention is there, reward your baby with praise. Learning language is not a quiz. There are never wrong answers, just opportunities for learning. Be kind, be gentle, be consistent, and repeat. The process of teaching your baby any new words requires many, many repetitions.

Bath Time Play

Continue to incorporate learning and vertical surface play into bath time. Hold up water toys, state what they are (i.e. duck says quack), and promote play (i.e. wash the duck with a washcloth, peek-a-boo with the duck, use a little bucket to pour over the duck to rinse, stack blocks for the duck to waddle up, bang the blocks together, etc.) You can even use baby soap foam and dab it on your baby's arm. Encourage them to rub it in by modeling it for them or hand over hand. Then repeat on different body parts as you label them.

Vertical Quadruped Play Position

While your baby is in the quadruped play position, introduce vertical toys that encourage your baby to reach and visually scan up and down, which is a skill needed for crawling and to transition up into kneeling.

Set a few puffs on your baby's tray and wait until they are finished. Next, while making the sign for more, ask, "Do you want more?" Gently guide their hands to sign for "more." After they sign for more with your guidance say, "Okay, let's have more." Repeat this a few times. On your third or fourth time, ask if they want more and provide three to four seconds of wait time before guiding their hands. If they make any attempt to move their hands toward midline, assume they are trying to make the "more" sign and make a big deal of it. Say, "Oh, you want more? Okay!" Remember: Wait time allows your baby to process and react.

Crawling Games

Play is much more mobile now; therefore, the focus of play continues to move toward development of movement patterns. But remember your baby is perfectly unique and will develop at their own pace. For example, if your baby is ready, they can work on crawling games; however, if they are not, continue to work on quadruped play activities from last month to strengthen their arms and legs for future crawling.

Fast crawl: Your baby might be picking up speed when crawling and even enjoy being chased around. Be silly and carefully crawl behind them saying, "I'm going to get you," tickling them or doing something silly when you reach them.

Crawl and carry: Once your baby is crawling, they will likely enjoy crawling with an object in one hand or sliding an object in front of them. Offer simple, flat items such as board books that they can easily push along the floor or hold in their hand. Put a toy animal on top and pretend the book is a train, "Chugga, chugga, choo choo."

Ready, set, go: Crawling after rolling items, such as a car or ball, is motivating to our little movers. Use different types of items so they can explore and observe how they move differently.

Warrior Crawl Challenge

Be creative and set up a safe crawling challenge with items from around your house. Some things you can consider using are a tunnel (or make a tunnel with a sheet over two chairs); foam wedges (or place a couch cushion on the floor and a pillow next to it with a bolster pillow or folded pillow under it to build your own wedge); pillows of various sizes; a sitting nest (or make your own with an old box, innertube, or similar object) filled with textured baby-safe balls and different-textured pieces (or take your single socks and make them into balls by rolling them in and together) all over the floor; and low-lying plush toddler chairs.

Different levels will challenge your baby's balance to help develop their vestibular system.

Different textures providing input through their hands, knees, and feet will enrich their sensory world.

Climbing

Your baby might also show interest in climbing stairs, so you must make sure you have gates at the top and bottom of steps. Prior to practicing stair climbing with your baby, work with them

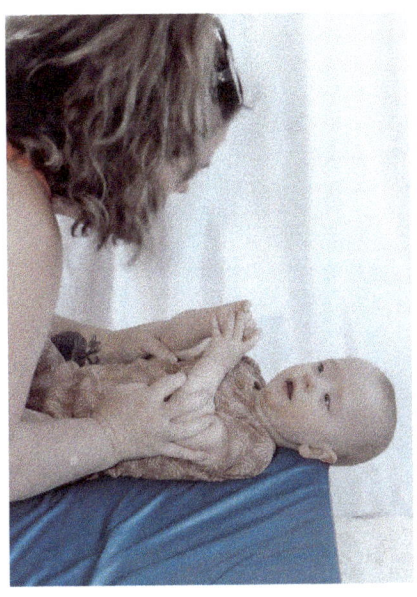 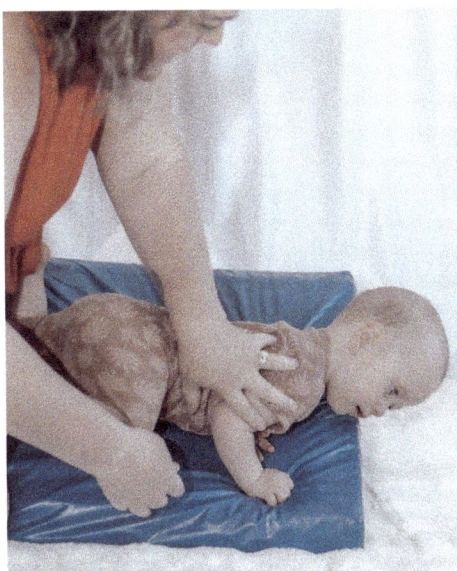 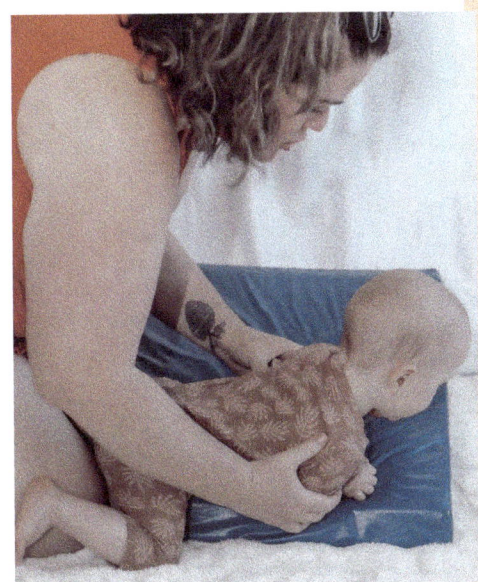

to get on and off your lap and child-sized plush chairs. Here are some tips on how to teach your baby safety on the stairs.

Encourage your baby to transition to kneeling at the bottom step, then transition to stand through half-kneel, advance hands to the next step, advance each knee up on to the first step,

and then transition to stand through half-kneel and repeat. Vary your hand position depending on where your baby needs support.

Initially, keep one hand on your baby's chest to prevent them from falling forward. Use toys or another caregiver a couple steps above to motivate your baby to crawl up the steps.

Standing

Your baby might enjoy cruising along furniture or walking as you hold their hands, with their arms up in the air and their scapula retracted (shoulder blades squeezed together) to stabilize their trunk. The standing position builds leg strength and endurance, and it works on your baby's balance for future walking.

Depending on your baby's motor control, they might still push up over both feet at the same time to achieve the standing position. However, when working on this skill, facilitate standing through half-kneel to help your baby develop the ability to shift their weight side to side and increase their core control.

Continue to provide your baby opportunities

to play at low surfaces. Vary the position of your baby's toys to encourage shifting weight and rotating.

Cruising

Cruising is when your baby moves laterally, taking side-steps. Couches with cushions removed are often the perfect height to practice cruising. Place a toy on the couch, slightly out of reach and to the side of your baby. Shake the toy to engage their attention and motivate them to side-step toward the toy along the furniture. Place your hands on your baby's hips to help them shift their weight away from the toy onto their back foot to enable them to lift the foot closest to the toy and take a step toward it.

A Note on Mastery

Mastery comes when your baby consistently demonstrates success with a skill. While your baby is still learning a skill, they might appear to regress in another area. This is normal, not cause for concern. True regression is only when a skill was mastered, but then your baby is no longer able to complete the previously mastered skill.

The height of a toy box may make it difficult for your baby to look in and retrieve toys at this age. Baskets, boxes, or even baby-safe handbags might be more easily accessible and fun for your baby to look in and sort through to find their preferred toys. Stable boxes are also another surface your baby might enjoy cruising along while looking in to see what toys interested them.

Eight Months Old

Fill in the answers to reflect on the past month and to track.

How do you feel?
_____

_____

What exercises did you work on?
_____

_____

What is your baby doing now?
_____

_____

What was your baby's favorite activity this month?
_____

_____

What questions do you have for your ob-gyn and your baby's pediatrician?
_____

_____

Notes:
_____

_____

_____

_____

Nine Months Old

© Jennifer Bainbridge

MOMMY MOVEMENTS

As you come into your own as a parent, understanding your baby, balancing your schedule, and reflecting on the little things that create big changes, our hope is that you are not just surviving, but thriving. Hopefully, the questions, second-guessing yourself, and the doubts are lessening, and the gut feelings that you know what's best for you and your baby are getting stronger. As you wake up each day, reminde yourself, "I am thriving!"

If you have been doing your Mommy Movements, the same is likely true for your body. You are more confident; you are feeling stronger. You are more aware of how your body was working for you during your pregnancy, and you are retraining your body back to the more efficient prepregnancy muscle patterns.

Postnatal Pelvic Floor Isolation Progressions

We each place different demands on our pelvic floor (PF), depending on our lifestyle. For example, sitting at a desk for most of the day requires different levels of efficiency of the PF muscles than a job that requires standing, lifting, and moving objects all day. Whether your exercise routine consists of slow, mindful movements like yoga or quick, ballistic movements like high-intensity interval training (HIIT) or CrossFit, your PF needs to be able to counteract the forces placed on it for you to remain continent and to thrive. Either form of exercise requires your PF to be able to predict the demands you place on it and adjust accordingly.

Though jumping jacks might not be in your daily repertoire, going to the trampoline park with your toddler might be. Though lifting heavy weights might not be for you, bending and lifting a 20-pound child quickly will probably be a daily event. That's why, regardless of your exercise routine, the pelvic floor isolation (PFI) exercises in this chapter are important for everybody for healthy, efficient PF engagement during everyday life activities. So don't just survive your daily routine, thrive by incorporating these PFI progressions to support your pelvic integrity.

Pelvic Floor Isolation Progressions

It is common to experience leaking when adding exercising elements back into your routine postpartum, especially during lunges, jumping jacks, and running, even if you do not leak other times. This occurs for a few reasons.

First, some leg and hip muscles are designed to help you with pelvic floor contractions (agonists), while other leg and hip muscles promote relaxation of your PF (antagonists). For example, when you squeeze your thighs together, you activate your inner thigh muscles (adductors), which help your PF muscles contract more efficiently. Think about it, when you really have to urinate, you probably cross your legs and squeeze with all your might. You are using your adductors to help you engage your PF muscles to prevent you from releasing urine. Similarly, when you engage your outer thigh muscles (or your abductors), you promote relaxation of your PF.

If you took a birthing class, the instructor might have had you in deep squat positions, which use your abductors to assist in relaxing your PF to facilitate the birth of your baby. You get the point: You can use muscles as helpers and hinderers when needed.

So what if you are exercising in a deep squat, activating your abductors while holding weights for resistance and have a full bladder? Well, if your PF muscles relax when your hips are open and your abductors are on, you are going to feel quite uncomfortable and might have to change your clothing. For this reason, you want to engage your PF despite the fact that your hip muscles are promoting relaxation. Make sense? Although you may use the helper muscles of your legs in some circumstances, you do want to be able to activate your PF in isolation (meaning by itself, also known as disassociation) when needed.

A second reason leaking might occur during exercise-type movements is because, despite working hard on PF contraction exercises, higher-level types of movement put more demand on your core and PF. So how do you address the great demand placed on your muscles? You train your PF to handle the challenges through PFIs, with your breath so you can manage the pressure you place on your body. These exercises teach your PF to stay engaged no matter what the rest of your body is doing, gradually learning how to counteract the pressures and demands placed on them.

The exercises that follow are a four- or five-step process where the PF is the first to contract or engage and the last to relax, while you perform different movements and breathe. At times, it might seem like the challenge of patting your head and rubbing your belly, but that is exactly the goal: a combination of dissociation and coordination of movements (the ability to do two different things at the same time on purpose).

Your nine-month-old is sure to be on the move, and so are you! These PF isolation progressions will help keep you safely on the go with your little mover.

Always get clearance from your healthcare team to perform exercises during pregnancy and postpartum. However, once you can perform each progression while maintaining your full breath, if you are able to find your stabilizers and without any fear of leaking, you can move into the next progression.

Holding your breath during any exertion is one of the main reasons that you might leak during an activity because it causes increased intra-abdominal pressure, which adds pressure to your bladder. However, it also puts stress on your PF muscles to counterbalance the pressure, adding to their work-demand. So when in doubt, exhale. Exhale on exertion, exhale as you lift something, exhale when you land or push off during a jump, and exhale when you bend or stand up out of a chair. Remember, the PF muscles work with your diaphragm, so an exhale helps to release your abdominal pressure and also works to engage your PF. This simple adjustment to your breath can make a huge difference.

Pelvic Floor Isolation Adduction

Lie on your back with your knees bent and a ball (or a pillow) between your knees. As you exhale, engage and maintain your pelvic floor contraction (PFC) by pulling up (gently close and lift), squeeze your knees on the ball, relax your knees, and then release your PF. Repeat this sequence five times.

Pelvic Floor Isolation Abduction

Lie on your back with your knees bent and an exercise band around your knees. As you exhale, engage and maintain your PFC, push your knees out into the band, relax your knees, then release your PF. Repeat this sequence five times.

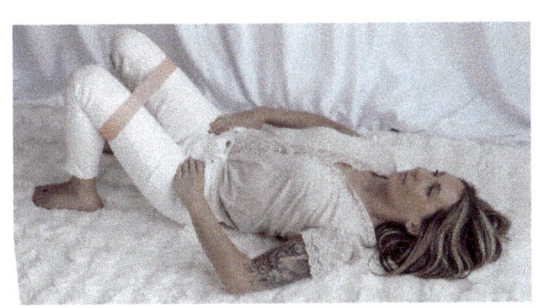

Pelvic Floor Isolation March

Sit up at the edge of a bed or chair with your feet hanging over the side or planted on the ground. As you exhale, engage and maintain your PFC. March your right knee up and then down, march your left knee up and then down, relax both knees, and finally release your PF. Repeat this sequence five times.

Pelvic Floor Isolation Leg Extensions

Sit up at the edge of a bed or chair with your feet hanging over the side or planted on the ground. As you exhale, engage and maintain your PFC. Extend one leg out and back and extend your other leg out and back. Relax your legs and then your PF. Repeat this sequence five times.

Pelvic Floor Isolation with Wall Squats

Standing against a wall, engage and maintain your PFC by pulling up (close and lift). Slide down the wall into a squat, stand back up, and then relax your PF. Repeat this sequence five times.

Jumping Jack Deconstructed Initial Cycle

Standing with your feet together, engage and maintain your PFC. As you exhale, move your right leg out to your side (abduct), return back to starting position, then relax your PFC. Repeat this sequence with your left leg. Repeat the entire cycle (one cycle includes the right and left leg) five times, resting your PFC between each side. Your goal is to work up to being able to engage and maintain your PFC while repeating this sequence three to five times per leg. Remember always move on the exhale!

Progression Challenge One: Jumping Jack Deconstructed Phase One

Repeat the exercise above, but this time as you exhale, engage and maintain your PFC as you switch between your right and left sides for one full cycle. (Stepping out to the right, returning to start, stepping out to the left, then returning to start is one cycle.) Relax your PFC after one full cycle. Then reengage and exhale, maintain your PFC, repeat another full cycle, and relax your PFC again. Repeat for five full cycles.

Once mastered, to advance, engage and maintain your PFC and on your exhale, hold it through two cycles in a row. (Your left leg steps out and back, then your right leg steps out and back for cycle 1, then your left leg steps out and back again, then your right leg steps out and back again for cycle 2, then relax your PFC only after two full cycles.)

Your goal is to work up to engaging and maintaining your PFC and holding it through five cycles in a row before you relax your PFC.

Progression Challenge Two: Jumping Jack Deconstructed Phase Two

Standing with your feet together, engage your PFC. As you exhale, jump both of your legs out to the sides (open/abduction), then relax your PFC. Reengage your PFC, exhale, jump both of your legs back to standing with feet together, then relax your PFC. Repeat this sequence five times.

Progression Challenge Three: Jumping Jack Deconstructed Phase Three

Repeat Challenge Two; however, this time jump your legs out and back together before you relax your PFC. Practice one jumping jack at a time and repeat a total of five times.

Progress Challenge Four: Jumping Jack Deconstructed Phase Four

Progress to two jumping jacks before you relax and reset your PFC. Continue to progress by adding on one more jumping jack each time you exercise, but only after you are able to engage and maintain your PFC throughout. Your goal is to build up to 10 jumping jacks.

BABY'S DEVELOPMENT

We are cruising along through this first year, and it's been so much fun! No matter what your baby's pace, they are moving along and progressing daily. Their progression might be so small that you may not see it, but it is there. Or your baby's progression might be so fast that you want to slow it down and just "embrace the baby."

Motor Development

As your baby's mobility continues to develop with each new day, they explore new perceptual concepts such as in/out, on/off, up/down—both in their play and in their environment. Your baby will continue to use a variety of sitting positions when playing with toys, but they won't likely sit in one place for an extended period of time. They will be busy crawling to explore and find toys and then experimenting with climbing onto and over obstacles. Your baby will attempt to climb up on a variety of surfaces and will learn through practice and problem-solving which objects are safe to climb on. Because they will fall and get out of sight easily as they develop these problem-solving skills, create a safe space for your baby to explore. All of their climbing helps them to develop motor planning as they reach with their hands and experiment with where to place their legs and how to move their trunk while maintaining their stability.

Your baby loves to climb up the stairs and might begin to lower themselves to crawl down the steps. Your baby is continuing to gain stability in standing, needing less support from their hands, and is squatting to pick up toys. They are beginning to cruise side to side (laterally), around corners, and turn to hold on to objects with only one hand. This month, they might even take forward steps while holding onto furniture and transitioning between two different surfaces, such as a couch and nearby chair. When you assist your baby as they walk by holding both of their hands, they will be most stable when you hold their arms above their head. Lowering their hands will challenge them more.

As your baby's gross motor skills are advancing in leaps and bounds, so are their fine motor skills. These important skills create the necessary foundation for later handwriting accuracy and success. Your baby still enjoys banging objects together and continues to develop their pincer grasp—the grasp they use when pinching things with their index finger and thumb. Your baby enjoys picking items out of a container and letting them go. You can work on your baby's mastery of body movements during your daily routines through simple tasks such as a cleanup game. Bring a storage bin over to your baby and model picking up and placing toys in. Make it a challenge for speed and accuracy by playing a song and ending your task when the music stops.

Your baby is learning to poke at objects, which is the start of isolating their pointer finger for future pointing, both near and far. Pointing is an important language skill that allows your baby to label objects in their environment. At home, you can encourage pointing at objects in books while reading and identifying them or by presenting two choices at mealtime with your baby pointing at their preferred choice. Outside, you can model for your baby how to point to such things as birds, trees, and planes, which will help promote and strengthen gestural communication.

The symmetric tonic neck reflex (STNR) might start to integrate between nine and 11 months old. Some signs of retention might be poor seated or standing posture, decreased hand-eye coordination, low muscle tone, W-sitting, and messy eating.

The spinal galant reflex is typically integrated now. Some signs of retention might be postural issues, hyperactivity, attention and concentration concerns, bedwetting (after they've been fully potty trained), decreased endurance, lower extremity coordination, and digestive issues.

Visual Development

Now that your baby is moving and grooving, they are using their vision and depth perception more than ever. As they continue to crawl, pull up, and stand, their improving visual acuity and depth perception help them navigate the world around them.

Because your baby is better able to see details now, they should be able to recognize family members by sight only, even if they are across a room. They should also be able to fixate on smaller objects, such as a small piece of cereal, buttons, and even crumbs on the floor, so scanning an area and babyproofing are critical.

Cognitive Development

Your baby is all about mastering their coordinated body movements and moving around their environment. Remember, as you enter new environments with your baby, think "safety first" and scan the environment for any potential hazards or small objects your baby might inadvertently put in their mouth.

Your baby continues to express their own preferences and dislikes, much to some chagrin for you. They continue to explore their impact on the world through cause-and-effect games. Your baby might start throwing toys and watching where they land and will still find fun in dropping objects, so take a deep breath when picking up the items they throw or drop repeatedly.

Your baby is able to focus more when you talk to them. They might now listen to and respond appropriately to simple commands such as "come here" and "no."

Now that your baby is more mobile, they will move toward an object to retrieve it, drag it with them, or carry it, then scoot. They will use whatever method they find most efficient and fun to bring toys along with them. Your baby might enjoy playing with toys that have wheels or move spontaneously when activated. They might even reengage a toy to activate it when the action ceases.

As discussed previously, irritability might increase during cognitive growth, as it often occurs with physical leaps.

Social-Emotional Development

Engaging your baby in play with friends is helpful now, with the understanding that they will not play together with their friend; rather, they will play next to another baby while each doing their own thing (parallel play). Because they are unable to interact effectively during play, they will play alone. But they will enjoy playing near other children, showing interest in what they are doing. Because babies at this age do not understand how to share, your baby might get easily upset if a toy is taken, or you might notice them offering a toy to their playmate but not releasing it. You can certainly practice sharing, but do not set your expectations high because your baby is not developmentally ready to understand this play concept.

Your baby might also start testing you this month during feeding and bedtime. For example, they might play games with their food and utensils, such as dropping them on the floor, resist going to sleep, or remain active as you transition to bedtime. Although it might be difficult, consider this stage as a time to work on your personal growth in the area of patience. When your baby pushes your limits, remember to keep calm and be consistent.

During simple relational play, your baby enjoys imitating you. Encourage your baby to imitate various daily tasks, such as brushing their hair, feeding themselves, and washing themselves. Also continue to encourage them to imitate you clapping and playing imitation games.

Now that your baby is more mobile, they will also enjoy exploring all over, so continue to be alert and have appropriate safety measures in place.

Self-Care Development

Your baby's independence can be most noted this month in their desire to self-feed and move to reach desired people or toys. Once your baby has good trunk control and is able to sit well independently, they will start to feed themselves with their fingers, enjoy holding and exploring utensils during feeding, and use a small cup with your guidance.

Your baby's bite reflex, which is a tight jaw closure with gum or tooth stimulation, is now starting to disappear, allowing your baby to begin establishing a more deliberate up-and-down biting response to food. Your baby's jaw isolation is improving, and they are able to take a couple consecutive sips before taking a breath.

Speech and Language Development

Your baby's receptive language continues to blossom between following simple directions and identifying more and more body parts. Your baby uses sounds individual to them, such as a a-a-a (protowords) to indicate that they want a specific item. By acknowledging your baby's communication attempts, you are encouraging their social development. Your baby continues to mimic the rhythm of conversation and might even attempt to sing along to their favorite song. Your baby chuckles and babbles when they are alone and might respond with increased attention or excitement when hearing familiar voices.

A Note on First Words

Your baby might say their first words soon. Look for consistent patterns of babbling, such as "mamama." Respond by giving meaning to the babble, for example by saying, "Yes! I am your mama." Protowords are transitional sounds that consistently represent a word for your baby. A protoword does not necessarily sound like the word itself. For example, your baby might use the sound a-a-a and point to indicate they want their lovey or say e-e-e when they want a drink from their cup. Encourage and affirm these protowords. Do not feel as if you need to correct your baby; just encourage them to keep trying to communicate.

A fun way to encourage your baby's use of protowords is to pretend that you know what they are saying during these playful babbles and have a conversation with them. Note the distinction between the two following conversations.

Below is an example of regular all-day talk where you convey your day to your baby, such as during a walk or making dinner.

Baby: "babadugabe"
You: "I agree. It is really hot outside today."
Baby: "pabutahahba"
You: "I don't think it is supposed to rain until Sunday."

Now, let's look at an example of a specific playtime activity where you simplify your language with play, being specific to what your baby is playing with, such as while looking at a block.

Baby: "babadugabe"
You: "Block. Do you want the block?" (Hold up the block.)
Baby: "pabutahahba"
You: "Stack three blocks! Up, up, up."

Increase your baby's understanding (receptive language) by giving them simple directions targeting basic concepts such as in, out, next to, besides, up, down. You can incorporate these into everyday routines such as by saying, "Let's put your dirty shirt IN the hamper" or, "Let's put your toys IN the tub. Your turn!" You can also begin to set up important routines that will help save you some sanity in the future such as "cleanup" time. At the end of each night, you and your baby put away all their toys together. Your baby won't do much; however, you can hand them a toy and point into the toybox while helping them place the toy in. Your baby might not get this concept right away, but as with everything, repetition and consistency are key.

Pacifiers and Speech Development

When overused, pacifiers impact your baby's lips and tongue, which in turn can impact development of speech sounds. Pacifiers should only be used when your baby needs to self-soothe. At nine months, it could become a habit. Watch for signs that your baby is using it throughout the day, during play, or other times when self-soothing isn't needed.

A pacifier mimics a premature sucking pattern, like your baby uses with your breast or a bottle. Using a pacifier too long can create an open-mouth resting posture (your baby's mouth slightly open, teeth pushed out shaped like a pacifier, and tongue low or protruding forward rather than lips resting in a closed position), which changes the oral cavity of your baby so that their teeth and gums grow around the pacifier. Studies suggest children using pacifiers above 18 months of age are more prone to their teeth being impacted.

The American Academy of Pediatrics recommends starting to wean your baby from the pacifier at six months due to some studies suggesting that pacifiers can also increase ear infections in babies over six months. Prolonged pacifier and other oral habits, such as thumb and finger sucking, can cause a narrow dental arch, which can make the baby more prone to upper airway obstruction.

As your baby grows, they need to explore different ways to move their tongue and lips by babbling. Also they need to gain information from the outside world through their mouth by mouthing objects. Babbling strengthens muscles and sound production, which aids in word formation and vocabulary. Pacifiers impede this natural development

Although at this age your baby's pacifier might continue to soothe them, consider teaching your baby to self-soothe during daytime hours with a toy, stuffed animal, or blanket in place of the pacifier. Limit your baby's pacifier use at this time to only during nighttime sleeping or wean them completely. Weaning your baby off the pacifier takes patience and time. It might be helpful to start by limiting the pacifier to use just during bedtime or having your baby leave their pacifier out for the "binky fairy" to help with weaning off the pacifier.

Developmental Play

Continue to challenge your baby by placing items just out of their reach to encourage them to move toward and obtain them. Your baby's early explorations of their motor abilities build the foundation for future whole-body coordination. Remember to observe the serve. Return with focus, attention, support, praise, communication, and taking turns.

PLAY POSITIONS

Sitting Play Position

Your baby continues to be more mobile each month, and that's wonderful because these continuous positional changes are essential for your baby's development. For example, your baby has been moving from sitting to quadruped (on their hands and knees), which facilitates the development of the palmar arch. The palmar arch development is important because it helps to refine fine motor skills and future handwriting skills.

Swing Time

Swinging on swing sets outdoors or in a blanket inside offers opportunities to expand your baby's interactive language skills, vocabulary, anticipation of play activities, and social engagement.

If your baby is over the age of nine months and sits independently, as long as you maintain direct contact with them, you might consider using a bucket seat swing with a five-point harness system. Whenever your baby is in a swing, always stand in front of them so you can keep them safe, see their face, and monitor their reactions.

Seat your baby in the swing, standing in front of them. Pull the swing slowly toward you; say, "Ready, set;" pause; say "Go" or "One, two, three;" pause; and release your grasp on the swing. While your baby is gently swinging, repeat a simple song or phrase, such as, "Look at baby, flying high, like a bird in the sky." After a few swings, grab the swing and hold it. Wait for your baby to gain eye contact, then use simple words, such as, "More swing? Okay! Ready, set" pause, "Go!" Providing wait time increases anticipation and joint attention.

Note: It is important to start out slowly in swings. The movement and feeling of swinging in the air is new to your baby, and every baby reacts differently. This might be scary at first for your baby because their vestibular system is still developing. If your baby is scared, consider either taking them out of the swing and trying again another day or simply keep hold of the swing and slowly bring them toward you and away from you. Work up to more movement at your baby's pace and within their comfort zone.

Swinging in a blanket can still be fun for your baby. Have your baby lie on their back in the middle of a blanket. If your baby prefers, you can have them hold a favorite toy. Recruit a family member or friend and each grasp an end of the blanket and lift your baby slightly up off the ground. Swing your baby from side to side in the blanket slowly, staying low to the ground. Pairing a song such as the alphabet song "A,B,C…" helps your baby begin to understand time and that activities have a beginning and an end. You can also pause swinging and omit a letter, waiting for your baby to make a sound or wiggle to encourage you to resume swinging. This interaction builds on the social play of that Ping-Pong interaction.

As your baby begins to express joy and comfort with gently swinging, you can increase stimulation of the balance system by slowly dipping one side of the blanket, causing your baby to roll gently, then alternate rolling side to side while on their back in the blanket. This type of stimulation can help your baby be less fearful of moving in their environment.

Standing Play Position

This month, your baby continues to thrive, seeing the world as we do in an upright position. They also begin to enjoy standing during play.

Inside and Out

This activity helps teach your baby how to shift their weight from one leg to another while bearing weight through their hands. Teach your baby how to get into and out of safe items, such as low boxes or bins no higher than your baby's knees.

When your baby is standing with their hands on the edge of the box or bin, help them to lift one leg and then the other to step in. Then assist your baby in stepping out by slowly shifting their hips forward on the side with their leg lifted. Repeat to the other side and marvel as your baby learns the concept of walking.

Caution: Never leave your baby unattended near a box or a bin and never use a box or bin with a lid.

Sensory Bin

If your baby is eating easily dissolvable foods such as puffs or melt-aways, you can place them in a container to make a sensory bin. Dissolvable foods are a wise choice because you don't need to worry if they put them in their mouth.

Verbally label the items as your baby picks them up, describe the dissolvable food, take cues from their facial expressions, observe them, and talk about what they are looking at.

If your baby is not eating melt-away foods yet, simply fill a container with toys of different textures, such as baby paper, extra-large pom-poms, or sponges, and talk about the toys as your baby picks them up.

Seek and Find

Object permanence doesn't only refer to your baby's ability to understand that you are still there when they don't see you. Yes, it's always fun to crawl behind the couch and pop up, exclaiming peekaboo!" to get that giggle going. Similarly, your baby loves playing with toys that are inside of an object, such as in a tissue box. While your baby is watching, pull out the toy, say "Boo" or "Hi," and place it back in. Engaging your baby's visual and auditory interest, you encourage them to retrieve the toy. Repeat this activity.

Over time, your baby will place the toy in the box and then go searching for it on their own. Later, your baby can also do this activity standing.

Nesting

Play with nesting items, such as nesting cup toys or household items, such as measuring cups or spoons. Hand your baby two or three of the items at a time—unnested. Model placing one item inside another. Start by placing the smallest one into the largest one to make it easy for your baby before adding the rest. This skill reinforces your baby's understanding of shape and dimensions of objects as they relate to one another.

Pointing Play

Pointing with one finger (finger isolation) is very important for your baby's hand dexterity and communication. Your baby will learn that pointing helps them to communicate with you about things they see in their environment. Pointing is important for both receptive language and joint attention.

When you point at something, take notice if your baby looks. To do this is simple. During a floor time activity, put an object approximately one or two feet from where you are playing. Hold up your index finger like you're indicating "number one" right in front of your baby's face. Once your baby focuses on your finger, move your finger slowly to an object one to two feet away, such as a teddy bear, shifting your gaze from your baby to the object. Once your baby sees the object, label the object with excitement, such as saying, "Teddy bear!"

If your baby does not follow your finger, move the object closer than one to two feet. You could also hold the object in your nondominant hand while holding up your pointer finger on your dominant finger having them only six inches apart.

Note: To encourage your baby's future pointing skills, wrap your hand around your baby's hand and allow the index finger to pop out and play with textured books or finger-tracing books; point to pictures in the books and label them and play with foods/textures.

Pinch and Pull

Your baby might find every dust bunny and hair on your floor now. They enjoy searching for and picking up small items, and in doing this, your baby is strengthening and coordinating the little muscles in their hands.

You can imitate these small finger movements by placing a piece of yarn inside of a straw and encouraging your baby to pull it through by moving it back and forth. (Never leave your baby unattended with yarn or string.) Tie a large knot on both sides of the straw so the yarn stays in. Once you model pulling the string back and forth for your baby, they will surely want to try it, too. Remember string, ribbon, or cords should be less than seven inches long.

Cause-and-Effect Play

Cause-and-effect play is enriching as your baby explores their world, learning rapidly about how their body can interact with their environment. Some examples of cause-and-effect toys are light-up toys that activate with the push of a button, pop-up toys, jack-in-the-boxes, and toy cars that roll. Because your baby loves to watch things drop, dropping light- or noise-activated toys is an excellent way to hold their attention.

If you want to change things up, you can teach your baby that every action has a reaction

in many ways that might even help you get through your daily to-do list. See the "Mealtime" and "Laundry" activities below.

Remember joint attention: Encourage your baby to engage with you during activities by gaining their attention and eye contact. Hold objects close to your face and interact with them enthusiastically once you gain your baby's attention. Eye contact is essential for your baby's social communication skills as they grow.

Mealtime

Fill a small container with toys and keep it in your kitchen. Use different-shaped toys (e.g. balls, blocks, etc.), so your baby can observe varying drop responses, and change your language as a result with "bounce" or "thud." Reserve it for use only during meal preparation or cleanup, which will keep your baby busy while you cook or clean.

For this activity, place your baby in their highchair. Give them the container to experiment with grabbing and dropping the toys.

If placing the container in front of them doesn't work, then try placing containers with toys on either side of them they need to reach and grab from.

To catch the items your baby drops, you could place boxes on the floor around your baby's high chair. You could even place an object in the box that will make the toys bounce up on impact, such as a ball that fits snugly in the box.

Laundry

While you are doing your laundry, provide your baby with a safe, small bin to play with next to you. Give your baby all those extra socks that you can't find matches for and model throwing them into their bin to encourage them to do the same. You can even fill the socks with toys and let your baby explore, feel, and find their toys, dump and repeat. Or switch laundry from the washer to the dryer or dryer to a basket, pull clothing out, hand it to your baby, and encourage them to drop it into the basket or cool dryer.

Cleanup

Bring a storage bin over to your baby and model how to pick up and drop toys during cleanup. Clear storage bins are helpful when it comes to teaching cleanup because they enable your baby to see what is stored where and offer an opportunity for your baby to learn objects names by pointing to and requesting specific items in the bin. Use this time to label items to promote speech and language by saying, "Clean up the blocks." Set a timer, sing, or play "The Cleanup Song" to provide a time and place for cleaning up.

"Clean up. Clean up. Everybody, everywhere. Clean up. Clean up. It's time to clean up the mess we share."

Switches, Faucets, and Bells

Hold your baby and encourage them to turn the light switches in your house off and on. When you go outside of your home or when visiting family or friends, encourage your baby to ring the doorbell. Even allowing your baby to help you turn your sink on and off prior to washing their hands is a cause-and-effect activity. Be creative and build cause-and-effect play into your daily routine.

Speaking of washing hands, start our hand-washing song with your baby now so they can start to repeatedly hear and learn the steps of handwashing.

Scrub, scrub, scrub your hands to make the bubbles come. Nails, palms, and in between. Scrub until they're clean.

Rinse, rinse, rinse your hands. Rinse the bubbles off. Swirling, twirling down the drain. Rinse the bubbles off.

Dry, dry, dry your hands dry them with a towel. Nails, palms, and in between. Now your hands are clean.

One Two Finger-Play Song

Finger-play songs, which are easily accessible on the internet, will help your baby with body awareness and development of motor skills. Search for songs with simple actions, such as the following, or make up your own:

One, two, I see you. (point to your baby)
Three, four, clap some more.
Five, six kick, kick, kick.
Seven, eight, arms up straight.
Nine, ten start again.

Dress-Up Pokey

As discussed previously, give your baby two choices of outfits when getting dressed, allowing them to play and feel the textures and anticipate the act of dressing. Talk about what you are putting on them, such as shoes, socks, headband. You might sing the "Head, Shoulders, Knees, and Toes" song or the "Hokey Pokey." Now try to change the words to involve the steps of dressing to further increase body awareness. Here is an example.

"You put your right arm in, you put your left arm in, to pull your T-shirt on, and shake your hands about. You do the dress-up pokey and put a smile on your face. That's what it's all about."

Add whatever verses you like, stand your baby up, and gently dance them all about in front of a mirror at the end to promote further body awareness.

If you're in a rush or haven't had your coffee yet and have no energy to be animated and sing, you can simplify things. Just say simple commands such as, "Arm up" to teach your baby to lift their arms and legs to help. As with all activities, allow your baby time to explore such things as patterns on clothing, textures of clothing, and sensations of brushing their teeth and hair.

Quadruped Play Position

Playing with toys on the floor, in the tummy time position, continues to be important; however, the quadruped position (on hands and knees) will likely be your baby's primary way of strengthening their core and upper body right now due to their eagerness to be on the move.

Crawling Expedition

Because your baby loves to crawl, continue to challenge them with over/under and in/out obstacles so they can work on strength, coordination, balance, visual motor skills, and body awareness and also activate their protective responses. In addition, combine more transitions between crawling, climbing, and standing by utilizing pull-up and standing stations.

You could make a baby obstacle course. Enhance their obstacle course with sensory and fine motor items, such as textured wall cards, mazes made out of painter's tape, block walls made of shoe boxes to knock down and build up, and/or puffs hidden in containers along the way. Use materials you already have in your home, such as an upside-down diaper box for a low toy station, to help on budget. Nurture your baby's listening and responding skills by saying simple commands during their expedition such as, "Come here," "Clap," or "Dance."

Change the obstacle course weekly by rearranging items or adding different toys. You can change the scenery by adding stuffed animals one might see in the jungle, on a farm, or in the sea.

Always be either actively involved or provide close supervision for your baby to safely explore their environment. Because your baby is so active now, they are more likely to pull things down on themselves, fall more frequently, discover outlets or fireplaces, and notice small objects on the floor.

When your baby shows interest in something that might be harmful, softly say, "No!" and guide their attention elsewhere. Learning the word, "No" is important for your baby's safety.

Standing Play Position

Your baby continues to learn and grow. Around this month, you'll find they enjoy spending more time playing while standing.

Standing Weight Shifts

Help your baby stand. While holding their hands out in front of them, sing an interactive song such as "Row, Row, Row Your Boat," and shift their weight forward and back to provide vestibular and proprioceptive feedback, which challenges their balance. Vary this activity by singing "Rock, Rock, Rock Your Boat" and shift their weight side to side.

Challenge Up

Your baby enjoys standing up to see their world in a new perspective, and this activity strengthens their legs, challenges their balance, and activates their protective responses. While your baby is standing at a stable surface, practice having them squat down to pick up toys from the floor and drop them into a container or bin. Change the location of the container or bin to different sides and heights to further challenge them.

Vertical Surface Stand

One way to challenge your baby in the standing position is to place them facing a vertical surface, such as a wall or a refrigerator. Because your baby can't lean or prop themselves when against a vertical surface, this enables full weight back through their feet. When this activity is new to your baby, position yourself next to them with your hand in front of their chest to protect them from collapsing forward and hitting their head on the wall. Using suction cup balls or magnets on a sliding glass door encourages them to pull them off and reach down and grab them off the floor or from you. Caution: Be sure the suction cups or magnets are large enough to not be choking hazards.

Cruising

While your baby is exploring in the standing position, motivate them to cruise by advancing toys along furniture and transitioning them to another surface, such as from the couch to a nearby chair. Setting up an ottoman or activity table next to the sofa or cruising surface provides opportunities to transition around the inside corner to a second surface, challenging their balance.

Supported Walking

Your baby needs to build strength and coordination before they start walking on their own. Once your baby is pulling to stand and cruising along furniture, they might want to walk with their hands held. Always follow their lead on this, presenting the opportunity to practice, but if they aren't interested or motivated to do so, try again another time. When playing in this position with your baby, it will be easiest for them to walk with their hands held above their head with you standing either in front of them or behind them. When your baby is standing with two hands held, shift their weight slightly forward to see if they begin to take a step.

As your baby continues to become more confident, coordinated, and stronger, you can start to lower your hands, which will lower their arms and hands, challenging them more.

Nine Months Old

Fill in the answers to reflect on the past month and to track.

How do you feel? _____

_____

What exercises did you work on? _____

_____

What is your baby doing now? _____

_____

What was your baby's favorite activity this month? _____

_____

What questions do you have for your ob-gyn and your baby's pediatrician?

_____

Notes: _____

_____

_____

_____

Ten Months Old

MOMMY MOVEMENTS

In her podcast, researcher and author, Brené Brown, PhD, mentioned a quote by psychiatrist and psychoanalyst Carl Jung that stuck with her as it relates to her life and her parenting: "The greatest burden a child must bear is the unlived life of its parents." Think about what that means and keep those words in your mind as you read on.

    As we have discussed many times throughout this book, mindset matters. In fact, did you know that, if you take two people born into the same circumstances and situations, if they both have the same resources provided to them, are the same age and gender, have lived the same lifestyle, and have a similar family unit yet two different mindsets, they will live extremely different lives?

If you let life happen to you, you will live an ordinary life that's small and within limits. You might exist, but you might not live.

On the other hand, if you can let life happen through you, you create your own life. So, ask yourself, "Am I doing what I love?"

Your goal this month is to pick one thing you are already doing or have been wanting to do with the sole reason being that you have chosen to do it because you love it, and remind yourself "I am doing what I love."

Postnatal Abdominal and Core Foundation Sequence Progressions Abdominal Progressions

You have laid the groundwork for healing, resetting core activation and stabilization strategies, and rehabbing motor patterns. It's time to combine the abdominal work and the pelvic girdle stabilization work that you have been progressing through to create a core workout in three primary ways.

The first way is in the Standing Position. The goal of Standing Position exercises is to work your abdominals without compromising the muscle strategies you've already learned and built upon, while in ways your body currently functions. In other words, the exercises make you stronger and immediately teach your body to translate that strength and utilize it during typical movement patterns you need daily.

The second way is with Ground Core work, for the crunch lovers out there. However, traditional crunches are not the focus. Rather, this is a similar but safer, more effective way to focus on your abdominal muscles.

The third way is Plank work. If you've been following the exercises correctly (and as always with clearance from your personal doctor), you are ready for these.

Standing Stability with Front Body Modified Crunch

Start in a Standing Stability Pose (see page 138). Bring your hands together over your heart (Hands-on- Heart Pose). Activate your upper belly muscles (under your rib cage), and while keeping your pelvic girdle stabilization (PGS) and the whole front body zipped up throughout the entire sequence, tuck your chin and round your shoulders to the tips of your shoulder blades (upper back) forward for a modified crunch. Inhale and on the exhale, return to standing. Relax and repeat five times.

Progression Challenge One: Standing Stability with Front Body Modified Oblique Crunch

Repeat the previous exercise, but this time, as you are bending forward, bring your left elbow toward your right knee, like a twist. Remember to always engage and maintain your PGS and whole front body. Inhale, exhale, untwist back to midline, return to standing, and relax. Repeat, twisting to the opposite side. Repeat this entire sequence five times on each side.

Standing Stability Upper Abdominal/Arm Resistance with Resistance Bands

Tie a knot in the middle of a resistance band and throw it over the top of a door, closing the door on the knot, so the two loose ends hang on your side of the door.

With your back against the door, grab one end of the band with each hand, starting with your arms at shoulder height. (You can progress to higher than shoulder height when you are ready.) Start in Standing Stability Pose, inhale, and on exhale engage and maintain your pelvic girdle isometrics (PGI), especially focusing on your pelvic floor (PF) and transversus abdominis (TA) sequencing. Inhale, exhale, and pull the bands down to your sides. Return your arms to shoulder height and relax. Reset your pelvic floor, lower belly, and pelvic girdle isometrics and repeat the entire sequence five times.

Progression Challenge One: Standing Stability Forward Bend

Start in Standing Stability Pose, holding onto the resistance band, with your back against the door, engaging and maintaining your PGI, especially focusing on your pelvic floor and TA sequence. This time, after bringing your arms down to your sides, pause in this position. Now inhale (remain in the same position) and as you exhale, while keeping your front body zipped up, bend forward at the waist as if you are leaning up and over a bar in front of you. Return to the Standing Stability Pose and relax. Reset your pelvic floor and lower your belly and repeat five times.

Progression Challenge Two: Standing Stability with Straight Arm Pulldowns

Turn around so you are facing the door. (This gives a different angle of resistance to your abdominals as you pull the resistance band.) Grab one end of the band with each hand, starting with your arms at shoulder height. (You can progress to higher than shoulder height when you are ready.) Step back so that you are one arm's length away from the door. Start in Standing Stability Pose, inhale, and on exhale, engage and maintain your PGI, especially focusing on your pelvic floor and TA sequence. Inhale while maintaining this position and on the exhale, pull the bands down to your sides. Return your arms to shoulder height and relax. Reset your pelvic floor, lower belly, and pelvic girdle isometrics (PGI), and repeat the entire sequence five times.

Progression Challenge Three: Standing Stability with Door Bend

While facing the door, grab one end of the resistance band with each hand, starting with your arms at shoulder height. (You can progress to higher than shoulder height when you are ready.) Step back so that you are one arm's length away from the door. Starting in Standing Stability Upper Abdominal/Arm Resistance with Bands (see page 192), inhale, and on the exhale, engage and maintain your PGI, with special focus on your pelvic floor and TA sequencing. Inhale while maintaining this position and on the exhale, pull the bands down to your sides and pause in this position. Now inhale, exhale, and bend forward at your waist as if you are leaning up and over a bar in front of you (see page 193). Return to standing, bring your arms to shoulder height, and relax. Reset your pelvic floor, lower

your belly, and remaining PGI and repeat the entire sequence five times.

Progression Challenge Four: Standing Stability with Block

Remember to always engage and maintain your PGS and zip up your abdominals with breath throughout the entire following exercise. Start facing the door in Standing Stability Pose, but this time place a yoga block under your left foot so that 75 percent of your weight is through your right standing leg. While engaging and maintaining your PGI, with special focus on your pelvic floor and TA sequence, pull the band down and hold for five seconds. Inhale and as you exhale, lift your left knee up off the block and then return your leg down to the block. Relax the bands back up, reset, and repeat five to 10 times on each side.

Progression Challenge Five: Standing Stability March

Start facing the door in Standing Stability Pose, engaging and maintaining your PGI, especially focusing on your pelvic floor and TA sequencing. Inhale while maintaining this position and on the exhale, pull the bands down to your sides. Now, hold the bands down and on your next exhale, march your left knee up to hip height, promoting both an upper and lower abdominal challenge. Hold for three to five seconds while continuing to maintain your PGI, breathe, and return your left leg to the floor; release bands back up and relax. Repeat five times on each side.

Progression Challenge Six: Standing Stability Leg Lift

Remember to always engage and maintain your PGI, zipping up your abdominals with your breaths as outlined above during this four-step exercise. Inhale while maintaining this position and on the exhale, lift your left foot off the ground in front of you so that all of your weight is through your right standing leg. Pull both bands down to your side and then relax the bands back up, while maintaining your single leg stance through your right leg. Rest, reengage, and repeat five to 10 times on each side.

Core Foundation Sequence Progressions

Review the core foundational posture on pages 102 to 104.

Progression Challenge One: Core Foundation

First, complete the core foundation abdominal series without a ball. Then, once that is mastered, work up to one of these options:

Option one: Place the ball under your lower back (sacrum) to challenge your mid to lower abdominals.

Option two: Place the ball under your middle back, between your shoulder blades, to challenge your mid to upper abdominals.

Progression Challenge Two: Core Foundation Table-Top Phase One

Lie on your back and bring both knees up to a table-top position (90 degrees at your hips, knees, and ankles). Inhale and on the exhale, engage and maintain your PGI, especially focusing on your pelvic floor and TA sequencing; tap your right foot down to touch the ground and then return to the table-top pose. Repeat this sequence with your other leg. Your goal is to complete the entire cycle for five repetitions per leg.

Progression Challenge Two: Core Foundation Table-Top Phase Two

Lie on your back and bring both knees up to a table-top position (90 degrees at your hips, knees, and ankles). Inhale and on the exhale, engage and maintain your PGI, especially focusing on your pelvic floor and TA sequencing as you tap both legs down to touch the ground and then return to table-top pose. Repeat five to 10 times.

Progression Challenge Three: Core Foundation Leg Extension Phase One

Lie on your back and bring both knees up to a table-top position (90 degrees at your hips, knees, and ankles). Inhale and on the exhale, engage and maintain your PGI, especially focusing on the pelvic floor and TA sequencing. Next, on your next exhale, extend one leg straight out so it is about 45 degrees from the ground, then return to the table-top pose. Repeat with your other leg. Your goal is five repetitions per leg.

The Nuture Notebook for Mom and Baby

Progression Challenge Three: Core Foundation Leg Extension Phase Two

Lie on your back and bring both knees up to a table-top position (90 degrees at your hips, knees, and ankles). Inhale and on the exhale, engage and maintain your PGI, especially focusing on your pelvic floor and TA sequencing. On your next exhale, extend both legs straight out so they are both 45 degrees from the ground and return both legs to table-top pose. Repeat five to 10 times.

Progression Challenge Four: Core Foundation Leg Extension: Part One

Sit on the floor with your legs bent in front of you, gently holding your legs under your thighs. Inhale and on the exhale, engage and maintain your PGI, especially focusing on your pelvic floor and TA sequencing as you lift both your legs into a table-top pose.

Progression Challenge Four: Core Foundation Leg Extension: Part Two

Sit on the floor with your legs bent in front of you, gently holding your legs under your thighs. Inhale and on the exhale, engage and maintain your PGI, especially focusing on your pelvic floor and TA sequencing as you lift both your legs into a table-top pose. Inhale and on the exhale, while still holding your pelvic floor and zipping up your abdominals and remaining PGI, extend your knees so your legs are straight out at a 45-degrees angle from the ground.

Progression Challenge Four: Core Foundation Leg Extension: Part Three

Sit on the floor with your legs bent in front of you, gently holding your legs under your thighs. Inhale and on the exhale, engage and maintain your PGI, especially focusing on your pelvic floor and TA sequencing as you lift both your legs into a table-top pose. Inhale and on the

exhale, while still holding your pelvic floor and zipping up your abdominals and remaining PGI, extend your knees so your legs are straight out at a 45-degree angle from the ground, and if you able, lift your arms to a V on either side of your head. (Don't let your shoulders shrug up toward your ears!) Breathe while maintaining pelvic floor and lower abdominal engagement. Hold for five seconds or three big breath cycles. Relax. Repeat this sequence five times.

Progression Challenge Five

Pick one of the following positions and complete the Progression Challenge Two while using a small exercise ball:

1. Ball under your lower back (sacrum) to challenge your mid to lower abdominals

2. Ball under your upper back between your shoulder blades to challenge your mid to upper abdominals

Plank Progression

Note: Building on the Pelvic Girdle Stabilization (PGS) Exercises, Phase Three, and foundational posture. (See page 120.)

Plank

Once you feel confident completing your PGS exercises, knowing you are pulling in the correct muscles rather than bulging outward or losing the correct core strategy, then and only then may you progress on to the plank. Start on your hands and knees with PGS, as in Pelvic Girdle Stabilization Challenge One in Quadruped (see page 121). Again, once you feel confident in your strategy, walk your hands out a bit more and repeat your PGI and breath in this position. Continue this progression until you are in Plank pose.

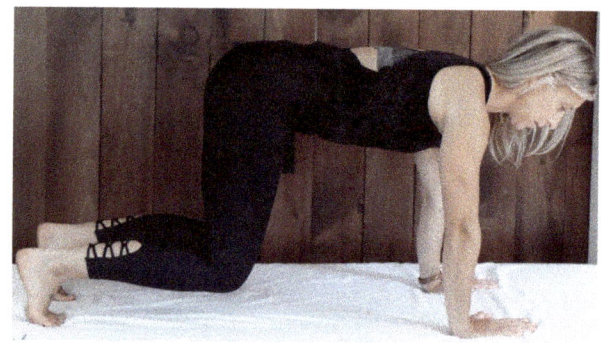

Here are suggested progressions for improving Plank hold times. These are just suggestions. You have to find what works for you. Never sacrifice breath, form, or sequence for progression.

Progression Challenge One: Hold each position for five seconds. Once you've

mastered each position for five seconds, start to increase your time to seven to 10 seconds each, and then to 10 to 15 seconds each, increasing incrementally an additional two to five seconds.

Progression Challenge Two: Starting on your hands and knees, progress just this position to 30 seconds, starting at five seconds for five repetitions and adding on in five-second increments at five repetitions. Once you've mastered that position, walk your hands out a bit and challenge just that position until you can hold it for 30 seconds or whichever amount of time you choose. Continue this way until you make your way into a full plank and are able to tolerate it for up to 30 seconds.

Side Planks

To transition from Plank to Side Plank, start in the Plank pose described above. Engage and maintain your PGI as always, then as you exhale, lift your right hand off the ground, slowly open your body so that your chest faces the right side of the room, and reach your right arm up to the ceiling. Your right leg will be crossed over your left and both feet planted on the floor. You are making a tripod: Your left hand is supporting you while your legs are straight out with your right foot placed slightly in front of your left foot. Keep your left side and your hips off the floor.

Side Planks Progression

Lie on your left side with your knees bent, propped up on le left forearm. Place your right forearm in front for stabilization. Engage and maintain your PGI. Inhale, exhale, and lift your hips up toward the ceiling, keeping your knees down. Hold for five seconds, relax, reset, and then repeat five times.

Progression Challenge One: Lie on your left side with knees extended (legs straight). Cross your right leg over your left so that both feet are planted on the floor. Prop up on your left forearm, with your right hand on the ground in front of you for stabilization. Engage and maintain your PGI throughout. Inhale, exhale, and lift your hips and your knees up toward the ceiling, keeping both feet planted down. Hold for five seconds, relax, reset, and repeat five times.

Progression Challenge Two: Lie on your left side with your knees extended and your legs straight). Stack your right leg on top of your left so that only your left leg is planted on the floor. Prop up on your left forearm, with your right hand on the ground in front of you for

stabilization. Engage and maintain your PGI throughout. Inhale, exhale, and lift your hips and your knees up toward the ceiling, keeping both feet planted down. Hold for five seconds, relax, reset, and repeat five times.

BABY'S DEVELOPMENT

As your baby continues to develop, they are learning to coordinate their motor, vision, and touch systems. They transition more smoothly between all positions now. In the midst of all this growth, you might feel as if you are raising a little teenager with bursts of attitude and continued testing of the limits.

Motor Development

Crawling is your baby's primary way to explore their environment now. They are likely trying to climb up onto furniture and toys. Once they get up, they can turn around with your help and sit down. They will need your assistance again to lower back to the floor feet first.

Your baby makes the transition from a half-kneeling position to standing with one hand on a surface with ease now. Leaning their body against surfaces while standing enables bilateral hand play until they progress to standing without support. They transition between squat, stand, and lowering to the

floor, experimenting with how much support they need.

From hands and knees, your baby might place one foot on the floor, then the other, pushing up into a squat and then further to a standing position in the middle of the floor. The aim here is mastering their center of gravity. Your baby can walk with one hand held or with one hand holding on a piece of furniture and might begin to take independent steps. Their first independent steps will likely be wobbly and lack control, but with time they will master this skill.

From this month, your baby's ability to keep their trunk in alignment with their head and arms at midline, when they are shifted off balance (righting reactions) are most observable, meaning your baby learns to upright themselves and keep themselves symmetrically balanced in standing against gravity.

Your baby is also learning the three-dimensional nature of objects and how they relate. Their motor precision is becoming refined through their pincer grasp, and they are starting to understand relationships of sizes and shapes and the purpose and function of labeling objects through language. Your baby desires to act on these gained skills and master their body, as seen through actions such as attempting to scribble. Watch out, walls!

Visual Development

Your baby's hand-eye coordination should be improving every day. Hand-eye coordination is important in many activities in which your baby will engage as they mature. If they are having difficulty with simple hand-eye coordination, consult with an eye care professional to make sure that their vision is developing normally.

Reading to your baby stimulates both their visual and cognitive development. At this age, your baby might start to participate in story time by spontaneously pointing to familiar objects in a book.

Cognitive Development

Your baby is listening to you more without becoming easily distracted. You can encourage them to pay attention to you by gently touching them to gain their eye contact before communicating to them. They have a better understanding of "No," and they are beginning to understand other verbal commands, such as "Up," "Come," and "Sit down."

Your baby is intrigued by unwrapping loosely wrapped toys, taking round pegboard style puzzle pieces out, and removing rings from stackable toys.

Social-Emotional Development

Your baby will continue to test you. Even though they now understand "No," they might still push your limits, seemingly misbehaving on purpose. They are testing you to observe how you respond to them just as a teenager will, particularly at mealtimes or bedtime. Try your best to be calm and consistent.

Encourage ongoing imitation and self-mastery during daily tasks, such as brushing their hair, feeding themselves, and washing. Also continue clapping and engaging in imitation games. (This interest can develop anytime between nine and 12 months.) Maintain safety measures to protect them while exploring.

Self-Care Development

Your baby might reach their arms and legs out to show involvement in getting dressed, and they are able to drink from a cup with less help from you. Remember the dressing songs discussed previously? Now your goal is to encourage your baby to lift their arms or their legs themselves during dressing. If they do not respond, touch the back of their hand or foot to bring awareness to that limb and encourage them to raise it.

Speech and Language Development

Your baby's lips, tongue, and jaw are becoming stronger, allowing more purposeful (volitional) movement, which provides new opportunities for speech production. They understand more with each passing day and have a receptive vocabulary of five to 10 words. They continue using protowords, and now they mimic the intonation and structure of conversation (varied jargon). You will hear patterns of exclamation, singing, questions, and even commands. Continue to observe your baby because they share a lot of information through nonverbal communication and sounds.

Ways to Increase Your Responsiveness

Label items and ask WH questions. Create conversation by labeling objects of interest and also asking WH (who, what, when, where, and why) and yes/no questions that you then answer. Learning language should not become a quiz. Therefore, avoid asking "What's this?" repeatedly. Look at the following conversation.

Your baby looks at a ball. You follow their lead and pick up the ball.

You: "Oh, wow! Did you see the ball?" (Hold up the ball.)

Your baby reaches for the ball.

You: "Do you want the ball? Here you go! Here is the ball."

Take turns. Taking turns shows your baby the back-and-forth of conversational etiquette. In the above example, your baby reached for the ball, and you returned the serve by giving your baby the ball. Wait and see what happens next. A simple look from your baby might indicate continued interest (i.e. their serve). Wait for observation of their serve before attempting another return (i.e. handing them the ball). Be patient and use simple language.

Expand and extend. This is important when your baby begins to say words. Repeat the word back to your baby and extend on what they say. For example, using the above conversation. If the baby says "bah" for the ball, you can say: "Yes, ball! Red ball." You can add another idea onto the simple sentence: "Should we roll the ball?" Adding onto your baby's simple words will help to model how to share ideas, explain things, and share feelings. Your baby responds to simple requests with gestures such as "come here" or "drink your water." When they hold out objects to show you, remember that it is important for you to acknowledge and talk about their "serve." Babbling continues to grow, and they might begin to have small "conversations."

Babies are little sponges, soaking up information about life all around them because each day brings new experiences. The mundane is exciting to them! A boring trip to the grocery store can become a lesson in fruits and vegetables, and going to a pet store is a chance to look at the fish. This can be a great opportunity to talk about colors and animals. Take a walk. Let them touch leaves and flowers; all this input will grow their vocabulary.

Remember joint attention, when you and your baby are attending to or paying attention to the same thing. You point to the light, your baby looks. Voila!—joint attention. A study from the American Speech and Hearing Association showed that your baby initially will look at items within their line of sight (visual field), and this eventually progresses to outside their visual field. This progression from within to outside the visual field might help with attention regulation, representational thinking, and social cognition, plus it might aid in language learning.

How can you help with this? Begin to point to objects within your baby's visual field.

Once they learn the idea of "point and look," begin to point to objects just outside of their visual field.

Developmental Play

Your baby enjoys and refines their independent movements, transitioning between laying on their tummy or their back, sitting, quadruped, pulling up to stand, cruising along furniture, crawling, picking up, banging, mouthing, pinching, and pulling various objects they want to explore.

PLAY POSITIONS

Standing Play Position

Some babies are very motor driven and might be on the go before others. Whether your baby is motoring along or not, they continue to require support. Your baby enjoys supported walking as well. Continue to hold your hands as low as you can. They may begin to be able to take steps with one hand held, as well.

Position Cruising

During cruising play, your baby might be ready to unweight one hand, turn, and reach. Position one support surface, such as a small activity table or ottoman, across from and parallel with another support surface, such as a couch. Place the surfaces close together so that your baby can place a hand on each surface.

Encourage your baby to transition between the two surfaces by placing toys on the surfaces. This transition will allow your baby to practice letting go of the first surface with one hand, while turning their body and shifting their weight to reach for the other surface. When your baby masters transitioning in close proximity, getting stronger and more confident, you can gradually move the two surfaces apart for a challenge.

Play-with-Me Obstacle Course

Your baby's love of exploring continues to explode as they eagerly seek out new adventures, so continue to vary the crawling surface sizes and firmness, provide pull-to-stand opportunities, and offer cruising surfaces in your obstacle courses to develop problem-solving skills, depth perception, and mastery over transitional movements.

Some examples of items you can use for an obstacle course are pillows, wedges, foam baby stairs (continue to practice safe stair climbing), play nests, tunnels, exercise texture balance discs, beanbags, stuffed animal chairs, boxes, and mats. It is not necessary to spend a lot of money and buy a lot of things. Be creative with safe things around your house.

There are so many fun ways to create obstacle courses throughout these next several months and even years to promote your baby's development, so keep obstacle courses in your play toolbox.

Use your baby's favorite stuffed animal, baby doll, or rolling toy such as a train to join them in the obstacle course. You can encourage your baby to bring it with them from the start or hide the toy somewhere along the course to find and take with them.

Place parts of an activity along the course to use with their favorite stuffed animal or doll, such as a baby spoon, bottle, and bowl that they can find along the way. Your baby can carry them along, and at the end of the course, you can imitate pretend play for your baby by feeding their favorite toy.

Set up different pretend play scenarios throughout the entire obstacle course to stop and play, such as standing at a low surface to scribble in a coloring book (imitate making dots on a paper for your baby), then crawling through a tunnel collecting puzzle pieces that you can then put in the puzzle for your baby when they get to the end of the tunnel.

Be silly and chase your baby around by crawling on your hands and knees to encourage them to change their crawling speed.

Standing

Your baby loves to pull to stand up and play in this position now, which strengthens their legs. You can facilitate standing play in many ways. For example, encourage them to stand and play with both hands engaged at a low surface, such as a play table. When your baby is progressing independently with standing at a low surface, introduce another toy to the mix to encourage independent standing with your baby letting go of the surface to play with the toy.

Standing at a mirror and singing songs such as "Head, Shoulders, Knees, and Toes" promotes body awareness. The mirror will keep your baby engaged because they love to watch themselves.

Place your baby with their back against a piece of furniture or a vertical surface such as a wall with their feet several inches in front of the wall. Encourage your baby to shift their weight forward and reach for you. This forward-weight shift over their feet will allow them to practice independent standing momentarily as they reach out for your hands. In addition, this shift is necessary for taking independent steps. Another way to change this activity is to position your baby with their back against you and encourage them to reach for a toy on a low surface.

Sit to Stand to Support

Sit on the floor. Position your baby on your lap, with their feet flat on the floor (short sitting), close to a support surface, such as an ottoman. Place your hands on your baby's hips and help them to transition from sitting to standing, then encourage them to reach out for the support surface. As your baby masters this transition, challenge them by providing them with less support so they are able to gain more independence. As with all activities, repeated practice will strengthen the skills required to complete such tasks.

Sitting Play Position

Your baby is able to sit more independently now, making them enjoy the sitting play position even more.

Unwrapped

While your baby is sitting, engage them in activities that incorporate the skill of unwrapping. Lightly wrap shoe boxes or other boxes or toys that you have with a light blanket. Model how to unwrap them and encourage your baby to try by starting to unwrap a small section.

Another way to practice is to put diapers on stuffed animals and dolls and encourage your baby to take off the diapers.

Puzzle Piece Retrieval

Your baby might now be able to remove puzzle pieces from age-appropriate chunky puzzles. Simple shape puzzles are best for beginners, and they facilitate visual motor explorations, social interactions, and language expansion. A circle is the easiest shape to remove and place back because it is cohesive the entire way around and doesn't require specific angles or edges to fit the piece into. Start with either a single circle puzzle, or if playing with a multi-piece puzzle, cover the other shapes so that your baby focuses solely on the circle. Demonstrate removing the circle and then label it, while tracing your finger around the edges, turning it, and rolling it along the floor.

After your baby has mastered simple shape puzzles, introduce animal puzzles. Identify the

most circular piece available, such as a round sheep, and remove it after hiding the rest of the pieces. Hold the puzzle piece up at your baby's eye level. Identify the animal and imitate the sound it makes to promote language. Let your baby hold it while you talk about it. When your baby is done playing with it, return it to its place in the puzzle. If your baby shows continued interest, guide their hand to remove the puzzle piece again. Observe your baby for cues on what they would like to do next.

For example, if your baby is not interested in removing or replacing the puzzle pieces, walk the sheep around on the floor saying, "Baa Baa." Put the sheep on your head and ask, "Where did it go?" Once your baby looks up, point to your head, and exclaim, "There it is!"

If you don't have a puzzle, you can use household objects, such as a cupcake tin with cupcake liners. You could also cut holes in a shoebox lid and divide a paper towel tube into several circles for the pieces.

Ring Stack

Encourage your baby to remove rings from a stacking toy by tilting the top of the stacker toward them, model removing one, say, "Off," give your baby wait time to process what you did, and then repeat. Sequential size order is not essential; in fact, initially, your baby might be able to get the rings off more easily if you reverse the stack and place the smallest piece on the bottom and the largest on the top. If at any point during this activity, your baby starts to remove the rings themselves, praise them.

In the future, encourage your baby to remove the rings independently by tapping on a ring or starting to slide the ring up.

Cup Exploration

To prepare your baby to drink independently from a cup, start with an empty one as discussed in the Six Months Old chapter. Model drinking from an open cup. Then offer your baby an empty, open cup on their high chair tray at the end of a meal so they can practice manipulating it with smooth coordinated control when bringing the cup to their mouth (graded control). Babies enhance their motor planning skills as they learn to grade and refine their movements with decreased spillage.

Here are tips for choosing and teaching your baby to use an open cup.

- Consider using small, clear, flexible cups.
- Try nosy-cups, which have a section shaped for nose clearance.
- Place a small amount of pureed food on the lip of the cup to motivate your baby to mouth the cup rim.
- Gradually add small amounts of thin liquids, such as water, formula, or breast milk.

The Nature Notebook for Mom and Baby

- Facilitate correct cup position and liquid flow by using the following steps.
  - Make sure you tilt the cup so that the liquid is at the top of the cup and is nearly spilling over the edge.
  - Bring the cup carefully toward your baby's lower lip.

Ensure your baby is leaning toward the cup with their chin slightly tucked, anchoring the cup to the corners of their mouth, and resting it on their lower lip and with their tongue under the cup (not in the cup) to help promote upper lip dissociation for sipping.

It is typical for babies to dump the cup on themselves and on their tray when they are starting to learn this skill, so be patient. Biting the cup is also common in the beginning. Starting to use a cup might begin earlier than many realize and for a variety of reasons, such as difficulties with sucking from a breast or bottle, muscle tone challenges, negative experiences with spoons, and even to promote lip closure needed for speech and language development. Defer to your baby's health care team on the best time for your baby to start drinking from an open cup.

If your baby sputters while trying to drink because they inhaled some water, don't be alarmed. Babies have a diving reflex that blocks off the airway when volumes of water are introduced, putting them at risk for inhaling. If your baby is coughing or making noise, they are passing air through the vocal cords, which means they are getting oxygen. With that said, if your baby is coughing and sputtering during drinking frequently, pause in challenging open cup drinking for a bit. Use this as a general rule to fine-tune your awareness and concern for a potential choking situation; however, seek medical attention immediately with any concerns.

Puff Play

Your baby can now pick up small items with their pointer finger and thumb, activating the pincer grasp. This advancement in their prehension (grasping with their fingertips) takes a lot of coordination among their hands, eyes, and touch senses. Consequently, you might see your baby squeezing, pinching, and picking with their thumb and index finger.

When you hand items such as puffs to your baby, model the correct finger isolation by diligently using only your thumb and index finger (pincer grasp). Remember to encourage your baby to grasp your pointer and thumb; they will then naturally work their hand up to your fingertips to grasp the

small object with their pointer and thumb.

If your baby is still struggling with this skill, place your ring and pinky fingers in their palm when they reach for a small item, which will limit the engagement of their other fingers, isolating their thumb and pointer finger only for grasping.

Color Play

Your baby enjoys watching you write or draw and might now even begin to imitate by scribbling. Typically, their initial grasping pattern will be with their entire palm. Sit with your baby in a location that works well for the both of you, such as on the floor inside or on a sidewalk outside. Place two different colors of baby-safe crayons (if inside) or pieces of sidewalk chalk (if outside) directly in front of your baby. This placement of writing utensils activates visual convergence (eyes working together) and allows them to use their preferred hand. Imitate dots with quick taps on the paper while repeating, "Dot." Your baby's first mark will likely be an accidental dot as they bang the writing utensil on the paper or pavement. Every action has a reaction, and in time your baby will recognize that by moving their hand they are making marks.

Reminder: If you are outside, make sure you are in a safe place, not behind cars, near a bee's or ant's nest, or on hot pavement. Talk to your baby about why you picked the spot you did by saying, "We are going to walk to the back porch because there are no cars, and it feels cooler in the shade." It is never too early to talk about safe practices in a healthy way that naturally instills it without inducing fear. Plus, it might also help remind you to be aware of your surroundings at all times while with your baby.

The terms imitation and copy might often be

interchanged during conversations; however, in the world of development, imitation is when one observes an activity being completed. For example, your baby observes you drawing a circle, then they imitate that circle by attempting to draw something similar, while your circle is still in sight.

On the other hand, copying does not involve observation of the process of an activity from beginning to end. Instead, it makes use of only the final product. For example, your baby copies a circle that they see on paper; however, they did not see how that circle was drawn.

With that understanding of imitation and copying, between 10 months and five years of age, your little one will work on prewriting skills in the following sequence: imitates scribble starting with dots by accidentally banging a writing utensil on paper (10 to 13 months), spontaneous scribble

(13 to 18 months), imitates vertical stroke (18 to 24 months), imitates horizontal stroke (24 to 30 months), imitates a cross (24 to 36 months), and copies a circle (25 to 36 months).

Container Play

Encourage your baby to purposefully put items in containers. This purposeful release is actually a developed skill in understanding depth perception—a future necessity for handwriting. This could be embedded into your routines during cleanup time, or you can use a receptacle such as a plastic food container, or a plastic meltable baby snacks container with a small opening in it. Model picking up pieces of baby food and dropping them in.

Various Play Positions

Peek-and-Point Excursion Play

Take your baby on a tour either inside your home or outside. First, point to objects within your baby's visual field, such as pictures in board books or photo books. Gain your baby's attention by slowly saying the word "Peek." Then pause and slowly move the page back and forth so you can spot an object and build your baby's anticipation. Quickly turn the page and say "aboo." You don't have to read the page or even talk about the main subject. For example, if there is a small mouse or butterfly on the page that your baby wouldn't have otherwise noticed, point it out. Say "Mouse, Squeak!" and lightly close your hand around your baby's hand to expose only their index finger. Point to the object again, encouraging them to use their finger. Do not force them to do this; simply keep repeating this type of play.

Some babies do not like the hand-over-hand technique, and that's okay. Your baby might respond better to it on your next attempt. Start pointing to objects just out of their visual field once they've learned the idea of looking around and then pointing.

Here are some Peek-and-Point Excursion Ideas. Outside, explore the things you see while walking with your baby, such as trees, flowers, butterflies, leaves, snow, door, window, and doorbells. Inside, explore the main room you are in, pointing to photos, pictures, people, and pets at your house or your friend's house. Other excursion ideas include animals at a zoo; insects, animals, leaves, and flowers on a walking trail; butterflies, flowers, benches, and garden art in a garden; and slides, swings, trees, and dogs at a park.

Make Music

Music is a great way to help your baby learn about their own body and what it can do. Your baby loves to listen to themselves making noise, whether with their own vocals or banging items together, and you are their biggest fan!

Gather safe objects around the house to make

pretend instruments, such as pots, pans, wooden or plastic spoons, plastic cups, and sealed plastic containers with dry pasta in them or toy instruments. Model tapping or banging on the instruments spontaneously and to a tune. Turn on some music and encourage your baby to explore along. Introduce the concept of tapping to the beat of your favorite song.

Up and Down

This movement activity will keep your baby engaged and challenge their sense of balance. Your baby must be able to sit up independently to complete this activity.

Place your baby on your lap, facing you and holding their hands. Slowly lift your knees up and down in rhythm. Simply say "Up" and "Down" with the movement or sing a silly made-up song.

Ten Months Old

Fill in the answers to reflect on the past month and to track.

How do you feel? _____

_____

What exercises did you work on? _____

_____

What is your baby doing now? _____

_____

What was your baby's favorite activity this month? _____

_____

What questions do you have for your ob-gyn and your baby's pediatrician? _____

_____

Notes: _____

_____

_____

Eleven Months Old

MOMMY MOVEMENTS

This month, "One of a kind" refers to both you and your baby. We are all uniquely made. You've read about the difference between doing things you should and choosing things you love. Doing what you love is the big picture. But let's take the big picture out of the equation today. Today is about the small picture. Are you loving what you are doing today? It might feel hard to stick with the choice of doing something you love if you aren't finding the joy and love in the small, daily steps needed to get you there.

Through this year, you have been reading about ways to bring awareness back to your body, how to reset your body, and most importantly, how to move your body. You know the muscle patterns and strategies that lay the foundation for efficient and safe movement. Now it's time to explore how to utilize them through the different forms of exercise you love, such as dance, yoga, strength training, and running.

How do you identify which forms of exercise work best for you? Ask yourself the following: What did I love doing before I had my baby? Does this still work for me? Does it bring me joy? The famous quote by Greek philosopher Heraclitus, "The only constant in life is change," refers to all aspects of life, including your exercise routine. For example, maybe doing yoga felt unfulfilling before you had a baby to care for, but now you find joy and strength in moving slowly, deliberately, and with intention and body awareness. Maybe last month dancing felt great, but this month HITT training feels better. Results are not seen in only one form of exercise; your plan can and should continuously evolve. Loving what you do means listening to your body and making changes based on your self-awareness each day. Finding the right movement routine for you should feel like a challenge, not a chore.

It might be hard to determine whether you truly love what you are doing because you've been doing it for so long or you are doing too much and simply running on autopilot. That's often the problem with parents. You may feel overwhelmed, with barely any time for yourself, and when you do give yourself a moment, it's typically something that is quick and fast. Remember: Movement is practice. It will not only benefit you but also those you love when you find a place and time for you, a type of movement—a class, a group, a meditation, a community, a life outside of your baby. The only way you'll know you've found the right "you time" activity is that you will feel full of love and joy when you do it. So if it sparks joy, put it on your to-do list every day. Take a deep breath and declare "I am loving what I do!" It will likely take time to get used to this idea, so be patient with yourself while you search to find what ignites you.

Postnatal Year End

As you follow through with the postnatal exercises that follow, be present in the moment and be proud of how far you've come. We hope some of these will fill you with joy. Consider everything that you have learned about the importance of muscle patterns and now incorporate your knowledge into all different types of exercises, from sun salutations to burpees. The beauty of your understanding of muscle patterns and progressing appropriately is that you can now bring those patterns into any type of movement that you love, even if it is ever-changing, and make it your own practice. Movement alone is a practice.

Side Lunge

Inhale and on the exhale, start in the Standing Stability Pose and progress through standing stability with a squat (see page 157). Once in a squat, keep PF and PGS engaged while shifting weight to one leg and stepping out to the side with the other leg, creating a side lunge. Next, even out your glutes (engage both gluteal muscles) and check in with other stabilizers (pelvic floor, lower abs, shoulder blades). Hold for one full breath cycle and while engaging and maintaining your PGI, return to squat. Keep holding your PGI while returning to the standing stability pose. Repeat on each side five times.

Progression Challenge One: Starting in a standing stability pose, inhale and on the exhale, engage and maintain your PGI and step out to your right side, bending your right knee to sit back into your seat. Your left knee is straight and extended out to the side as if you are lunging on your right side only. Reengage your PF and PGS and return to standing. Repeat this sequence five times on each side.

Standing Stability with Lunge into Warrior 1

Start in the Standing Stability Pose, always engaging and maintaining your PGI throughout this series. Inhale and on the exhale, shift your weight to one leg and step back with the other leg, lightly bending your front knee, while keeping your back leg/knee extended in a modified lunge. Both feet should be facing forward, with your front heel down, and your back heel raised and pushing down through all five toes.

Once you are in this modified lunge, raise both your arms overhead, keeping your shoulders down and away from your ears, into a Warrior 1 position.

Even out and engage both gluteal muscles and check in with your other stabilizers (pelvic floor, lower abs, lats/lemons). Hold for one full breath cycle. Now, while keeping PGI engaged, return to Standing Stability Pose. Repeat on each side five times.

Progression to Side Lunge or Warrior 2

Throughout this entire sequence, always engage and maintain your PGI. Start by transitioning from Standing Stability Pose into Warrior 1 position. Keep your feet/legs in place but turn your torso and hips open toward the side of your back leg. Bring your arms down, placing one arm facing forward over your bent leg and your other arm facing backward toward your back leg. Stretch through both arms, like arrows reaching toward both the wall in front of you and the wall behind you. Keep your shoulders down and away from your ears. (Your "lemons" are still turned on.) Your front foot should face forward, with your back foot pointing in the direction of your torso with the heel down. Even out and engage both gluteal muscles, while checking in with your other PGI (pelvic floor, lower abs, lats/

lemons). Hold for one full breath cycle. Return to Warrior 1. Hold for one full breath cycle, return to Standing Stability Pose. Repeat five times per side.

Push-Up Breakdown Progression One: Quadruped

Start on your hands and knees, positioning your hands into fists to protect your wrists if preferred. Engage and maintain your PGI as you bend your elbows on your exhale, lower your chest and core down to the floor. Relax your PGI for one breath cycle. Now inhale; on the exhale, reengage and maintain your PGI as you straighten your elbows, pushing your chest and core away from the floor. Relax your PGI and then repeat the sequence five times.

Push-Up Breakdown and Progression Progress Reminder

You should not move on to Planks or Push-Ups until you have mastered the Pelvic Girdle Stabilization Exercises in Quadruped (hands and knees in month 10). Use these isometrics in quadruped as a guide to progress to those harder and more core-demanding exercises. If you progress to those exercises (like Planks) before you are ready (i.e. able to do these five isometrics in quadruped without losing one of the holds or "doming" on your abdomen) you can be causing more harm to your abdominals or pelvic floor than good. However, once you have mastered this position, you will be able to progress towards Plank and Push-Ups safely. For example, over time, walk your hands out farther and farther, mastering a new modified quadruped position each time until you have reached Plank. If you walk your hands out to a point that is too challenging to maintain and stabilize all five of these isometrics in a balanced way, that is a sign that the position is too difficult for you currently, and you should back up to the previous position until you have mastered it enough to try again.

Push-Up Breakdown Progression Two: Repeater

Complete Progression One as previously learned and practiced; however, now you are ready to continue to hold your PGI while straightening your elbows and pushing your chest and core away from the floor without resting in between. Repeat two more times (three-repeater total, all while continuing to hold and engage your pelvic floor/PGI). After three full repetitions, relax your pelvic floor/PGI.

Push-Up Breakdown Progression Three: Position Change

Any of the push-up progressions may be performed now in different positions to challenge your body in different ways.

Incline on a dresser/counter/table.

Incline on a bed or couch (a softer surface; this is typically more challenging than a stable surface like a dresser/counter/table).

Extend your legs out to full push-up on the floor. Remember to move on the exhale, especially when pushing back up!

Deconstructing a Burpee: Walking Burpee

Start in Standing Stability Pose. Engage and maintain (or reengage if you need breaks) your PGI throughout this entire sequence. Inhale and on the exhale, slowly squat and then continue squatting until you lower your hands to the ground in a low crouch. Inhale and on the exhale, step one foot back and then step the other foot back until you are in a plank position (push-up position). On your next exhale, step one foot back up to its same-side hand and then your other foot back up to its same-side hand,

positioning you back into a low crouch. Slowly rise up into a squat, return to Standing Stability Pose, and relax your pelvic floor.

Progression One: Repeater: When you are

ready to repeat the entire cycle more than one time without relaxing your PGI in between cycles, it is time to add another cycle that week.

Jumping Burpee

Start in Standing Stability Pose. Engage and maintain (or reengage if you need breaks) your PGI throughout this entire sequence. On the exhale, slowly squat and then continue squatting until you lower your hands to the ground in a low crouch. Inhale and on the exhale, jump your feet back into a Plank. Inhale and on the exhale, jump back into a low crouch and then return to standing and relax your pelvic floor.

Progression One: Repeater: When you are ready to repeat the entire cycle more than one

time without relaxing your PGI between cycles, it is time to add another cycle that week.

Progression Two: Jump: On the exhale, jump straight up at the end of your burpee, meaning after you return to standing.

Overall Goal: Progress accordingly, giving yourself reasonable time (ideally at least a week) to master each progression in the sequence. Repeat any of the burpee progressions in a more fluid motion, without stopping to reset between each step, all while maintaining your PGI throughout. Remember to exhale on your exertions!

Sun Salutation

Stand at the edge of your yoga mat, keep your feet together, and balance your weight equally on both feet in Standing Stability Pose. Engage and maintain your PGI throughout this exercise unless otherwise noted. Open your chest and relax your shoulders.

Inhale, lifting both arms out to the sides and then overhead. Exhale, bringing your palms together in front of your chest and into prayer position.

Inhale, lifting both arms in a forward upward motion and then overhead, while keeping your biceps close to your ears. Exhale and stretch forward, bending downward from your waist,

reaching your arms to your shins or ankles or the floor, and into a forward fold. You may bend your knees, if necessary, to bring your palms down to the floor.

Inhale and reset your PGI while sliding your hands up your shins, flatten your spine, and look straight out ahead of you. Exhale, relaxing back down into a forward fold.

Inhale, reset your PGI, and step your right leg back as far as possible. Lower your right knee to the ground while your left foot is between your palms (knee is bent to a 90-degree angle). Exhale,

reset your PGI, take your left leg back, and bring your entire body into a straight line (PGI in Plank pose). Stay in Plank for one full breath cycle: inhale and exhale, while holding PGI.

Inhale, reset your PGI, and lower your knees to the ground. Exhale, slowly bend your elbows, and lower your chest to the ground.

Inhale, position your hips slightly off the ground (bearing weight through your thighs), straighten your elbows, slide your chest forward, and open your heart. Remember to keep your PGI engaged, especially your latissimus dorsi/lat. Exhale, untuck your toes so they are pressing into the mat.

Reset your PGI, and press down into your toes to perform PGI with down dog prep (DDP).

Inhale and hold PGI with DDP. Exhale and drive your pelvis and hips back and up into a downward-facing dog (DFD). Stay in the DFD for one full breath cycle: inhale and exhale.

Inhale, reset your PGI, and step your left foot forward and between your hands into a modified Standing Stability Pose with a reverse lunge, while looking up. You may keep your right knee on the ground as needed. Exhale, reset your PGI, step your right foot forward to meet your left, lift your tailbone to the ceiling, slowly straighten your knees, and bring your arms up overhead to a Standing Stability Pose.

Inhale, maintain your PGI, bring your arms together, then over your head, and slowly lower them down to Prayer Pose, in front of your heart.

BABY'S DEVELOPMENT

Your baby is nearing the end of their first year, and you are probably marveling at how slowly the days went yet how fast the year flew by. You made it through sleepless nights, feelings of uncertainty, nursing or bottles, exhaustion, and emergency diaper changes. Even though there were difficult times, you have fallen in love with the moments you shared with your baby. Pat yourself on the back; you are a stronger version of yourself!

Don't stop here; keep plugging away. Every year with your baby, is amazingly different, requiring a boundless amount of love, encouragement, and support from you—the amazing parent. How do we know that you are amazing? Because you picked up this book, demonstrating that you genuinely care about your baby's well-being and that you want to be the best parent you can be.

Reflect on your baby's milestones with the certainty that you've helped them grow. Embrace your accomplishments together.

At the end of this month, your amazing, one-of-a-kind baby will be a year old. Now grab a box of tissues and get prepared for those first-year pictures. If you are using a professional photographer, schedule the appointment now. Keep track of your photo ideas; there are so many creative first-year photographs from smashed cakes to ones with a favorite stuffed animal.

Motor Development

Your baby is exploring and climbing on a variety of surfaces, transitioning in and out of sitting, crawling, bear walking (hands and feet), tall kneeling, and half-kneeling smoothly. They are working on transitioning to stand in the middle of a room through pushing up from hands and feet (plantigrade) and standing without support to play. When standing independently, it is normal for them to use a wide base of support, perhaps locking their joints into the extension to gain stability. They are lowering themselves to the floor by squatting but still may end up falling into sitting if they lack control or move quickly. Walking with both hands held, one hand held, or even taking some independent steps enables them to experience learning in an entirely new way.

Because your baby is still working on taking independent steps, it is typical for them to take short, quick ones with a wide base of support. They often use a high guard posture: arms up and shoulder blades squeezed together (retracted) until they gain the necessary control to master walking. Even after they begin to take independent steps, they may return to crawling when they want to move quickly or are in an unfamiliar environment. Crawling may still be their primary way to explore.

Your baby is using both their hands together consistently, and you might feel that a hand preference is becoming noticeable. They might also use a palmar-based grasp on a crayon and orient the crayon toward the paper to color. With supervision, the use of large broken crayons is helpful to facilitate the development of a grasp on a writing utensil. They supinate their forearm (turn their hand with their palm facing up). Your baby might now be starting to attempt to blow kisses or to play peekaboo with their hands now that they are beginning to rotate their forearm, which in turn helps them to flip their hand palm up and palm down. Your baby might show an interest in stacking blocks now instead of simply knocking them down.

Visual Development

Your baby's vision has changed so much over the past year! Although their eyes will continue to develop over the next few years, many aspects of their vision are at the level of an adult's. As your baby begins to move around their world more, they use their eyes to view objects around them and to judge how far from them an object is located. Pointing and naming objects will teach them auditory and visual associations to identifying things. If your baby has not had an eye exam with a pediatric optometrist yet, then now is the time.

Cognitive Development

Your baby will enjoy scanning for items and placing pegs in matching holes. Your baby might exhibit dance-like movements in response to music being played. Your baby can now express themselves with a variety of different gestures to communicate their wants and needs.

Social-Emotional Development

Your baby's social-emotional self might not differ much from the past couple of months. They may continue to test, or just start testing you, in various ways as previously discussed, including bedtime, feeding, and other routines such as diaper changes. Your baby might hold out a toy for you but refuse to let it go on purpose. They likely enjoy playing near others, watching others, and imitating others. Modeling behaviors, actions, and activities during play promotes engagement, learning, and imitation. You are your baby's role model, and they want to repeat what you do.

Self-Care Development

Your baby's oral motor skills are progressing to a rotary chewing pattern. Their adeptness with self-feeding improves as they gain better awareness of their body in space and their ability to smoothly coordinate (grade) their motor control and motor planning. Your baby might have been able to drink from a cup as early as 10 months, or they might still be working on that skill.

It is typical for your baby to want to exercise some control. Finding ways to foster their sense of control through offering choices can help to reduce the battles of wills and allow your baby to feel autonomous while you are still structuring their environment.

Speech and Language Development

Your baby has changed your life in so many special and unexpected ways. Can you even recall life before they arrived?

Because your baby's speech and language development are picking up speed, they are playing with a variety of sounds throughout each day. Your baby babbles in all the sounds of your native language. English sounds develop in the following order from easiest to hardest: b, m, p, d, t, n, g, k, w, h, f, v, th, s, z, l, and r. This does not necessarily mean that your baby will be producing all of these sounds in words. Coarticulation (the effect one sound has on another within a word) increases the demands of coordinating your baby's lip, tongue, and mouth movements. The above sounds are listed as a reference, but these sounds have the potential to develop within words up until age eight.

Your baby is comprehending more and beginning to understand life and their daily routines. They probably imitate simple actions, such as waving or placing a block into a box after you. Your baby will look at and point to pictures with

When a baby focuses on a new skill, it often appears as if they have regressed in another. That perception is false, though. It is typical to have pockets of growth that then take a back seat to a newly forming skill. For example, it is normal for your baby to neglect speech and language gains while they are starting to walk because their focus and energy have turned toward the newly emerging skill. True regression is when a skill has been fully mastered and then completely disappears. If your baby is starting to walk, you might feel as if their gains in speech development have regressed.

you. They have a lot of energy and want to enjoy all that life presents them.

When you talk to your baby, they respond in their own sweet jargon. Continue to pay attention to those "serves" (what they are looking at, such as a dog), engage them (point at the dog), and comment ("Look! It's a dog"). Don't worry about being perfect; your baby neither cares nor knows the difference. The more words they are exposed to the better because at this point your baby's receptive language is much larger than their expressive language.

Your baby is very social and loves to smile at both familiar and unfamiliar people. Their listening skills continue to develop as they respond to their name, to the word "no," and even to sounds that are heard and not seen (such as someone dropping something in the kitchen). Your baby might respond to music by shaking their head or dancing.

Developmental Play

Because your baby is motivated by movement, they want to explore everything, and you are the leader of their adventures. Remember, pairing simple, functional, positional words (up, down, next to) with their associated actions will help your baby know what to expect while building critical vocabulary.

While engaging in the play routine you have established with your baby, remember to use the serve and return play interaction, which we call Ping-Pong play.

PLAY POSITIONS AND MOVEMENT PATTERNS COMBINED

Squatting

You might observe your baby squatting to play because it becomes easier as their strength continues to increase. If they still require help, hold their hands or support them around their torso to encourage transitioning in and out of squats, depending on the level of support they need. Either way, providing them with low-seating options, such as a soft stuffed animal chair or a baby chair, and positioning toys on the ground while they are standing will promote this position.

If your baby is standing independently, challenge them by handing them two toys to hold and play with. Standing at a windowsill and looking outside might provide the optimal play height, provide opportunities for speech and

joint attention ("Look! It's a bird!"), and be motivating too.

Transition Up

Transitioning to stand in the middle of a room will allow your baby to continue to practice walking after they lose their balance and fall. This transition occurs through hands and feet (plantigrade). To encourage this transition to occur while your baby is crawling, stabilize their trunk with your one hand/arm and use your other hand to help them place one foot, then the other foot flat on the floor. Now that your baby is on their hands and feet, help them shift their weight back over their feet by holding them around and gently applying weight back through their hips while lifting their hands off the floor to come up to a standing position. You might feel like you are doing most of the work initially, but

with practice, your baby will learn how to move their body and complete more of the transition themselves.

Walking Variety

Because all babies develop at their own, perfect pace, it is common for there to be a big range in abilities at this time. Your baby might not be walking at all, or they might be walking with one or both hands held. They might even refuse to hold your hand or try to run away. Keep in mind that they are still wobbly, so of course, they do require you nearby to keep them safe even if they are walking independently. Remember that because each baby develops differently, you want to continue with activities in prior chapters if your baby hasn't mastered them yet.

If your baby is walking with hands held, continue to encourage them to walk with hands held to explore and move around your home. As you feel your baby getting more stable and needing less support from you, let go of one hand to encourage them to walk with one hand held. They might only take a few steps before looking for your other hand when you begin to practice.

If your baby is walking with one hand held at this time, you can challenge them by holding an object in your hand for them to hold onto, such as a doll, stuffed animal, or their favorite toy. This technique is useful when they

are transitioning from hand-held to supervised walking.

If your baby is taking independent steps, provide a safe, low surface to step up on and down from, while holding their hand, to challenge them in yet a different way.

Giving your baby a small, baby-safe bag to carry around for collecting items is yet another challenge for the independent walker.

Maze Cruise

This activity is fun for the cruiser or independent walker. Remember the past month how you set up two support surfaces parallel to each other? Now move them further apart to see if your baby will let go of one surface momentarily while shifting their weight to reach for the second surface.

After they are having fun cruising or walking

between the surfaces, use that same concept to make a short maze by lining up parallel furniture, foam pads/play yards, or large cardboard boxes/diaper boxes closed, flipped over, and sturdy to create a small maze for your baby to cruise and walk between. Do not use any furniture that your baby can pull down on themselves. The skill you are working on will dictate the placement of the

toys. For example, if you are working on cruising, you will line up lightweight toys along both sides of the maze to allow your baby to practice going back and forth between parallel surfaces, as well as cruising along one surface.

If your baby is walking independently, you will want to put a toy in their sight and at the end of the maze to motivate them to walk forward to the end of the maze.

Your baby may even be able to hold a small baby-safe bag/purse on their shoulder or elbow to place the toys in and take with them.

Wall Stand and Advance

Position your baby standing with their back to a wall and encourage them to reach out for you like last month, but rather than staying still, slowly move back to encourage them to take an independent step as they reach out to get to you. You may use toys to motivate them, or if you feel more comfortable positioned next to your baby rather than in front of them, practice the prior activity only until you are ready.

Puzzle/Obstacle Course

Puzzles continue to be an essential toy because they effectively develop gross, fine, and visual-motor skills and may be played in a variety of play positions. Spread puzzle pieces around a room in clear view or throughout an obstacle course. Crawl, squat, or walk around with your baby to find the puzzle pieces. Continuing to introduce crawling or propping up on your forearms will strengthen the shoulder muscles and arches of your baby's hand, which directly

If you haven't already gated off stairways, now is the time. Because your baby is so mobile and may also attempt climbing, having a safe, gated play area is helpful. Close supervision and precautions are still required for the next several years, but having a gated area will allow you to safely put them down for a couple of minutes. The areas should be inspected every time you place your baby in them. Check the area for broken toys and small items that can pose a choking hazard; make sure you've enclosed space away from windows, cords, or anything your baby can pull down on themselves. Carpeting should be secure to prevent your baby from pulling it up or apart or chewing on it or its pad. Even books can pose a choking hazard.

translates into better prewriting skills. If your baby enjoys carrying around a baby-safe bag or push toys, you can incorporate them too. The most age-appropriate puzzles are chunky ones in varied shapes, such as simple ones that mirror circles, rectangles, squares, or basic animal shapes. Chunky puzzle pieces can also be used for pretend play. For example, a zoo animal puzzle piece can be used for a pretend day at the zoo. Shoeboxes make great pens that can be stationed around the room. You can both explore the different animals, incorporate speech sounds, such as monkey sound "oo-oo-oo," collect them, and return them to their puzzle. In addition, puzzles with small pegs attached and corresponding animal-to-sound activation facilitate the understanding of cause and effect and the use of the pincer grasp.

Don't be discouraged if your baby is only able to remove puzzle pieces. Developmentally,

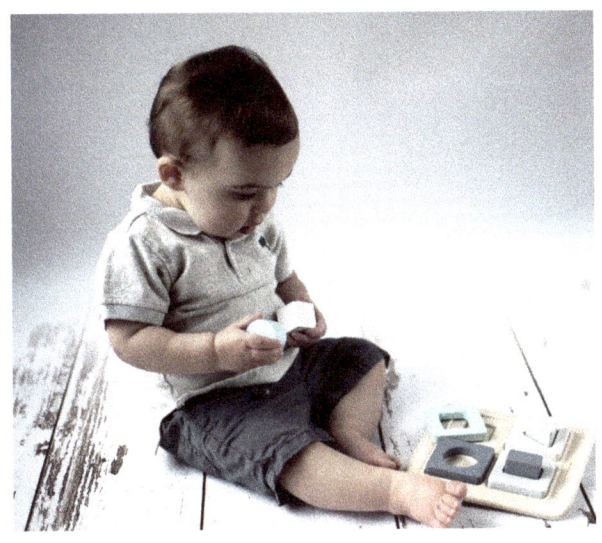

a simple circle puzzle piece is the easiest and first to master. Remember, you do not always need to buy toys; instead, you can use household items such as a cupcake tin and cupcake liners, a child's cookie cutter and a box, or other baby-safe objects to encourage putting in and taking out.

Bounce to the Beat

Model dancing behaviors for your baby to help them understand that there are different movement patterns. Encourage your baby to emulate dance-like movements in a variety of their favorite positions by holding them around their torso and gently bouncing them up and down, moving them side to side, shimmying them, helping them to weight shift, clapping, or patting—whatever fun, gentle movements you can think of. Music with a strong beat will work best.

Crossing Midline Play

Crossing the midline is a critical developmental milestone that is often forgotten. It is important to encourage your baby to play in ways that foster their ability to cross their arms and legs over the midline of their body because this helps the left and right sides of the brain coordinate with one another.

How do you do this? There are many options to promote crossing the midline. Be creative and keep the following technique in mind. Position your baby's toys strategically to encourage exploration of their hands and fingers at the middle of their body, as well as to facilitate reaching across the middle of their body. Set up toys to the right side of your baby and use hand-over-hand guidance to show your baby how to reach across their body with their left arm to retrieve the toy. You may need either to hold and stabilize their left hip gently so they don't turn their entire body or to put a toy in their right hand so they do not reach automatically with it.

Another suggestion is taping a piece of paper on a table or wall. Place a thick crayon at your baby's midline and allow them to adaptively grasp it with their preferred hand. Encourage scribbling either independently or through hand-over-hand guidance. Model coloring on the side of the paper opposite to the hand in which they're holding the writing utensil.

Allowing your baby to carry a small, baby-safe bag while exploring also facilitates crossing the midline. If they are carrying the bag on their left side, encourage them to pick up objects they find with their right hand, cross over their body, and place them in the bag.

Crossing the midline is important for motor planning, communication between both sides of the brain, development of body awareness, and more, all of which are needed to complete future tasks, such as coloring and getting dressed. Remember to foster crossing the midline with both the right and left sides of your baby's body.

Complete the following activities with the goal of incorporating sensory fun with the act of crossing the midline.

- Paint with yogurt on a food tray, smearing or drawing lines from the left to the right and vice versa.

- Use measuring cups or spoons, allowing one hand to stabilize a baby-safe cup and the other to scoop and dump dirt or water in.

- Play with baby-safe sidewalk chalk on the sidewalk or fingerpaint at an easel. Place the paint or chalk on the side opposite of your baby's coloring or painting hand to encourage crossing over the midline.

- Trace on a bathtub or shower wall in the steam or with washable art utensils.

- Make hand impressions in mixed media.

- Place large, baby-safe blocks in a homemade sensory bin (i.e. cooked pasta in a container) and then find them, stack them, and knock them down.

High-Five

Why high-five? Because helping your baby to explore the versatility of using their forearm in coordination with their hand is important, and that is what a high-five does. Hold your hand in different positions, such as down with your palm facing up, and use hand-over-hand to guide your baby's hand down for a high-five. Hold your hand with your palm facing out in front of them and guide them to high-five your hand. Have fun with it by holding your hand in different positions and guiding their hand to yours saying, "High-five." Reaching for items such as a rattle to shake, twist toys to play shake and twist, or a play mallet toy to hammer also promote both palms up and forearm coordination, which is needed for up-and-down motions.

Let It Go

Though reciprocal back-and-forth play is not necessarily typical at this age, it can still be introduced to develop social play skills because it helps to decrease rigidity. This reciprocal play helps to decrease the rigidity of how your baby typically plays and introduces flexibility through others taking the lead in play. Hand a toy to your baby and prompt them to hand it back to you, using simple terms such as, "Give please" or, "My turn." Immediately hand it back to them so they see that they will get it back. Repeat. Think of this activity as the baby version of the game Hot Potato. As they understand the concept of letting toys go and

taking turns, you can expand on the vocabulary and say something such as "uh oh," and drop it into their hand, engaging back and forth by being silly. After your baby has mastered this, recruit family or friends to sit in a circle, passing toys around and dropping them.

Popping Popcorn

Work on your baby's language expansion and social development with a small blanket and small sensory balls or something you have at home that you can use in lieu of the balls. Hold one end of the blanket and have your baby or someone else hold the other end. Quickly move the blanket up and down. Say "Pop, pop, pop!" while popping the balls up in the air. Target the words pop, balls, more, look, up, and down. When a ball falls off the blanket, it is a great receptive language opportunity. "Where did the ball go? Can you get me the ball, please?"

Handprint Art

Marking the first anniversary of your baby's birth is right around the corner, and you don't want to forget hand or footprint art. There are a lot of creative options both to create a birthday keepsake and to promote sensory play. Here are some fun ideas, but be encouraged to explore and discover your own inventions.

Create a family painting with both you and your baby's handprints based on your interests. Find a paint you are comfortable with. Use a paintbrush to apply it on your baby's hand or spread paint on a paper plate and dip their hand into it. Place your baby's handprint on a trial surface first and then on the surface of choice for your actual artwork. For example, each of you makes one handprint on a canvas or paper of your choice. Either let your baby scribble and play on this paper after it has dried or turn it into a painting, such as a scene of your favorite season or your favorite animals.

Start a handprint book. Each year, place your baby's handprint in the book and let it dry. Label it with the date, write some things they love on the page, and let them scribble on it. In future years, they can add their own unique touch to each handprint after it has dried. When they get older, they can even add words to it and turn it into a story.

Advance this activity by tracing your baby's hand with a marker or pen. Next, paint the same hand you traced. Last, use hand-over-hand to place your baby's handprint within the boundaries of their traced hand. As they get older and their visual-motor skills improve, repeat this activity, challenging them even further by encouraging them to trace their own hand, paint their own hand, and place their painted handprint inside the drawing.

The Nuture Notebook for Mom and Baby

Routine-Based Activities

Creating routines is important in the development of two key ingredients for learning: relationships and repetition. Routines provide consistency, security, and predictability throughout your baby's day. Although routines can vary from family to family, knowing what will happen next helps to increase your baby's self-control and reduce power struggles. For example, providing a predictable schedule for waking, eating, and playing at the same times every day will help to decrease the chances that your baby will become hungry or overtired.

Researchers have identified a few different types of routines. Baby-led routines take cues from your little one as to structure and time versus parent-led routines, in which you create your daily schedule. A combination of both relies on using signs from your baby while incorporating your input. According to research, parent-led routines are most effective for babies and toddlers. Keep in mind that because every family is different, you need to do what you feel is best for your family.

Incorporating routine-based play activities into your schedule will always be your most efficient use of time, enabling you to embed consistent, specific developmental play into your day.

Cook with Me

Stock a small low drawer or bin with plastic bowls and spoons, measuring cups, and any other baby-safe, kitchen-related items. Encourage your baby to pretend to cook alongside you. Engage your baby through modeling (i.e. mixing ingredients) and talking to them about what you are doing (i.e. "mix, mix, mix"). Measuring cups continue to be developmentally stimulating because your baby can scoop with them and stack them. They can explore in many ways, from banging a plastic spoon against a bowl to pretending to pour them into empty containers and boxes. Always keep safety in mind. Be sure your baby is far from the danger of fire, the risk of being splashed with hot items, pulling items down on them, choking hazards, etc.

Time to Brush

Brushing your baby's gums and teeth is important for their oral health, particularly because of the sugar in breast milk and formula. You started this practice shortly after they were born, so they are likely used to it and may even want to try to brush their own teeth. Provide your baby with their own baby toothbrush to hold while you brush their teeth so they can begin to experiment with this skill. Sing a song while brushing your baby's teeth (i.e. the alphabet, making sure to sing each letter clearly and evenly paced, rather than rushing through l, m, n, o, and p). When you are done brushing your baby's teeth thoroughly, hand the toothbrush to them, encourage them to try to brush, and sing the same song. Always gently brush your baby's gums and teeth first to ensure they are getting the proper dental care.

Mealtime

Your baby enjoys finger foods and their independence with self-feeding. To promote the use of baby utensils, consider reverse chaining. This technique is when you introduce a spoon to your baby and then let it go. Give wait time and encourage your baby to remove the spoon from their own mouth. You can also preload the spoon with food for your baby and encourage them to bring it to their mouth independently. This works best with foods that adhere to a spoon, such as yogurt or pudding. Your baby will slowly learn to introduce the spoon into their mouth independently and master self-feeding using baby utensils.

Name It Game

During a diaper change or at bath time, ask "Where is your belly?" and point to your baby's belly. "Where are your toes?" And point to your baby's toes. This helps increase both expressive language and receptive language as well as body awareness.

IT'S A WRAP

While this first year was undeniably one of the most critical years in your baby's development, every year is amazing and different, offering a multitude of opportunities for love, encouragement, and support from you. During difficult times in parenthood, be kind to yourself, trust yourself as a parent, and breathe. Obviously, you genuinely care about your baby's well-being and want to be the best parent you can be.

Thank you for allowing us to join in the excitement and development of your baby's first year.

Auditory Development

Contributed by John M. Page, PhD

Audition, which means hearing, is so vital to human development that a chapter in this book is devoted to understanding it. Audition (hearing) supports speech and language development, working memory, cognition, socialization, attention, alerting, orienting, tracking, sorting, sequencing, inhibition, and binaural interaction.

Development of the auditory system begins at birth and is different for each individual, with full development expected during the preteen years (puberty). The brain is flexible and capable of change. Auditory development creates change in the ear (the organ of hearing) and the auditory reception areas in the brain. Lack of stimulation of these neurological areas could lead to deterioration of function.

We actually hear with our brains, not our ears. The structurally normal ear communicates with the brain by sending appropriate signals through speech to the brain, where speech interpretation takes place. The ear performs 10 percent of the work, whereas the brain performs 90 percent.

The ear must provide the brain with appropriate, high-quality signals. For example, the ear hears three individual sounds in the word "c-a-t"; then the brain attaches meaning to the combination of sounds to form a complete word, also called labeling. How well the ear "talks" to the brain determines how well the brain will understand what was said. Therefore, the ear must provide a clear signal for correct interpretation.

The following example will help you understand this concept: The next time you listen to a song, try to pick out individual instruments; this exercise illustrates the task of the ear, hearing each individual instrument. On the other hand, the brain listens to the song function as a whole, not individual instruments.

Another example demonstrating the importance of signals is how your ear discriminates the phrase "26 sheep" from "20 sick sheep."

During normal maturation without ear infections or hearing loss, hearing develops in proportion to the complexity of both stimuli and the tasks. For example, we are able to hear in the presence of background noise, discriminate one speech sound from another (p/b), and learn foreign languages. The ultimate goal of audition is to receive and utilize spoken language. We "speak" because we hear (think ear infections,

A newborn hearing screen is recommended to be completed in the hospital after your baby is born.

hearing loss, and deafness). We also speak as we hear (think speech delay, accents). The speech production of many speech-delayed children improves as their awareness and knowledge of everyday speech sounds improve. Auditory development is the beginning of speech and language development.

Now consider the significance of the following developmental milestones that might not be on your radar. When your baby hears speech sounds and responds through behaviors, such as eye-widening, head-turning, and a change in sucking behavior, these nonauditory behaviors can be indicators of normal or near-normal hearing sensitivity, recognizing the presence of sound. Your baby is startled in response to the sudden onset of sounds, such as noise from sound-producing objects. The discrimination of familiar and unfamiliar voices shows that your baby is beginning to process auditory differences. Cooing sounds are your baby's first vocal milestone, enabling them to work toward their next vocal milestone, babbling. As your baby begins to use their auditory feedback mechanism—realizing they can hear themselves—babbling will start to disappear, turning into imitations of what they hear. This developmental process reveals that babbling is a precursor to speech and language development as your baby learns to repeat what they hear. Deaf babies stop babbling around six months of age because due to hearing loss they have no auditory feedback mechanism.

Providing high-quality auditory stimulation encourages auditory neurologic development, and the good news is that you have all the tools at your fingertips. The human voice is the best form of auditory stimulation, provides a good foundation for speech development, and offers a multitude of riches: soothing, calming sound, sound discrimination, emotional contact, bonding, and excitement.

From newborn to about two years of age, the auditory nerve becomes surrounded by a fatty material called myelin. This encasement enhances the nerve function in the brain. Eliminating fat from your baby's diet can impede the development of myelin. Although the sense organ of hearing fully develops at birth, the auditory nerve is not. The myelinization process supports auditory nerve development. Of course, you should follow the guidance and advice of your medical care team regarding your baby's diet.

The following indicators point to a partially developed nerve.

- **Pseudo hearing loss:** A hearing loss, as determined by audiometry, might be indicated; however, as the auditory nerve matures, the baby shows lower and lower hearing levels, indicating that the nerve is maturing.

- **Delayed speech development:** In some cases, speech delay lessens as the auditory nerve matures, sending improved signals to the brain for processing.

- **Overreaction to loud environmental sounds:** As your baby ages, this startle response lessens. You can see your baby covering their ears as protection. If your baby continues to be disturbed by loud sounds, it reflects their neurologic makeup, not pathology. If these behaviors persist, other considerations, such as sensory sensitivity, should be discussed with your baby's pediatrician.

- **Otitis media:** An infection and fluid buildup of the middle ear, can interfere with speech and language development. In normal hearing, the eardrum vibrates as a result of sound stimulation, thus sending signals to the brain to be interpreted. If the eardrum does not vibrate properly due to fluid in the ear, the brain receives an unclear signal and must work extra hard to decipher it and assign an appropriate meaning.

EAR INFECTIONS

If your baby has recurrent ear infections before the age of 2½ years, they are at risk for interruption in the development of cognition, social interaction, and receptive and expressive language. In some babies, minor disruption in the sensory input will affect auditory language development. The time this disruption occurs can determine the cognitive aspects that are affected. Some high-level cognitive language will develop despite the disruption of sensory input. Otitis media distorts sounds, thus providing the brain with incomplete and incorrect signals. Under these circumstances, the brain has to work overtime to organize and interpret signals that generally are devoted to other brain functions.

If your baby is experiencing ear infections, you can help them process the auditory signals better by increasing vocal loudness, making good visual contact while speaking, and being aware of background noise. Such efforts can help offset the effects of otitis media. Children prone to otitis media will have recurrent disease, with 20 percent of the bouts being silent—showing no signs.

Some babies do not do better after bouts of otitis media because the speech has changed. They cannot learn speech because of the speech itself—the content and the arrangement of speech sounds within words.

By now, you likely see the critical relationship between the developmental process of audition and speech and language because audition maturation reflects speech development.

AUDITORY STIMULATION TIPS

The following suggestions are based on the knowledge that your baby has normal hearing. This determination is made during the newborn hearing screening conducted while your baby is in the hospital after birth. You would have been informed if your baby did not pass the screening.

- Speak to your baby in the same volume you would use during a regular conversation.

- Vary the pitch of your voice when you want to provide additional stimulation.

- Look at your baby as you speak or sing to them to encourage eye contact.

- Vary your facial expressions to add to the richness of the auditory stimulation.

While engaging with your baby, be aware of background noises, especially from a television, which can produce many different voices and varying loudness levels. When your voice competes with background noise, your baby must work to determine what should be attended to and what should be ignored.

Understand development so you can facilitate future auditory, speech, language, and communication success. For example, nouns appear first, followed by verbs, followed by two-word phrases.

Language forms become more sophisticated with increasing age. By age four, your baby possesses all the necessary language rules to speak in the adult form. The rest is just a matter of time.

INTRODUCTION OF FOREIGN LANGUAGES

It is best to start speaking to your baby in a foreign language if that's important to you after your baby has turned three months old. As auditory development occurs, your baby will learn to discriminate sounds among numerous speech sounds known as phonemes. Research has shown that a typical developing baby can distinguish among various phonemes and language forms. The earlier, the better certainly rings true when a nonnative language is spoken in the home.

Dental Care

Contributed by Kimberly DeWire, DMD

The key to optimal oral health during pregnancy is prevention, which starts before conception.

DENTAL CARE BEFORE AND AFTER PREGNANCY

The hormonal changes during pregnancy result in a heightened response to the toxins produced by the bacteria routinely found in the mouth. Incidentally, pregnancy gingivitis or periodontal disease (periodontitis), formally known as pyorrhea (gum disease), can be a result. Clinically, gingivitis presents as inflammation of the gum tissue and increased bleeding of the gums during brushing, flossing, and dental cleanings. In severe cases, this inflammatory response can lead to or exacerbate bone loss. The bone holds your teeth in position, so when bone loss occurs, you might experience the mobility of teeth, drifting and migration of teeth, and an overall increase in bacteria and inflammatory factors. Comorbidities like diabetes or autoimmune disorders will be more challenging to control with elevated inflammatory factors.

Preventive dentistry during pregnancy can be accomplished safely, including dental exams, x-rays, cleanings, and minimal fillings. If more complex treatment, such as root canal, extractions, crowns, or bridgework, is required, it should be limited to the second trimester or deferred until after delivery.

People often think, "It's just my teeth." The issue with this thinking is that teeth are attached to the rest of your body through bone, tissue, and blood. The mouth is the pathway into your body through the digestive, respiratory, and circulatory systems. When there is an issue in your mouth, especially a bacterial one, this problem can quickly enter into or be transferred to other areas of your body.

When there is inflammation, the body brings blood to the area to increase fighter cells, causing an increase in bacteria levels in the bloodstream. In severe cases of infection, the bacteria can travel to other organs and the developing fetus. For this reason, obstetricians typically advise seeing a dentist early in your pregnancy to address any potential issues. Studies have shown that a mother with gum disease is more likely to have a preterm, low-birth-weight baby, which is why many insurance companies cover additional dental cleaning during pregnancy.

Many dental problems, such as periodontitis, are preventable with current evidence-based practices and care provided in dentistry.

DENTAL CARE FOR YOUR BABY

Tongue-Tie

At birth, your baby should have an oral exam by their nurse or pediatrician. In very rare cases, babies can be born with teeth, but more importantly, they might have a condition known as a tongue-tie, which occurs when the tongue is securely fastened to the floor of the mouth by a membranous fiber called a lingual frenum. If your baby has a tongue-tie, you might notice they have difficulty latching on during nursing, resulting in issues with feeding for your baby and significant pain for you while nursing.

Tongue-tie can pose other development issues relating to speech and airway incompetence. If you feel your baby might have a tongue-tie or you have other concerns regarding nursing, contact your lactation consultant or your baby's pediatrician for a proper diagnosis. Tongue-tie can be surgically corrected.

Routine Oral Care

After feedings, whether with breast or bottle, wiping your baby's mouth out with a clean washcloth is essential. The sugars found in breast milk and formula can cause early childhood cavities once teeth start erupting or growing into the mouth; therefore, it's a good habit to get into early. The last evening feeding before putting your baby to bed is the most crucial time of the day to wipe out your baby's mouth. Never put your baby to bed with a bottle in their mouth or within your baby's reach from their crib.

Once your baby's teeth start to erupt, you should brush them with a small-headed, soft-tissue brush. Baby toothbrushes come in many shapes and sizes for ease of use.

Some parents are concerned about the use of fluoride. However, fluoride, a mineral like iron, is good for our bodies in appropriate doses. Studies have shown that fluoride is most effective in a topical manner and is only effective systemically while teeth are developing.

When using fluoridated toothpaste, dab only a tiny smudge or smear on your baby's toothbrush. Swallowing a little bit from the toothpaste smear is suitable for your baby's developing teeth; however, excessive fluoride can upset their stomach and cause vomiting. Toothpaste specifically made for little ones has a pleasant taste that encourages cooperation with brushing and provides topical benefits for optimal dental care.

> *The American Academy* of Pediatric Dentistry recommends that babies see a dentist at one year old or within six months of the eruption of their first tooth.

Teething typically starts around six months, but there is a wide range; it can occur sooner or later (even as late as 12 months). Typically, teeth erupt in the following order:

- Lower front teeth, followed by upper front teeth
- Lower first molar, followed by upper first molar
- Lower canine, followed by upper canine
- Lower second molar and lastly, upper second molar around age two

There is no way to identify whether your baby will handle teething well or have a difficult time, and unfortunately, there is no magic solution to ease the discomfort of teething.

Teething

Teething can frustrate parents, but rest assured, it will pass.

Amber necklaces are not recommended.

Also, topical gels should be used with caution because they are short-acting, require repeated applications, and are ultimately ingested by your baby without any way of knowing the amount swallowed.

The safest way to provide relief to your teething baby is to give them over-the-counter ibuprofen or acetaminophen in a dose recommended by their pediatrician. Numerous studies show the effectiveness and safety of these medications.

WHEN TO TALK WITH YOUR BABY'S DENTIST

The American Academy of Pediatric Dentistry recommends that your baby see a dentist at one year old or within six months of the eruption of their first tooth, whichever comes first, for parent education, assessment of your baby's oral health, and preventive treatment. Early childhood cavities are detrimental to your baby's development and need to be addressed early or, better yet, prevented.

Subsequent visits should be every six months or sooner if the dentist is monitoring any specific concern.

Acknowledgments

We are so very grateful for the many amazing people in our lives. It has taken a village to create this book, faith to bring us together and carry us through this learning endeavor and accomplish this publication.

The Nurture Notebook family: I am so thankful and inspired by this amazing and talented group of professionals.

Dr. Sonja Burmeister, my dear friend and colleague, was the first person to start this journey with me. She inspires me daily with her grace, faith, commitment to higher education, and entrepreneurial sense.

Dr. Julie Spencer, her contagiously optimistic personality made it impossible not to become an immediate friend. Her faith, resilience and entrepreneurial intellect is an inspiration in my life.

Jaime Henry-Heimer, another dear friend has blessed me with her constant support and creativity: This awe-inspiring friend constantly challenges herself with technology, new endeavors in both continued education in speech and language and entrepreneurship.

Dr. Erin Jenewein, her dedication to the book, her profession, and the children she serves is outstanding.

Registered dietitian Alison Unger has been a breath of nutritional knowledge, and we are so grateful to her! Thanks also to Danielle Kinney for persevering through hardships to stay dedicated to the book and team.

Lactation consultants Beth Kushner-Giovenco and Jolie Maehrer have been friends for years and were immediately enthusiastic to volunteer their time and professional expertise to our book.

Tracy Walters, Licensed counselor, without hesitation contributed a chapter to support the well-being of moms.

Dr. Kim DeWire is another dear friend who inspires me and has supported me throughout my parenting years. This real life Wonder Woman enthusiastically jumped on board to contribute a chapter to support moms and babies.

Dr. John Page, a dear friend who we are grateful for his kindness, compassion toward helping others, his years of dedication to the field of audiology, and his eagerness and expertise to contribute to our book.

Briana Davis, this dear friend has encouraged me with inspiring words, her faith, eye for creating stunning photography, and entrepreneurial spirit.

Jennifer Bainbridge, an amazing and talented photographer who excitedly jumped on board, focused and prompt, ready to support this book as we worked hard to finalize everything in the final weeks.

Jennifer Bright and Bright Communications

team, thank you for their enthusiasm, perseverance, teamwork, support, and dedication to getting our book finalized, published, and in the hands only moms all over has been a blessing. Jennifer and her team went above and beyond to bring our book to fruition.

I cannot express my gratitude enough to the entire *Nurture Notebook* family. Your friendship, fearlessness, optimism, and persistence will forever inspire me. I adore you all with all my heart.

Thanks to my three daughters for blessing me with motherhood and challenging me to be the best version of myself every day. I love the three of you with all of my heart. I'm so proud of each of you.

I'm so thankful for my mom. She is my best friend and the ultimate awe-inspiring mother, who I strive daily to emulate. She has been unwavering in her love and support from day one of this project, which started in 1978. From inspiring words to help around my house, to being present and spending time with us has been invaluable. I love you.

Thanks to my husband, Jason, for giving me the gift of time to complete this project and being a supportive father to our children— from waking up with our girls so I could sleep to driving them all over the United States for their travel sports and all the in- between. I love you.

I'm grateful for my father, for teaching me that you can start new endeavors at any age in life and to never give up. I love you.

Thanks to my MIL and FIL, for all their support throughout our 20 years of marriage and for being wonderful grandparents.

Thanks to my brother, Steve and his family for their continued love and support.

My Aunt Missie, for her love and support. She was the first one to volunteer her time to edit the huge undertaking of our book.

Thanks to my Aunt Leslie for her love and being another cheerleader on my team.

I am so appreciative for Kathleen Donohue, for being such an attentive and supportive business mentor.

Thanks to Vincent Prinzi, Albert Longden, and Richard Sands for your guidance and support as well.

Mitchell Scheiman, OD, PhD, FAAO, FCOVD, for his support when meeting with me at the beginning of this endeavor and introducing me to Erin Jenewein, OD

Josh Berk, an amazing author and friend, who has given us guidance and support. Cynthia DeLuca, another fabulous author, for her guidance.

Thanks to Andrea, Jessica, Peggy, Alli, Alexis, Jenna, Alisha, Ali, Dave, and ALL my dear friends, new and old, who have always listened and supported me through all my different life journeys, including this one.

Many thanks to all the moms who let us share their first year with them through photography.

Dr. Geetika Verma, I appreciate her support and time reading through the book.

Cindy Brown, Lisa Jones, Carolyn Herrlinger of Childrens Dyslexia Center of Allentown for letting me bounce ideas off of them.

My friends Tom and Rachel for their friendship for helping with our Bio photo and videos.

Alisha for helping with the my work caseload during all this chaos.

Our second editor Gayle Crist and everyone else who has supported us. Thank you! You have all been a blessing in my life. I have much love and appreciation for you all.

About the Authors

The Nurture Notebook includes contributions from more than a dozen medical experts in a wide range of fields, including:

Bottom left to right:

- Kim Bandi, OTR/L (pediatric occupational therapist), founder of The Nurture Notebook, director of Valley Family Therapeutics, Orton-Gillingham practitioner, and photographer
- Julie Spencer, PT, DPT, PCES (women's health physical therapist, pregnancy and postpartum corrective exercise specialist), co-founder of The Restoration Space
- Emily Cupples, DPT, pediatric physical therapist
- Briana Davis, Jennifer Bainbridge, and Kim Bandi, photographers, capture the first year of life, providing visual guidance for the exercises and activities.

Top left to right:

- Jolie Maehrer, RN, BSN, IBCLC (lactation consultant)
- Kim DeWire, DMD (Doctor of Dental Medicinie), owner of DeWire Dental
- Jaime Henry-Heimer, MS CCC-SLP/L (pediatric speech and language pathologist), owner and CEO of Radical Speech Therapy Solutions
- Alison Unger, MPH, RDN, LDN, CDCES
- Sonja Burmeister, OTD, MSPA-C (physician's assistant), OTR/L (pediatric occupational therapist), EICP-OT Certified Specialist in Pediatric Early Intervention, certified autism specialist, owner of Valley Family Therapeutics, co-owner of Connective Interventions, co-founder of MyHealthcareKit
- Beth Kushner-Giovenco, RN, BSN, IBCLC (lactation consultant)
- Danielle Kinney, homeschool mom, founder and CEO of The Confident Baker

Not pictured:

- Erin Jenewein, OD, MS, FAAO, diplomate-binocular vision, perception, pediatric Optometry Associate Professor Pennsylvania College of Optometry Salus University
- John Page, PHD, audiologist
- Tracy Walters, MA, LPC (licensed professional counselor)

Visit TheNurtureNotebook.com for extensive biographies of our team.